SHOGHI EFFENDI
Recollections

SHOGHI EFFENDI
A drawing by Reza Samimi from a photograph taken during
the first months of his Guardianship

SHOGHI EFFENDI

Recollections

by

Ugo Giachery

MCMLXXIII
GEORGE RONALD
OXFORD

ISBN 0-85398-051-9

This humble work is dedicated to my
dear wife Angeline whose love for Shoghi Effendi
and utter dedication to the Cause of Bahá'u'lláh
are far greater than my own.

Contents

CONTENTS

List of Illustrations

The author wishes to thank the Audio-Visual Department, Bahá'í World Centre, Haifa, Israel, for kindly making available twelve of these illustrations.

x

Preface

THE date of November 4th, 1957, will remain for the author of these *Recollections* the day of anguish, of sorrow and bewilderment. In a modest hotel in the city of London, the earthly, fruitful life of Shoghi Effendi, the Guardian of the Bahá'í Faith, came abruptly, and unexpectedly, to an end. To the writer, it was as if the light of wisdom, solace and righteousness had been extinguished forever: something similar to an apocalyptic darkening of this planet.

A radiant and useful existence had suddenly ceased, leaving a multitude of co-religionists throughout the world stunned and grief-stricken. It was an unequalled and widespread feeling of despair and irremediable loss that filled the hearts with a poignant pain that could never cease; the end of an age of comfort and assurance, of light-hearted joy, the joy of one's adolescent years, when dreams, aspirations and idealism came into existence from the tranquil life revolving around the unity of the family, with its power of love and security, the source of our inspiration, fortitude and strength.

The greatest gift received from the Omnipotent, during my lifetime, was the privilege of being closely associated with Shoghi Effendi for a number of years. No words will ever be able to describe the depth of my devotion and of my abiding love for him, nor the transformation I underwent under the influence of his warm and tender affection; an influence that changed my character, my outlook on life, my habits, and opened my eyes to the unending vista of new aspirations and horizons.

In later years, I have felt the urge to communicate to others the power of his love; thus the decision to write down some of my observations and experiences. It is a recollection, however inadequate—an effort to render him due justice and to recall for others the life of such a unique and precious personage. I sincerely trust that future scholars will undertake to produce a detailed life history of him whom I consider to be the 'true man of the century'.

Much merit for my efforts goes to my dear wife, Angeline, who with her encouragement and patience has guided me to the completion of the manuscript. Deep thanks and appreciation go to our dear friend Beatrice Owens Ashton, for her many suggestions and the reviewing of the text, to Marion Hofman for her skilful editing, and to the painter Reza Samimi for his extraordinary and moving crayon portrait of Shoghi Effendi. My sincere thanks go also to the hosts of friends who have urged me to put in writing what I have verbally expressed in Bahá'í gatherings in various continents of the world. It is my hope that the reading of these *Recollections* will enkindle and strengthen, in the hearts of many, a deep love and admiration for Shoghi Effendi, that we may all dedicate our lives, as he did, to the service of the Cause of God which he so greatly loved, and that we may emulate him in placing such services ahead of any personal motives or restraint.

UGO GIACHERY

PART I

The Personality of Shoghi Effendi

I

An Appreciation

MY direct association with Shoghi Effendi, the Guardian of the Bahá'í Faith, was a unique, once-in-a-lifetime experience of the deepest spiritual import that can only very inadequately be described or explained in words. It began in the spring of 1947, after my wife and I had returned to Italy, and it lasted a little more than ten years.

In the early 1920's the Guardian had been, at least to the Western Bahá'ís, an almost intangible figure, the symbol of an institution functioning on an extra-human plane, incomprehensible from any rational approach. I knew him first through his letters and messages to the Western world. At that time my knowledge of the East was confined to acquaintance with a few Persian Bahá'ís who had migrated to our part of the globe and had acquired many Western habits and characteristics. Reports from Bahá'ís returning from pilgrimages to the World Centre of the Faith in 'Akká and Haifa were at times vague, at times contradictory, and not always illuminating. Those pilgrims who had earlier been in the presence of the Master, 'Abdu'l-Bahá, were reticent; they spoke with compassion of the bereaved members of His family and grieved at the emptiness left by His passing in November 1921. Other pilgrims mentioned details of the life in Haifa, of its beauty and repose, making reference to Shoghi Effendi as a scholarly youth who had an extraordinarily brilliant and cultured mind, and as a kind, loving, gentle and hospitable host.

In those early days of the Guardian's ministry, when the basic institutions of the Administrative Order were being forged into shape one by one, with much labour and great travail, it was indeed difficult to understand Shoghi Effendi's unique station, aims and efforts. The great body of the Bahá'ís, the world over, was like a new-born babe whose sight is not yet adjusted to the new world into which he has come. The old believers, in East and

West, were slowly recovering from the extremely severe loss of their beloved 'Abdu'l-Bahá and from the shock of what appeared to them to be an irreparable vacuum in the affairs of the Cause. The newer believers were trying with difficulty to become part of the as yet dimly understood administrative pattern. When we read the early messages of Shoghi Effendi now, we can see how immensely vast was his vision and how wise and far-sighted are the plans outlined in his letters and communications. All his counsel, as he led them on the way to an understanding of Bahá'u'-lláh's universal conception of World Order, is expressed by Shoghi Effendi in words charged at first with patience and expectation and then with a surge of unbridled hope, underlined, however, by a shade of indefinable sadness. Was this due to the loss of his beloved Grandfather, 'Abdu'l-Bahá, or to the immensity of the tasks ahead?

I am certain that the echo which sounded then in my heart was resounding similarly in the hearts of countless Bahá'ís everywhere. When Shoghi Effendi's first messages appeared, followed soon by his translations of some of the Sacred Writings, it was clear that a new style came into bloom, a new standard was set, and a perfect balance was achieved between the poetic and flowery Eastern languages of the original texts and the rationalistic Western idioms. I vividly remember spending long hours reading and living every word, feeling the joy of being part of some reality which reflected an unseen world as yet unknown to most human beings, from which emerged, with ever-increasing brilliancy, Shoghi Effendi's personality. In later years when I was fortunate enough to meet him in person, I was grieved to notice what a heavy toll his gentle body had paid during the decades of writing and translating. As time passed, Shoghi Effendi's personality arose in crystalline clarity to an ever greater magnitude, establishing him as a true beloved in the hearts of the believers and as a leading and unique world figure. Historians and scientists of the future will eagerly investigate the life, activities and achievements of Shoghi Effendi, and prove to a perhaps still disinterested and unbelieving world all the spiritual and eugenic factors that blended into the making of a genius.

Shoghi Effendi's love of learning, his eagerness to know and understand, a refined artistic taste combined with a great ability to do things, the remarkable energy he possessed, all these, together with much common sense and such superior spiritual powers that all who came into contact with him were subjugated by his love, made it clear that the striking qualities so evident in his maternal Grandfather had appeared in him to the fullest extent. His indomitable will imposed a self-control which is seldom found in others. During the first crucial months of his stewardship following the passing of 'Abdu'l-Bahá, when he found himself appointed Guardian of the Bahá'í Faith, undoubtedly he must have relied on this self-control to adjust himself to his new life, to bid farewell to his youthful dreams, to his fondness for sports (tennis and Alpine climbing), submerging all worldly desires, interests and feelings—normal emotions in a young man of his age and rank—into nothingness. As to his remarkable energy, suffice it to say that his ability to work uninterruptedly for long hours was amazing and bordered upon the marvellous.

He was of a gentle nature, his manners were cordial, remarkably loving and aristocratic, and his memory was extraordinary. He could remember names, dates, places and circumstances with a clarity that commanded respect and admiration. He knew the history of the Bábí and the Bahá'í Revelations from their inception, while at the same time his full, comprehensive and detailed knowledge of the world and its nations, peoples, governments, religions, history and culture was outstanding.

With regard to his appearance, my first impression was one of wonder. His gentle, graceful figure was enhanced by the power and authority which emanated from him; his broad forehead, his fine hazel eyes filled with light, the harmonious oval shape of his dear face, with his dark hair and small moustache, the consuming fire of his gaze, the small well-shaped hands, the striking purity and innocence and integrity which emanated from his whole being, all made a perfect vehicle for the tremendous forces of the spirit which were channelled through him.

His apparently delicate body was charged with such vitality

that he could work month after month, year after year, without any appreciable interruption. If one came near to him, one could feel this great vitality, almost like an electric charge, radiating from him upon men and things, and when his particularly well-modulated and resonant voice eagerly and passionately expressed the depth of his thoughts, the fascination was complete and captivating.

Early in 1947 I was practically unknown to him but, because of a fortunate coincidence which placed me in Italy at that time, I was charged by him with the mighty task of securing the carved marble and other materials for construction of the outer structure of the Báb's Shrine on Mt. Carmel. My personal relationship with the Guardian hitherto had been limited to a few letters and some cablegrams, most of which concerned personal matters. After the work on the Shrine began, in April 1948, directives came with frequent regularity, and I soon learned that alertness, speed and accuracy were wanted by him at all times. Then I well understood the tone of urgency which had become the keynote of most of his messages.

Those were difficult days in Italy, a country whose economy had been shattered by a disastrous war. My efforts therefore had to be multiplied if I wanted to keep pace with Shoghi Effendi's eagerness. As I redoubled my efforts, my recompense became greater. Never before in long years of business activity had I received such a recompense! A flow of appreciation, of tender and abiding love, of undeserved praise and gratitude came my way almost every day, for well over nine years. My life was transformed: the greatest joy and elevation came to me from a gentle and noble hand that penned letters and cables in words loomed with the indestructible threads of superhuman love—words which revealed to me what a treasure the world possessed!

As time passed, my activity expanded: more duties and more trust were placed upon my person. By then I was well aware of a tremendous power which originated at the World Centre of the Faith and was bountifully infused into my being by him whose word and wish had become my law. Finally, in the early spring of 1952, when my longing could be repressed no longer, a cablegram came: 'Welcome to Haifa'. Hasty and feverish preparations were completed in a few days and then I went on wings.

II

Pilgrim Impressions

I HAVE now only a vague memory of what happened or what I saw in the hours until I met Shoghi Effendi that evening of the middle of February 1952.

Those Bahá'ís who went on pilgrimage during the lifetime of Shoghi Effendi will remember the air of expectation which reigned all day until the coveted moment when, at dinner-time, one was ushered into the Guardian's presence. It was a custom to let the newcomer precede everyone else to the dining-room of the Western Pilgrim House—an oval-shaped room at the northern end of the lower floor of the building. When my time came that evening, friendly, eager hands led me down the staircase into a large empty hall and through another room to a clear glass door of the French type which opened into the dining-room. Those loving hands literally pushed me through the door into the room where a large table was set for the evening meal. At the far north-eastern side of the table, almost facing the door, sat Shoghi Effendi, his handsome face absorbed in deep thought. A few seconds elapsed as I paused, unable to utter a word or a cry, while my heart was ready to burst. He was wearing a dark steel-grey coat and on his head rested a black tarboosh of unusual height and shape. He lifted his head in my direction and then I met his luminous penetrating gaze. As he rose to greet me a broad smile illumined his whole face, while his eyes seemed to probe my innermost being, as if searching for proofs of love and trust.

The most affectionate words, the sweetest tongue in the world could not reproduce the eloquence of that smile, nor could the deepest thinker of this earth have analysed the loving understanding that radiated in it. I cannot relate the emotion I felt on going near to him.

'Welcome! Welcome!' he said, with a gentle and yet compelling voice. 'At last you have come.' And with a rapid and unforeseen motion he embraced me with such a tenderness that for a time I felt I was in the arms of all the mothers of the world.

Satisfaction and contentment filled my heart; unable to utter a word and yet electrified by all the love expressed in this gesture, I had to steel myself not to fall at his feet. A strong urge to embrace him, again and again, to make myself inconspicuous, small, humble, was overpowering me. But Shoghi Effendi must have sensed this perplexity within me, and guided me to a place at the table. As soon as I was seated and had regained my control, I had the feeling that finally I had reached home. After so many years I cannot recollect all that Shoghi Effendi told me. Expressions of praise and gratitude were flowing from his lips, and my embarrassment and blushing must have been quite evident to the other guests at the table.*

This feeling of nothingness in his presence never left me. Even years afterwards, whenever I came near him, there was an overwhelming force that filled my heart with joy and awe, with the certainty that even my thoughts were visible to him.

As I have stated, we saw Shoghi Effendi nearly every evening at his dinner-table in the Western Pilgrim House. Every day, when the hour approached and our anticipation could scarcely be bridled, minutes became unending hours until the Persian maids of the household appeared unobtrusively and swift as winged messengers, to summon the assembled pilgrims and guests to his presence. My personal experience extended over periods of weeks and, at one time, of months, and yet night after night my meeting him was the source of new emotions. Whenever he came to the table he brought with him a feeling of ecstatic excitement which replenished my soul. Invariably I was filled with a wondrous sensation of continuity and safety, with all contingent matters fading into nothingness, as I anxiously gazed at the remote but serene expression of his endearing face. Had I served him well that day? Had my modest collaboration brought him relief and solace? Was I worthy of his consideration and love to continue to serve him? These were the questions that assailed me whenever I

* See Appendix II for letters written by the author to his wife in Rome relating his first meetings with Shoghi Effendi.

11

came into his presence. These daily contacts, however, assured my fears and left me nourished, hopeful and eager.

The dining-room of the Western Pilgrim House,* which was located at 10 Persian Street, in Haifa, was at the extreme northern end of the ground floor of the building. On the south side of the room, French doors permitted access from a central hall which was connected with the kitchen. At the west end of the dining-room, a door communicated with a small antechamber used by Shoghi Effendi to enter or leave the dining-room. On the east side, a small door led to another small room used at that time for storage of household implements. Between this door and the south-east corner there was a built-in bookcase, which gave the dining-room a slightly oval shape. In this bookcase were many volumes from the Bahá'í literature and a geographic atlas, kept at hand to be used, very often, by the Guardian. On the north wall, several windows opened on the little garden outside. The dining-table was rectangular and, when fully extended (as it usually was after the pilgrimages began again in the winter of 1951–2), left barely enough space for chairs and for passing around the table.

The Guardian never sat at the head of the table. This place was reserved by him for guests whom he wished specially to honour. When no such guests were present, the Hand of the Cause, Mrs. Amelia E. Collins, sat there. Shoghi Effendi invariably sat at the eastern end of the north side of the table, with Rúḥíyyih Khánum at his right. Hands of the Cause, members of the International Council, and pilgrims sat around the table in places designated by the Guardian. The room was well lit at night, and during the winter months was agreeably heated by a portable kerosene stove.

On entering the room, always after the Guardian had been seated, one became surcharged with intimate joy and assurance. His radiant smile always expressed his welcome. Night after night here was the most perfect setting for a symposium of love, of universal planning, of understanding, and of action. The stream of noble words, the flow of thoughts, ideas and plans, coupled with his far-reaching vision, probing into the immediate and the distant future, were exciting and ultra-stimulating. I believe that,

* At present the seat of the Universal House of Justice.

year after year, every person who sat at his dinner-table was changed, immediately and completely, as if touched by a magic wand. That person's inner life and his approach to life, renewed by the sublimating love of the Guardian, were undoubtedly transformed in a way that no other person could ever experience. I, myself, have never been alone or unhappy again. He imparted something to my spirit that levelled all obstacles within myself, and he opened avenues of freedom and heavenly vistas among all children of man. It was as if we were sitting in the hall of the highest ranking university in the world, where the instructor was enlightening us on any subject the human mind could conceive, imparting a plenitude of knowledge, compassion and wisdom. I shall never forget those evenings and, as days go by, my link of love and gratitude to Shoghi Effendi grows stronger and stronger.

The towering spiritual perception of Shoghi Effendi always astonished all who met him for the first time, and this spiritual strength which he so abundantly possessed greatly enhanced his physical body. He had a refreshing directness that deeply stirred one's faculties; he asked many questions of everyone, and listened carefully to everything he was told. At times his conversation was far beyond the questioner's range, and more than often he was simplifying his reply, keeping it on an understandable level. It is said that 'man is a total of what he knows'; the greatness of Shoghi Effendi has been proved by the immensity of his knowledge. I cannot further elucidate this point because of my own limitations, but I shall try to portray his extraordinary stature by reviewing here the monumental structure he erected during the thirty-six years of his ministry.

Shoghi Effendi's actions were always founded on the solid blocks of divine inspiration, while the simplicity of his environment and of his personal life gave him an aura of great stability. He possessed the perfect clarity of vision that comes from supra-normal simplicity, and because of this he countered any form of ambition, indulgence or neglectfulness with his unfailing faith and stability, with the nobility of his purpose and the unwavering discipline of self-sacrifice, instilled in him from his childhood by his beloved maternal Grandfather, 'Abdu'l-Bahá.

In the Master's house, at 7 Persian Street, Haifa, which was also Shoghi Effendi's home for many years, on entering the large sitting-room one sees over a table on the left-hand side the portrait of a child's head which is arresting and fascinating. It is like the head of a cherub made by a great master and it reminds one of the school of Leonardo da Vinci, although I believe it is a skilfully arranged enlargement of a photograph. The size of the head is almost natural and its beauty moves and touches one very deeply. It is Shoghi Effendi as a child. He may have been four or five years of age at the time. Innocence and wonder are depicted on that dear face. The very large, almond-shaped eyes seem to look at one inquiringly; there is an expression of anticipation and eagerness in the whole countenance, as the lips are slightly parted, ready to utter an exclamation of surprise or marvel. I have looked at that picture for hours during the meetings of the Hands of the Cause which at times have been held in that room. Many questions have rushed to my mind: What was Shoghi Effendi like when a child? Was he aware of his great destiny? What was his character?

Shoghi Effendi was born in 'Akká, Palestine, in a house which still stands inside the fortress-city, quite close to the Most Great Prison. He was the son of Díyá'íyyih Khánum, the eldest daughter of 'Abdu'l-Bahá, and of Mírzá Hádí, an Afnán, a descendant of the Báb's family. Because most of those who lived with him, in the same household, have passed away long ago, there are only a very few persons living today who can remember Shoghi Effendi as a child. Mme. Laura Dreyfus-Barney* related to me the following:

'I was permitted, at the beginning of this century, to visit the Master in 'Akká, which at that time was a Turkish province. This happened during the critical years 1904–5 when 'Abdu'l-Bahá was constantly under the menace of being exiled to the far-away desert of Fízán in Africa, and I was privileged to have my interviews and conversations with Him while I was living in His household. Shoghi Effendi was at the time a child of seven or eight years of age. He was rather small for his age, but very keen and

* The compiler of *Some Answered Questions*.

14

attentive. When not engaged in his early morning studies, he followed his Grandfather ['Abdu'l-Bahá] wherever He went. He was almost like His shadow and passed long hours seated on the rug in the manner of the East, listening, quietly and silently, to every word He uttered. The child had a remarkably retentive memory and, at times when guests were present, the Master would ask him either to recite some passage from Bahá'u'lláh's Writings, which he had memorized, or to chant a prayer. It was very moving to hear the limpid, crystal chanting of that child, because all his being and soul were engaged in communion with God. Eagerness was ever present and animated him like a flame of fire in all he did.'

'Abdu'l-Bahá Himself was conscious of the potentiality already evident in the child; He made His Will at that time and appointed Shoghi Effendi His successor—the Válíy-i-Amru'lláh. To a believer who asked if He would have a successor, the Master replied:

'Verily that infant is born and exists and there will appear from his cause a wonder which thou wilt hear in future. Thou shalt see him with the most perfect form, most great gift, most complete perfection, most great power and strongest might! His face glisteneth a glistening whereby the horizons are illumined!'[1]

There is no doubt that the choice of 'Abdu'l-Bahá's successor had been made quite early in the life of Shoghi Effendi; although he himself was not aware of it, the Master had absolute faith in the character and capacity of His little grandson. That Shoghi Effendi was not aware of the Master's choice is certain. In December 1954, when my wife and I were on pilgrimage to Haifa, the Guardian turned to her one evening at dinner, and said, without any apparent motive except to answer the question she had been wanting to ask for days:

'I want you to know that the Master neither in writing nor by word of mouth intimated that I was to be His successor, nor left any written instruction as to the manner in which to conduct the affairs of the Cause; I had a tumult in my soul and find my way step by step.'

III

His Spiritual Virtues

HIS GREAT FAITH

OF all the characteristics that Shoghi Effendi possessed, the one that I believe was at the very core of his personality and was deeply rooted in his soul was the immense faith he had, his complete reliance on the efficacy of Bahá'u'lláh's Revelation. He clung to His Teachings with a tenacity that cannot be likened to anything. His whole being was permeated with the power of the Revelation, and this is the reason that all who came near him or in contact with him felt so safe, so assured, so regenerated. For the same reason, scheming individuals who inclined towards evil-doing or deceit could not remain long in his presence and went away frightened, bewildered and chastened. During my years of association with Shoghi Effendi I experienced, over and over again, the power emanating from his belief, a power that removed difficulties, brought unexpected happy solutions and paved the way to better and greater achievements.

Counterbalancing this characteristic there was a tremendous aversion to unfaithfulness and Covenant-breaking. During one of my longer stays in Haifa, from the end of March to July 1952, the 'old' and 'new' Covenant-breakers, emboldened by the end of British administration in Palestine, devised a plan to wrest from the hands of the Guardian all the possessions of the Faith in the Holy Land, by challenging the authority conferred upon him in the Will and Testament of 'Abdu'l-Bahá. Their machinations were intended mainly to harass Shoghi Effendi in the hope of bringing him to Court, where they could inflict on him publicly all kinds of humiliations through the use of legal cavils and the like. The affair lasted about three months, and of course ended with full victory for him, but what he suffered it is impossible to describe. The sacredness of the Institution of the Guardianship was not only challenged but was attacked for the purpose of creating confusion and turmoil in the rank and file of the believers. His great suffering was for the sacrilege being committed against this Institution of the Faith. It was so abhorrent to him that he felt physically ill, as if 'a thousand scorpions had bitten him'. During the most crucial days of this sorrowful experience, one night after dinner he spoke to me alone for several hours. His indignation was immense. He reviewed the tragic history of all that had happened since the days of the Bábí Dispensation, the sufferings inflicted on Bahá'u'lláh by Ṣubḥ-i-Azal (Mírzá Yaḥyá), the perfidy of Muḥammad-'Alí against the Master, the situation that arose in 'Abdu'l-Bahá's immediate family in the years which followed His passing, and all the acts of treachery and disobedience perpetrated by infamous followers in whom both the Master and himself had aforetime placed their trust. Often visibly grieved and filled with anxiety, he would say to me: 'You must know these things'; 'I want you to know these things'. These phrases he repeated several times during the course of the conversation. Many things he said I cannot repeat now, but they gave me a feeling of anguish and, I may say, of fear, because I became conscious that the Divine Covenant was assailed with vehemence by ruthless, satanic people, and that while the mass of the believers throughout the world were unaware of this grave danger, he, Shoghi Effendi, single and alone, was its defender, protected only by the armour and shield of his faith in God and His Covenant. The image passed rapidly through my mind of this new David battling single-handed against a ferocious, deadly monster, with all the terrors of the wilderness around him. He mentioned to me by name, one by one, the unfaithful members of his immediate family, their disobedience and obstinacy. He spoke also of the intrigues and disobedience of some followers who later had begged for forgiveness, with 'puny and pitiful excuses'. 'I am only the Guardian of the Cause of God and I must show justice,' he said; 'God only can show them mercy, if not in this world, in the next.' After a pause he looked at me silently for a while and then added: 'But if they repent the Guardian would know their sincerity and pardon them.'

During this entire conversation shadows of sorrow and dismay, like heavy storm clouds, passed over his luminous face. I could sense all the time the inner agony of his soul and the suffering of his body. A surge of unbounded love filled my heart. What would I have given to restore his happiness and tranquillity! How much I loved this Defender of the Covenant, this Sign of God on earth, the inspirer of every noble thought among the children of men! I had to control myself not to take him in my arms, to shield him from any further suffering, to assure him that for every Covenant-breaker there were thousands and thousands of believers who, like me, were ready to shed their blood if that were demanded!

THE GUARDIAN AND THE MAN

At this point I would like to illustrate still another of the spiritual virtues of Shoghi Effendi, which I had noticed before but which, during that vital conversation, became evident in all its strength and delicacy; namely, the capacity to separate himself as a man from Shoghi Effendi, the Guardian of the Cause of God. When he spoke of the labours, duties, plans, present and future, the inspirations, the decisions of the Guardian, he was so impersonal that one could have believed he was speaking of another person. This endeared him even more, because to find such a balance of humility and greatness, of objectivity and selflessness coupled with a fertile, creative and poetic mind is one of the rare happenings in thousands of years. I have used the word delicacy, because in all his thought and action there was no affectation or remote trace of pride or vainglory. An illuminating example of this is to be found in one of his masterly letters, *The Dispensation of Bahá'u'lláh*, in the section on the Administrative Order wherein is described the station of the Guardian.[2]

Another notable instance of his impersonal identification with the Guardianship—due in part to the great respect and reverence he had for that divine Institution of the Faith decreed by its Founder—is the terse and extraordinary cablegram to the Bahá'ís of the United States in answer to a congratulatory message on the occasion of his marriage to a North American believer.*

* Mary Maxwell, formerly of Montreal, Canada, daughter of the martyr of the Faith, May Bolles, and William Sutherland Maxwell, Hand of the Cause of God. The marriage took place in the Holy Land, on 25 March 1937. She was given the title Amatu'l-Bahá Rúḥíyyih Khánum by the Guardian.

This cablegram is one of the most beautiful and moving messages sent by Shoghi Effendi and shows the high degree of his love for the people of the American continent and his delicate sensitivity. Many times since the cablegram was made public, I have thought of the bounty thus bestowed upon the American people, for which they ought to be proud and grateful for ever. It reads as follows:

'Deeply moved by your message. Institution of Guardianship, head cornerstone of the Administrative Order of the Cause of Bahá'u'lláh, already ennobled through its organic connection with the Persons of Twin Founders of the Bahá'í Faith, is now further reinforced through direct association with West and particularly with the American believers, whose spiritual destiny is to usher in the World Order of Bahá'u'lláh. For my part I desire to congratulate community of American believers on acquisition of tie vitally binding them to so weighty an organ of their Faith.'[3]

Where can one find such nobility, expressed in a language that perhaps our generation is unable to understand and fully appreciate!

HIS HUMILITY AND SELFLESSNESS

Humility of a kind not yet known elsewhere was one of Shoghi Effendi's many unique virtues, a humility which came from the conviction that man's faculties are not self-created but are a precious trust from God, not to be displayed or used overbearingly or with vanity. And yet he emanated true pride and dignity, such a regal dignity that raised him far above any man I have yet met or known.

When conversing with him, one could strongly sense this feeling of humility, while his ample brow and penetrating eyes reflected an inner light born of faith, courage and determination. One could feel an awareness that was amazing and rendered one speechless.

Shoghi Effendi's selflessness was not only outstanding but exemplary. He never placed his personal interests or desires ahead of his functions as Guardian. Those who were near to him inevitably felt that his life was something to be fully expended in the service of God and humanity, in a dedication unlike that of any other human being. When close to him I always felt the powerful process of his sublimation to the reality of the unseen world, while his body was there, near to me, like a visible, finely-tuned musical instrument whose melodies, imperceptible to the human ear, vibrated unseen through the ether.

He was always ready to give comfort, verbally or in writing, to encourage, to praise and to stimulate to such a degree that one felt the urge to place at his disposal life, time and possessions within the range of one's capacity and emotional exaltation. This was the essence of his detachment from worldly things. The less he thought of himself, the higher he soared in the sphere of spiritual authority and prestige. This was perhaps the secret of his tremendous attraction and influence upon those who came close to him.

HIS INVOLUNTARY CONNECTION WITH THE DIVINE SOURCE

If one were to relate in detail the manifold aspects of the personality of Shoghi Effendi which like facets of a perfectly cut gem reflected the rays of divine light and inspiration, many volumes would not suffice. I firmly believe that psychologists will come to agree with the point of view that while human beings, generally, react in a voluntary or semi-voluntary way to circumstance, situations, inspiration and even to what may be considered illumination from the Divinity, Shoghi Effendi, like a sensitive instrument connected to the Source of all powers, reacted involuntarily to the most imperceptible spiritual impulse which activated his organism, making him capable of executing and discharging all functions and responsibilities related to the Cause of God without the slightest probability of error.

This analysis, made at the very first meeting with him, explained to me clearly and conclusively the meaning of divine guidance and infallibility—two things that Shoghi Effendi could not voluntarily choose or control. During the spring of 1952, as already stated, when owing to his graciousness I was allowed to remain in the Holy Land for several months, the opportunity came to observe him systematically and under various conditions.

It generated great delight in me to do so, because it was like exploring an enchanted land where one passed from wonder to wonder, from surprise to marvel. The joyful part of it was derived from the simplicity and normality of the environment and from situations which permitted these observations without hindrance and under the most favourable circumstances.

It was Shoghi Effendi's habit, in the early afternoon, to interrupt his work on his correspondence and to be driven from the house on Persian Street to the Eastern Pilgrim House on the slope of Mt. Carmel, close to the Shrine of the Báb. At that time (spring 1952) the construction of the superstructure of the Shrine was progressing with some difficulty because the architect, William Sutherland Maxwell, had recently passed away,* and the building contractor was seriously ill. I therefore welcomed the opportunity to assist the head-mason in many details of the construction that were well known to me, since all the marble had been carved in Italy under my supervision. This permitted the opportunity of spending many hours at the Shrine, and although it was accepted that one would not intrude upon the Guardian on such an occasion, I would notice him from a distance, pacing the entire length of the northern gardens deeply absorbed in thought and absolutely unaware of his surroundings. He would then enter the Shrine for prayers, remaining for quite some time, after which, slowly retracing the paths of the garden, he would return to his automobile to be driven home. The atmosphere of peace and repose which eternally hovers over the gardens and around the Báb's Shrine, combined with the sacredness of the Spot, certainly offered him a haven from distress and physical exhaustion, so that all his faculties were regenerated by the power of divine inspiration and guidance. At night, when at dinner, his dear face, like an open book, would reveal the process undergone during the day, and his warm and enthusiastic conversation would confirm, without any doubt, the new heights scaled in the world of realities.

A few times I had the great blessing of being permitted to accompany Shoghi Effendi to the Shrines of Bahá'u'lláh in Bahjí and of the Báb on Mt. Carmel. As we walked along the

* In Montreal, Canada, on 25 March 1952.

paths of the gardens, I was very close to him, and there came a feeling I cannot well describe. He walked with much dignity and grace, his fine intelligent face glowing with an inner light; his steps, well-measured and rhythmic, seemed to bring his feet scarcely in contact with the path, as if he feared to disturb the sanctity of the ground on which he trod or to break the harmony all around him. During my lifetime I have met several kings and many great personages in the scientific, political and ecclesiastical worlds, but never have I had the feeling of rapture and bliss that I felt in those unforgettable moments when I was so close to Shoghi Effendi. I could feel that although his body was with us (as on all these occasions a small group of believers was following him), his mind and spirit were rejoicing in the infinite realm of reality where no time, space or human frailties exist. The joy that overcame me on such occasions was as if I had reached the highest pinnacles of freedom and of true immortality. I could have laid down my life then and there without regret or sorrow, so immense was the flow of divine grace that enveloped me.

The first of these occasions was the anniversary of the Birth of the Báb. The few Western Bahá'í men who were in Haifa at the time (spring of 1952) gathered with other male believers of Haifa, 'Akká and Nazareth in the hall of the Eastern Pilgrim House on Mt. Carmel, to await the arrival of the Guardian.* When he came we had readings and chanting of prayers in Persian and Arabic, and then he led us to the Shrine. He walked ahead, slowly, with the utmost dignity, his head bent slightly forward in reverence. I received the impression that he was greatly moved by the majestic tranquillity of the surroundings and by the importance of the occasion. I walked after him, joyously, free from pains and cares, breathless as a runner nearing his goal, anticipating the moment when I could prostrate myself at the Holy Threshold of the beloved Báb's Tomb. In the incomparable beauty of the gardens, the outer world had vanished, leaving only a feeling of complete peace and contentment.

In those days the superstructure of the Shrine of the Báb was

*This Holy Day is celebrated in the Near and Middle East according to the lunar calendar.

but half erected; only the colonnade and the octagon were finished, and feverish efforts had been made the previous week to put into place the wrought-iron balustrade of the octagon section for this particular celebration. Shoghi Effendi stood at the door of the Shrine and anointed every one with attar of rose as we passed him. When the last had entered, he came in and prostrated himself, trying to contain his tears which were streaming from his eyes. When he rose, he stood silent for a moment, and then intoned a chant with such sweetness as cannot be expressed in words. His voice rose and fell with varied degrees of tonality, expressing sorrow and joy, exaltation and hope. I became unaware of place and time, transported on the wings of the chant to a remoteness filled with joy, into a stillness of space far above the toil and suffering of man, where I heard the hum of the universe in all its immensity. There and then my soul was eternally linked with Shoghi Effendi, the purest channel between man and eternity, between all the Prophets of God and His children.

Some time later the commemoration of the Ascension of Bahá'u'lláh gave me another opportunity to be with him. This time the group gathered on the lawn by the north-west corner of the Holy Tomb in Bahjí, sitting in a circle out in the open, in the balmy spring air laden with the perfume of orange blossoms. Readings and chanting of prayers preceded an address given by Shoghi Effendi, who from time to time would translate into English some of the salient points of his talk, which he gave in Persian. Afterwards he had oranges and tea served to us, and as the darkness of the evening began to descend, giving a uniform mellow tint to men, trees and all objects, he led us to the nearby door of the Shrine of Bahá'u'lláh. Shock-like waves were running up my spine and a tremendous feeling of awe overtook me as I stopped to be anointed by the Guardian. He stood at the door with a gentle smile wreathing his luminous face, which the joyful expression of his eyes enhanced. All lights inside the Shrine were ablaze in great glory. Slowly we advanced one by one to the Holy Threshold. When I placed my forehead on the hallowed ground I felt that my soul was being sublimated in the Glory of the True Father. When I arose, dazed by this unearthly experience, I gazed again at Shoghi Effendi; he was absorbed in heavenly rapture, and his face radiated light, beauty, purity, joy and strength. The time spent inside the Shrine listening to the golden ringing tones of his chanting was the greatest recompense I could receive from him whom I loved so imperfectly yet so immensely. These episodes remain unforgettable and constitute now the richest rewards of my association with him.

My love for the Guardian had blossomed into a tenacious unbounded devotion which can never be experienced again with another being. He was the eternal student of the greatest book of all, the human heart. Well he knew how to direct the overwhelming flow of love which his unsullied and pure heart was capable of emanating in ever-increasing quantity. Its origin was his great love for God, which reflected itself in his embracing love for all mankind. It was through his love for God that he accomplished the greatest effort the human intellect can make: to investigate the cause of this most sublime emotion and shape it for the benefit of the entire world.

HIS EAGERNESS

Another of Shoghi Effendi's characteristics was his eagerness. As early as my first meeting with him, I became aware of this burning flame within his soul, for it was manifested in the emphasis of his speech, in the penetrating and searching gaze of his intelligent eyes, in the swiftness of his action and in the rewarding smile with which he recompensed those who acted promptly. The phrase so often repeated verbally and in his immortal messages, 'Time is short', reveals the pressing needs of humanity and his concern about the realization of God's plan on earth during the normal span of man's life. This phrase was addressed to every believer, without exception, spurring everyone to an eagerness similar to that which he possessed. I have no doubt that future historians of his life will identify and assemble all the threads of the incredible texture of deeds woven on the loom of intuition, wisdom and divine guidance, to show the world that during the selfless, steadfast and active life of Shoghi Effendi he accomplished what no ordinary man could accomplish in many more decades.

HIS PERSEVERANCE

Perseverance was one of Shoghi Effendi's most noble qualities, and taught me many a lesson. I learned much from him in pursuing and accomplishing any given task. It is part of human nature to give up when attempts fail at the beginning; only a few persist in an endeavour when beset with obstacles of all sorts. His instructions to me, always to go or appeal to the highest authorities, to seek always the best, to accomplish things in the shortest time possible, and to persevere under all circumstances, became my second nature while I was privileged to work for the Cause under his personal guidance. In nearly every letter I received from him over a period of many years, the word 'persevere' is repeated. It had the power of a talisman for me, because such an exhortation was undoubtedly seconded by his love, well-wishing and prayers. How could anyone fail when he, 'the Sign of God on earth', was himself spiritually linked with the recipient of such a message?

Were I to relate all the difficulties, some nearly insurmountable, that I met during the years of supervising production of the carved marble and other material needed to construct the Báb's Shrine and the International Archives, I should have to write at much greater length. In nearly every case I did not trouble the Guardian with these obstacles. Clad with the armour of perseverance, in the certainty that his prayers were following me, and that in God's ledger the assent had been granted, I knew that the impossible could be accomplished. And it was, thus bringing him infinite joy.

Had the friends the world over well understood his plight, and the meaning and power of that exhortation, much more would have been accomplished and every goal would have been fulfilled. Like 'Abdu'l-Bahá, he offered up his soul, his life and his possessions in the path of God, devoting every moment of activity during thirty-six years of his stewardship in order to bring forward, as early as possible, the knowledge of Bahá'u'lláh's Revelation to all mankind. It was through his wisdom, initiative, directives, courage, example, dynamism and perseverance that, when his noble soul left this world on that fateful 4 November 1957, the map he had completed only the day before was able to record, like a graphic summary of his life's activities, the amazing

25

development accomplished in less than five years—years which implemented and fulfilled all the activities of the previous thirty-one years of his Guardianship. That map, as was the case with some previous ones, was drafted by his own hand, and embodied his analytic talent and geographical acumen. It will perpetuate throughout Bahá'í history the memory of his fruitful, precious and distinguished existence.

HIS GENEROSITY

The word generous is derived from the Latin (*generosus*) and signifies, literally, 'of noble birth' or 'magnanimous', but in its everyday usage it denotes liberality and munificence, both of which are qualities of magnanimity, or a regal character. Magnanimity and munificence ('great liberality') are virtues possessed by Shoghi Effendi. His greatness of mind and nobility of soul, his bearing and comportment, his apparent aloofness and reserve, which placed him in a lofty and intangible realm, were part of his birth-right and noble blood which went far back to the Sásáníyán dynasty of Persia (A.D. 226–651).* However, although his manners were reserved—an absolute condition for the prestige of his exalted rank—his heart was living, warm, pure, noble, tender and generous. The warmth and love that emanated from his innermost being were like a magnet that attracted and subjugated all who came close to him.

To be generous is one of the greatest qualities man can possess. It is rare to find on this earth an individual as generous as was Shoghi Effendi. A man usually accumulates, during his lifetime, possessions that he rarely shares with others, because the criterion of giving for the joy of giving is a celestial virtue; it has not yet become man's second nature. The generosity of Shoghi Effendi was reflected in his everyday life, in his writings, in his conception of a better world, and in the power of inspiration and leadership which permeated through him into the world-wide affairs of the Cause. What a heavenly quality he possessed! He always considered the needs of others before even thinking of himself. This was true not only for the spiritual wealth which was his greatest

* See Appendix IV.

heritage, but also for material things as well, which he never sought, wanted or desired for himself. On that evening when he spoke to me alone, he mentioned that after the reading of the Will and Testament of 'Abdu'l-Bahá, when he found himself appointed Guardian of the Cause of God, he told the assembled members of the whole family that he renounced, then and there, the ownership of any estate, possessions and chattels that would be his rightful inheritance. Looking back in retrospect and examining rapidly the events which took place from that fate-laden day in November 1921, to his passing in November 1957, we can readily understand and marvel at this act of true generosity.

Many instances could be related, of which I was an eye-witness, when this flow of generosity was not only overwhelming but even electrified all those present, to the extent that they wanted to emulate him, forget themselves and offer their wealth, services and their lives, for his use in the Cause he loved so deeply. As already mentioned, Shoghi Effendi possessed the uncommon virtue of not coveting any earthly possession; all his wishes and desires were directed towards the enhancement and prestige of the Faith of which he was the Guardian.

Pilgrims to the World Centre came and went, and nearly every one brought him gifts upon which love, dedication and esteem were engraved in indelible letters. They varied from personal objects to valuable financial contributions. All were accepted by him with infinite grace and dignity but the personal objects were usually passed along to the local believers and the pilgrims, while the contributions were allocated to the various projects for propagation of the Faith in all parts of the world, or for embellishment of the Holy Places, or to help the needy. While practising the utmost economy in his personal expenditure (the simplicity of his wardrobe bearing witness to this), he would contribute large sums to worthy causes outside the pale of the Faith. I well remember going one day to Jerusalem, at his request, to present to the rector of the Hebrew University a sizable donation from Shoghi Effendi for the support of its activities.

Any plan he initiated for the development of the Cause was invariably supported by a substantial contribution to inaugurate its practical execution, and to encourage the Bahá'ís to do likewise and so assure its success. It would be impossible to enumerate the wide range and size of his contributions that supplied the vital lymph to hundreds of projects. As a random example, the following is cited from his message to the 1946 Convention in the United States, which inaugurated the Second Seven Year Plan:

'Pledging ten thousand dollars as my initial contribution for the furtherance of the manifold purposes of a glorious crusade surpassing every enterprise undertaken by the followers of the Faith of Bahá'u'lláh in the course of the first Bahá'í century.'[4]

The reader may wish to peruse all of Shoghi Effendi's messages, to note how much he contributed to foster teaching plans, to establish endowments, to purchase national headquarters and Temple sites in every capital city throughout the world, to complete the Bahá'í House of Worship in Wilmette and initiate construction of other Temples in Africa, Australia and Europe—and these are only part of the enterprises which were blessed by his generosity. It is impossible to forget the expression of true joy which illumined his dear face, and the shining light in his eyes, when suddenly, at the dinner-table in Haifa, he announced a new plan and the extent of his own financial support. This writer, personally, was the recipient of Shoghi Effendi's generosity—his spiritual guidance, his encouragement and praise, his unbounded gratitude for services rendered, expressed in kind, warm and loving words written by himself in several dozens of letters. These are positive testimonies of Shoghi Effendi's great liberality and consideration; and there are many thousands of believers who were beneficiaries of his munificence! Some mementoes given to the writer by Shoghi Effendi are being treasured as the living part of an indissoluble chain of love, esteem and unfading memories.

IV

His Literary Gifts

GIFTS! Shoghi Effendi possessed many, and it is difficult to state which was the most remarkable, but one of his greatest talents is seen in his use of both the English and the Persian languages in his writings and translations. His untiring efforts, and the difficulty of his task in enlightening the masses of the believers, both in East and West, can only be fully realized by the conscientious observer who will, carefully and painstakingly, undertake the spiritual adventure of reading the vast and impressive collection of his letters, his translations from the Holy Writings of the Faith and his immortal, chronological history of the Faith known by its title *God Passes By*—all of which establish a notable epoch in English literature. To know Shoghi Effendi's literary work is to know and love *him*, to penetrate deeply into the discovery of his personality and the world of reality in which he lived.

As I stated at the beginning of this appreciation, I first met Shoghi Effendi in the greatness of his spiritual stature through his letters, which came to my attention towards the end of 1924, long before I met him personally in my visit to the Holy Land. In early youth I studied English, and for reasons yet unknown to me, I was so attracted by the freedom of expression which this language offers that the entire course of my life was influenced. When I was in my early teens, in Italy, one of my English teachers for whom I had great admiration and affection urged me to read Shakespeare, Byron and Shelley; my partiality for the English language was inflamed.

When I first read some of Shoghi Effendi's early messages to the American Bahá'ís, I was struck by a high sense of purpose, a sublimity of intention and a feeling of chastity (in the wide meaning of the word). It is difficult now to convey an idea of the emotions aroused by their beauty and the impact of their vision which, like sudden showers in the desert, enrich the arid nature of man with something rewarding, refreshing and precious. Later on, when it became feasible, I searched also in his earlier writings, when he wrote for 'Abdu'l-Bahá or translated His Tablets to the Western Bahá'ís, most of which were published in the *Star of the West*.*

Before proceeding it may be well to consider the titanic task which confronted Shoghi Effendi when he assumed the function of Guardian of the Faith at the beginning of 1922. To organize the affairs of the Cause, scattered over the continents of the globe, with the purpose of erecting on unassailable foundations the Administrative Order of the Faith—the forerunner and pattern of the World Order of Bahá'u'lláh—Shoghi Effendi had to provide instruments for the use of those (few they were at that time) who would carry out his instructions. This he did mainly through patient, inspiring and illuminating letters of guidance, letters which unfold to a sceptic, unbelieving and slumbering humanity the majestic and almost incredible plan of redemption for the whole of mankind. These letters, like liquid fire running from his pen, express the fullness of his feelings and emotions with a sense of assurance and inevitability. This fire permeated all his writings until his very last messages. The way he always expressed himself with dignity, care and refinement touched the hearts of the readers as would the harmonious notes of a musical composition. After a few years he undertook the translation into English of the major Writings of the Faith, a difficult task which must be considered one of his greatest gifts to present and future generations of Bahá'ís.

In addition to his translations, his voluminous correspondence by mail and cable with National Institutions of the Faith, as well as with individual believers, absorbed much of his precious time, limiting considerably his rest and relaxation.

Furthermore, we must remember the friendly relations he maintained in brilliantly conceived letters to the authorities of the British Mandate in Palestine and, after 1948, of the State of Israel,

* An official organ of the Bahá'ís of North America, which was published in Chicago and Washington, D.C., from 1910 to 1933.

activities which greatly enhanced the prestige of the Faith, as did his communications with outstanding leaders and personalities in various countries of Europe.

I have no doubt that what he accomplished during his thirty-six years of Guardianship was the systematic unfoldment of a well-conceived, broad plan which he must have envisioned at the very beginning of his ministry; he was also confronted early in 1922 with the necessity of making known his interpretation of the Holy Writings. His communications thus became the best fruits, the pure gems, of his spiritual and creative work. This one facet of his immense activity fills one's heart with great joy and will act as a stimulus and an inspiration to yet unborn generations of believers.

As a writer Shoghi Effendi achieved a degree of brilliancy that cannot be equalled. He dealt with an intangible subject in a way no other writer can ever approach, for lack of the spiritual stature which he possessed. His pen penetrated the most remote by-ways of human feelings, bringing tears to the eyes and gripping the heart with a variety of new emotions. Moreover, in his translations, his use of the English language reached the highest form of epic. Because his life had been interwoven with sacrifice, suffering and renunciation, his mind became a pure channel for the spirit; he could translate in ample rhythms, in masterly phrases, the mysteries of the subconscious in a flow of inspiration which poured forth from divine sources.

To be able to understand Shoghi Effendi's work, one must realize what animated him to accomplish the titanic task he did. The laws of genetics will perhaps prove that, as the great-grandson of Bahá'u'lláh, he had inherited many virtues and noble characteristics which made possible his grasp of far greater powers than are available to the average human being, as well as a discernment and spiritual penetration seldom encountered in the most brilliant writer or statesman.

But the true animating forces which permeated all his writings can be placed in three classes. The first was his great vision. With all his passion and zeal he projected himself into the far, far distant future, visualizing the blessings which the World Order

31

of Bahá'u'lláh would bring to mankind. Often we saw his dear face illumined by the glow of an inner consuming fire, reflecting the glory of this Order, while with a gentle and convincing voice he would tell of the five-hundred-thousand-year Cycle over which Bahá'u'lláh's Revelation would extend its shield and supremacy.

The second force was his unfaltering conviction of the ultimate triumph of the Faith of Bahá'u'lláh. Shoghi Effendi's life was not an easy one, but not even for an infinitesimal instant did he ever hesitate or delay. 'If I should be influenced by the chaotic condition which exists in the world,' he said one evening at the dinner-table, 'I would remain passive and accomplish nothing.' It was at the crucial time of the post-war period when nearly all countries of the world were in want of statesmanship. This unbounded conviction made him a tower of strength, a haven of refuge, and provided him with the power to accomplish things which by human standards would be considered extremely difficult, even impossible.

The third animating force was his faith in the accomplishments of the Bahá'ís throughout the world. This was one of the most real and precious sources of power to him, almost a talisman, something to be found only in the Bahá'í Faith. Shoghi Effendi was a part of the great body of believers; he was like the lymph in the human body. He was well aware that the co-operation of the believers was essential to the unfoldment of Bahá'u'lláh's divine plan for mankind. Verbally and in his written messages he strongly conveyed his acknowledgement of this active partnership of the believers in whatever he did. It was deeply moving to hear him say: 'We have accomplished this'; 'We shall do that'. There never was the least trace of personal pride in all his accomplishments. Happiness and joy filled his heart at a new victory, but all the credit and praise were given to the believers.

It must be said, however, that at times he was saddened by the actions of individuals, and he suffered deeply from the inertia which occasionally seemed to dampen the ardour of the Bahá'ís in one continent or another. But his faith in their obedience, devotion, activity, will and virtues, as a world-wide community, never diminished and afforded him much satisfaction, encouraging him to *dare* even more.

Many pilgrims will remember his saying at the dinner-table: 'I have told them to do this; now it is no longer in my power, it is in their hands, and they must accomplish it.' The things hidden in the future he keenly sensed, and all things he did or planned were far in advance of his time.

Perhaps it is worth while to examine one aspect of the whole question of holy and theological writings, in order to understand better the prodigious accomplishments of Shoghi Effendi in the field of man's religious evolution.

Until fairly recent times, Judaic and Christian scriptures have either remained unavailable in their original languages or have been translated into now dead languages accessible only to a few scholars and to part of the clergy. Latin, for example, has been the dominant language for nearly eighteen centuries and is still used almost exclusively in the liturgy of the largest Christian Church throughout the world. It is thus easy to realize that a tremendous vacuum has existed in the knowledge of the faithful concerning the tenets and practices of their religions.

Bahá'u'lláh's Writings were revealed partly in Persian and partly in Arabic. Shoghi Effendi, with his deep enlightenment and keen realization of the situation just described, initiated a new era in religious literature, for without delay, after 1922, but at great physical cost, he translated, within the very first century of his Great-Grandfather's Revelation, a large number of His Writings into English, a language now widely diffused and almost universally spoken. The Faith of Bahá'u'lláh has spread rapidly to all parts of the world because Shoghi Effendi made the dissemination of Bahá'í literature an essential objective throughout the thirty-six years of his Guardianship, and contributed his matchless translations from the original texts, which in turn have been translated into hundreds of other languages. 'Abdu'l-Bahá had prepared him for this work by enabling him to master some European languages, English being his favourite.

Everything Shoghi Effendi did had but one purpose, which was the result of his far-sighted vision directed always to the future. He was aware of man's limited opportunities during the normal span of human life, but for him the establishment of a granitic foundation for the New World Order of Bahá'u'lláh was most vital and impelling. One can perceive, by studying his writings, that this glorious goal was ever present to his mind, as the sun would be to a celestial navigator. Shoghi Effendi laid this foundation by erecting, step by step, the Administrative Order of the Faith. It was like raising the steel framework of a mighty sky-scraper almost single-handed; he encouraged, praised, welded, reinforced, consolidated, with the endurance of an untiring construction engineer. To him the body of the Faith was the mass of believers from every land, climate, culture, language heritage and background. The Administrative Order was the gigantic structure which bridged differences, bringing unity in diversity, harmonizing habits and alien cultures, cementing unbreakable links of amity, forging unprecedented, inconceivable and durable spiritual alliances.

If we ponder even briefly on the development of the Bahá'í Faith since 1922, we cannot but marvel at the swiftness of events and the strength of this mighty administrative structure that reaches into every continent of the earth. And if we look at the causes of irreligion today and the crises in which all major religious groups find themselves, we realize immediately that lack of a universal administrative order, such as is possessed by the Bahá'í Faith, has been a major factor in their deterioration. The flow of the dynamic spirit of any faith can be assured only by renewal of its vitality (as the coming of spring does for nature and for man), by the administrative process which the Bahá'ís so diligently and regularly observe, in the local, national and international elections of the governing bodies of the Faith.*

The early letters of Shoghi Effendi, written under the direction and instruction of the Beloved Master, immediately after the First World War,† are precious ones because they reveal his mature literary mind and his whole grasp of the delicate and vast implica-

---

* Called Spiritual Assemblies (local and national), and the Universal House of Justice (international).
† Published in *Star of the West*. (See footnote p. 30.)

tions of the spiritual influence he later was called upon to exercise on the entire body of the believers. The wealth of his literary vocabulary, the concise and expressive style, distinguished his writing again and again from that of the many other secretaries 'Abdu'l-Bahá had at different times. It is revealing to compare these early letters with the messages Shoghi Effendi sent as Guardian of the Cause in later years to the Bahá'í world, at an ever-increasing tempo, and to note how the later blossoms had the same colours and fragrances as the early buds.

The whole body of Shoghi Effendi's interpretations, translations and literary works would be a real challenge even to a seasoned critic who wanted objectively to penetrate and describe the avenues illumined by the splendour of such a mind, in order to establish standards that could be compared to the characteristics of world-famous writers. It has been said that Shoghi Effendi's aspiration as a youth was to translate the Bahá'í Writings into English. At the same time he had a tremendous sense of history. Indeed, some of his analyses of events of the nineteenth and early twentieth centuries so brilliantly presented in *The Promised Day Is Come* place him not only among the *élite* of the world's historians, but also in the front rank of men of *belles-lettres* in this century. The culture he possessed, the refined education of his sensibilities, and his passion for reading and observing, concurred in developing and perfecting his style, which acquired a structure and a particular physiognomy that became well known to Bahá'ís the world over.

TRANSLATIONS

In his translations of the Bahá'í Sacred Writings, Shoghi Effendi's style and form do not differ from those of his own free writing. They reach always the highest level of poetic prose, interwoven as they are with images, rhythm and lofty concepts. Generally speaking, some writers see and reproduce objective images of things; others express emotions produced in themselves by these images. Shoghi Effendi, however, having the most perfectly balanced temperament, could combine these two qualities and reproduce in his writings both images and emotions. In

35

illustration it would suffice to consider his translation of Nabíl's Narrative, *The Dawn-Breakers*, and his own historical narrative *God Passes By*, to evaluate the power of his style, the potency of his prose and the gripping pathos of his narration.

Much more could be said about his unique translations, such as those of the major Writings of Bahá'u'lláh: *The Book of Certitude*, *Epistle to the Son of the Wolf*, *Prayers and Meditations*, *Gleanings from the Writings of Bahá'u'lláh*, and others.* To translate from one language to another is an art which requires knowledge, imagination and perfect mastery of both languages involved. For many years I struggled with translation into English from Italian, and vice versa, so that I well know the tremendous difficulties encountered in retaining the style, form and character of the original text—the hallmarks of the personality of the author— in the process of transferring these characteristics into another language that possesses a different grammatic structure and may, at times, lack the corresponding noun or adjective or verb used by the author. There are words in one language that cannot be translated into another because they actually do not exist. If we but consider therefore, from this point of view, Shoghi Effendi's translations into English from either Persian or Arabic—two flowery languages so rich in imagery and abundant in synonyms, the structure of which is so different from any modern European language—we can then better understand the immensity of his labour and the greatness of his accomplishment.

Classical English, as used by the luminaries of English literature, is quite different from the style evolved by Shoghi Effendi to convey the mystic and heavenly meanings of prayer, praise, adoration, aspiration, tranquillity, contentment, fulfilment, joy and the inevitability of God's will. His translation of the prayers and meditations revealed by Bahá'u'lláh is like the mystic chanting of the Orient with all the fragrance of the exotic land of their origin, moving as by a mysterious impulse on the capable wings of the versatile English idiom. It is the highest form of poetry instilled with the divine substance of exaltation and anguish, of sorrow and hope. My pen fails to render due homage to such creative work,

* See Appendix III.

which brings joy to the hearts of countless followers and friends of the Bahá'í Revelation.*

ORIGINAL LITERARY WORK

In Shoghi Effendi's own writings, the flowery language of his translations is transformed into a poignant prose containing a high note of urgency and finality. He makes use of long sentences as a means of penetrating into the depth of the reader's soul, and it becomes evident that the writer, being so attentive, so precise and so well informed, uses the long sentences not casually but with a definite artistic intent and to fulfil a specific expressive function. Long sentences are similar to monologues with oneself. They are full of passages and discourses, and are yet objective, detached and peculiar to the writer who plunges himself into and lives in his subject matter, thus giving it a life from within.

For instance, *God Passes By* is a flaming narrative. The character and qualities of the innumerable personages in it spring from the personages themselves and not from the author's fantasy. Like a precious and veritable gift from God, Shoghi Effendi's writing is an infinite, passionate cry from his innermost noble soul: the need to relate with great force and vehemence, without pause or rest, the greatest epic of the millennium. One can well sense that the underlying element of urgency is motivated by the inner impelling need to proclaim it, without delay, to all mankind.

The same standards of excellence appear in all Shoghi Effendi's writings, his messages, his letters—too many to mention here. Some one, some time, will diligently make a complete collation of whatever flowed from his great pen. Then from this *opera omnia* his personality will appear in all its perfection and beauty, as a figure carved from the purest marble by Phidias or Michelangelo.

AS HISTORIAN

I have already mentioned Shoghi Effendi's keen interest in history. It is befitting to his memory to illustrate further the fertility

---

* The interested reader may consult *Prayers and Meditations by Bahá'u'lláh*, which contains one hundred and eighty-four of these matchless translations.

of his mind as it manifested itself in his interpretation of past
world events and of man's wisdom and unwisdom manifested
over the centuries. Night after night, at dinner, when pilgrims
from many parts of the world partook of their evening meal at the
Guardian's table, there flowed forth in his talks a succession of
clear, accurate statements on facts and events ranging in time
from the early days of biblical history to that very day. These
revealed the depth of Shoghi Effendi's knowledge of the history
of the world and of the alternate advances and reverses of mankind. They also revealed the adaptability of his views and deduc-
tions as related to demography, statistics, nations, races, creeds,
traditions, arts, and aspirations of the peoples of the world. It
was always a delightful surprise to hear him talk with such
authority and exactness on historical matters which covered the
whole earth. Having myself received a European education based
mainly on the Greek and Roman cultures, I was astounded at
the broad as well as profound wealth of information he possessed and used with such care and acumen in discussing crises
and situations whose background went far back into the past.
In both his writings and his table talks Shoghi Effendi felt the
need to assert with assurance the signs of the new victories
achieved through the spiritual flowering of a new Dispensation. Well he knew the causes of events. In the depths of
his thoughts and with the keenness of his perception, he
conceived them as a whole, and related the saga of inspiring
and electrifying happenings in his poetic, concise and vigorous
style.

His knowledge was by no means limited to the history of the
great religions of the world, but included as well the circumstances of the rise and fall of all great civilizations since men started to
record them, and, in particular, the situation of the world since
the advent of the Bábí Dispensation. The crystal clarity of his
grasp of the whole field of human endeavour was always evident
in the way he related events of the past to problems and needs of
the present and the future, and kept myself and those privileged
to be in his presence spellbound and spiritually filled to capacity.
Many nights I sat at the table eagerly anticipating the silver

stream of eloquence that flowed from a seemingly fathomless spring, with a dazzling brilliancy. Much, very much indeed, I learned during those fleeting months. It was a daily experience that reinforced and consolidated my link with the one who was skilled in the use of all the instruments needed to heal the ills of the world. As a master of pragmatic history, he indicates in all his writings the way to correct mankind's errors of the past by applying Bahá'u'lláh's regenerating remedies, and he foretells the difficulties that would result from neglecting to apply these remedies.

I have already mentioned some of Shoghi Effendi's writings, but I would refer the reader to all of his works, to appraise in their fullness his foresight and wisdom, which illumined the occurrences of the past in the light of the present day's needs and aspirations.

Outstanding as an example of his historical perspective is the Introduction to *The Dawn-Breakers*. It contains a concise and brilliant history of Islám, to inform the reader concerning the forms and elements which concurred to set the stage on which the deeply moving drama of the Báb's Revelation was played. Many a time, during his table conversation, to illustrate some points, he would accurately quote from that particular book, or from *God Passes By*, or some other of his writings, often showing surprise or perplexity at the limited information, or lack of it, of some of his listeners. The footnotes of *The Dawn-Breakers*, some of which are in French, are another example of his talent in the field of historical research. To appreciate the tremendous background of knowledge he possessed at the time of his translation of that book, it suffices to glance at the titles and authors of the fifty-five books he consulted, as listed in the Appendix. In addition, one finds in his own handwriting the genealogy of the Báb, showing connection with Bahá'u'lláh's descendants, and presented on a fivefold sheet of paper twenty-six inches long.* The genealogy is prepared with scrupulous care, and shows the ramifications of the families, including names known to every Bahá'í as well as names unknown to the average believer, but which Shoghi Effendi brought to

* The genealogy appears only in the American edition.

mind with great facility.* Always amazing was his inexhaustible memory and the ease with which he recalled episodes, placing personages in their proper positions, with all their particulars of names, backgrounds and degrees of relationship. It was like reliving the spellbound days of my childhood when my aged and learned tutor would narrate the legendary feats of Greek mythology, with gods and people brought alive by his fascinating word pictures.

In Europe it is customary to mention our ancestors with pride, as a means of establishing a social status befitting our heritage and, all too often, our ambitions. Shoghi Effendi, on the contrary, was reserved about his unique ancestry and, as far as I can remember, never made any reference to it, as if it were a precious possession to be jealously and secretly guarded, but unconnected with himself. The type of authority based on lineage and tradition, such as existed among the crowned heads of the past, and still exists among the few remaining rulers and heads of religion today, was quite alien to Shoghi Effendi's nature. He accepted the Guardianship, not as a mere hereditary right but as the most priceless trust any human being could receive. In this lay the substantial difference between himself and the disaffected members of his immediate family.

The accurate, scholarly arrangement of the genealogies of the Báb and Bahá'u'lláh, with their many details, and their precise transliteration implying a perfect command of Persian and Arabic, should suffice to convince any reader of the high merits and qualifications of Shoghi Effendi as a true historian.

CORRESPONDENCE

We cannot leave this subject of Shoghi Effendi's writing without mentioning another of his activities which engaged him for long hours, greatly taxing his health and strength. I refer to the enormous correspondence he had to carry on with believers

* See Appendix IV. The genealogy of the Báb is also to be found in *The Bahá'í World*, vol. IV, facing p. 234, and in vol. V, facing p. 203. An even greater labour, the genealogy of Bahá'u'lláh, also in Shoghi Effendi's handwriting, is included in *The Bahá'í World*, vol. V, facing p. 205. It is printed on a sheet of paper forty-six inches long, folded eight times.

throughout the world who wrote to him directly on thousands of different and, alas, at times immaterial subjects. For years he carried on this correspondence alone, assisted by a member of the immediate family or others. After his marriage in 1937 his wife, Rúḥíyyih Khánum, proved herself the most efficient helpmeet to him and assisted him in this onerous task. Every day, however, it claimed more and more of his energy.

All the letters he has written—and they may number many thousands—are the essence of equity, wisdom and spirituality and are, at the same time, literary gems.* His letters demonstrate that he was a true sovereign, the most noble person of the twentieth century. He never denied the light of his wisdom and of his warm rewarding love to anyone who wrote to him. Those pilgrims who visited the Holy Land during the later years of his ministry became familiar with the sight of one devoted believer who, early in the morning, would return from her first visit to the post office in Haifa with a large basketful of correspondence addressed to the Guardian.

When inquirers presented personal problems, Shoghi Effendi would answer in such an objective, kind and regal manner as to strengthen their faith and give them new hope. He would relate each problem to its wider aspect and thus lift it, and the inquirer, to a broader vision.

The thousands of questions put to him, either from the Institutions (the Administrative bodies) of the Faith or from individuals, were promptly and explicitly answered. On any given subject, concerning any aspect of the Teachings, of the Administration, or on personal problems, the answers, even at intervals of many years, were identical in concept. After the Guardian's passing, when I entered his room as one of the Hands of the Cause of God who went there to search for any directions he might have left, I was exceedingly surprised to find there was no master file or copies of letters, and to realize that the constancy of his answers was another of the unfathomable prodigies of the incredible mind

* The Universal House of Justice, in their Statistical Report entitled *The Nine Year Plan, 1964–1973*, pp. 8–9, state that they have record of Shoghi Effendi's replies to some 26,000 letters. They hold, in originals or authenticated copies, 14,430 letters which he wrote.

and guidance of Shoghi Effendi. This constancy was and is proof of his vast, complete, orderly and deep knowledge of the Sacred Writings, of his steadfast adherence to the principles and laws of the Faith, and, above all, of that conferred infallibility inherent in his station of Guardianship.

This characteristic is not the singular trait of an ordinary man but is an exemplary firstness, in the realm of objectivity and justice, of a human being who received his strength and vision from the unexplorable world of the Spirit. He possessed principles and virtues that were sublime and memorable; his actions could not be limited by the indetermination that often springs from the happening itself, but must be considered a unique bounty from God the Almighty.

It should be emphasized again, that he bore this tremendous burden of carrying on correspondence with the whole world on all the affairs of the Cause single-handed and alone. His heroic individuality was epitomized by this great virtue.

Moreover, in addition to answering the flood of correspondence directed to him, there are letters, messages and cablegrams addressed by Shoghi Effendi to the National Spiritual Assemblies of the Faith throughout the world, as well as his equally voluminous correspondence carried on with the Institutions of the Faith and the friends in Persia. For the Orient he used a loftier, more deeply spiritual and mystical language which lifted the hearts of a people who, for centuries, had been downtrodden and oppressed. Today his supplications, which are of the highest and most perfect beauty, are chanted by the believers there. They represent the agony of his own soul for the long-suffering and unfortunate brethren of the land of his ancestors.*

Had we a thousand lives to live, we could never fully repay Shoghi Effendi with enough love and gratitude for the beauty, inspiration and perfection of his literary work.

HIS ARTISTIC INGENUITY

The deep interest Shoghi Effendi had in geography and history has already been mentioned, as well as his vast knowledge of the

* For the genealogy of Shoghi Effendi, see Appendix IV.

world. Before his eyes he kept perpetually a wide vision of victories in the making and of victories he planned; like a strategist, he used maps of two hemispheres, singling out continents, nations, regions, islands and localities to be conquered with the blessings of the Faith of Bahá'u'lláh, the Faith which he so nobly represented. He possessed unrivalled ingenuity in making advantageous use of these maps that presented the whole globe at a glance and, with the deep insight of a true leader, he would make his plans on them, marking them with a variety of symbols and colours to reveal at sight the world situation of the Cause of God. Nothing escaped him. Everything was accurately recorded with the precision of a research scientist.*

The word ingenuity has been used, because Shoghi Effendi was richly endowed with the ability to devise ways of presenting his ideas with beauty, grandeur and prestige, as well as with durability and effectiveness. This talent will become more evident in all its magnitude when his monumental conception for beautifying the World Centre of the Faith in the twin cities of 'Akká and Haifa is considered.

Twice it was my good fortune to handle the reproduction of two maps which Shoghi Effendi made to show to the Bahá'í world the goals and progress of the Ten Year Crusade: the ten year international Bahá'í teaching and consolidation plan, 1953–1963, and the victories won during the first five years of this plan, 1953–1958. The original maps entrusted to me for reproduction were drawn by Shoghi Effendi's own hand. They represented the entire world, including the Arctic and Antarctic regions. By the ingenious and artistic use of well-conceived lines, colours, circles and other symbols, Shoghi Effendi presented on these maps (each one thirty-eight inches by twenty-two inches) the whole content of hundreds of pages of printing.

The first original was brought to me in Italy by a pilgrim returning from the Holy Land in the latter part of 1952. It had to be reproduced in time to be annexed to the booklet *The Bahá'í Faith 1844–1952: Information Statistical and Comparative*, to be published

---

* It was at his suggestion that informative maps of the progress of the Faith appeared regularly in *The Bahá'í World*, beginning with vol. V (1932–1934).

simultaneously in London and in Wilmette. It was also intended for the Intercontinental Teaching Conferences held in Kampala, Chicago, Stockholm and New Delhi in 1953, and for the twelve National Bahá'í Conventions held in April of that same year. Knowing the reluctance of the Italians in general to print anything of which the Church of Rome may disapprove, I had to move wisely and cautiously to find a printer in Italy who would undertake to carry out the project without fear or eventual regret. After some unsuccessful attempts, when I was turned down for incredible reasons, I was able to locate a firm which agreed to execute the work. Map printing is an art in itself. It requires special machinery which at that time was not readily available in a country that was slowly recovering from the ravages of a disastrous war. It is interesting to recall the curiosity of various men assigned to the work at the printing plant. They asked me veiled questions at every opportunity but were unable to understand either the importance or the future world significance of the contents of such a map. They felt they were working on something special and, although I had clearly explained the nature of the design, they always suspected that its scope was far beyond its simple and obvious purpose. There is a law in Italy which requires that three copies of anything printed in any manner or form be sent to the police. Thus the conscience of the workers was quite assuaged.

As soon as the first copies of the first map came off the press, a sample was sent to Shoghi Effendi. It was swiftly acknowledged with a cable of thanks and praise. Instructions for a second printing were received in the spring of 1953, thus necessitating my presence in Italy and preventing my taking part in the Intercontinental Conference held in the United States.

The second map was prepared by Shoghi Effendi during the summer months of 1957. It was his practice to gather information continuously, which he kept up to date in his copy of the statistical book already mentioned, interpolating new pages to keep the flow of additions in systematical order. Later, in November 1957, when I saw his book after his passing, it was double its original thickness. He had been so pleased at the development of the first four and a half years of the Ten Year Crusade that, in his message of October 1957 (which was to be his very last), he called for the holding of five Intercontinental Conferences in 1958. At this time the second map, depicting the victories with true originality and accuracy, was to be presented.

When, on 4 November 1957, the light of the world was dimmed by his passing, and I rushed to London at the request of Rúḥíyyih Khánum, the map had just been finished. On entering his room, the day after his passing, I saw it lying on two small mahogany tables that had been drawn together to make the necessary wide space available. Coloured pencils, pens, penknife, eraser, rulers and a compass were lying to the right of the map, just as he had left them when, in the late afternoon of the previous day, turning to Rúḥíyyih Khánum, he had said: 'The map is now finished'.

The next morning he winged his flight to the Kingdom on High, but the map was there, to testify to his love for mankind and to what he had created to bring about its unity.

With my eyes filled with tears and with agony in my heart I beheld the noble handiwork of the peacemaker, the healer of humanity, the mender of divisions, the architect of the immediate first steps that would usher in the World Order of Bahá'u'lláh in all its glory. Rapidly, with the speed of light, my mind raced back into the recesses of time, to the divisive forces that had brought mankind to the present abyss of antagonisms, conflicts and despair. Christianity, which had come to the world as a light in the deep darkness of paganism, began its decline early in its history, when theological differences brought the first divisions. Through the centuries the manipulations of men weakened the structure of that Holy Faith and its unity, culminating in further fragmentation brought on by the Reformation and the irreconcilability of the many sects of one original Revelation. No leader of Christianity, or of Islám, had ever made a definite and clear plan for the permanent unity of mankind based on love and understanding in the spirit of dedication to one God. But there, in that dimly-lighted room, was irrefutable proof that the first steps in a world-wide fusion of nations, races and creeds had been successful, and that Bahá'u'lláh's divine design of global unity had been at work under the directives of its able and dedicated leader and Guardian, Shoghi Effendi. Wherever men had become divided, separated, disunited or disconnected, the gentle healing hand of Shoghi Effendi had planted the seeds of unity, co-operation, harmony, hope, faith and virtue.

In the following months this second map was copied by hand, and taken to the various Intercontinental Conferences of 1958, where it was exhibited to the friends. Then it was again entrusted to me for printing in Italy, to be available in time for the Centenary Jubilee in London, 28 April to 2 May 1963, and to be annexed to the statistical book* compiled by the Hands of the Cause of God in the Holy Land. This time it was an inventive and sympathetic printer who did the work with keen interest and swiftness.

The genius of Shoghi Effendi is evident when one looks at the infinite details, the variety of colours and symbols used to give at first glance the incredibly vast results of the first five years of the World Crusade.

In considering some of the world events which have taken place since Shoghi Effendi's passing, we cannot but marvel now at man-made plans and events which clearly appear to be the aftermath of his vision. These maps clearly show the practical unfoldment of Bahá'u'lláh's World Order, with all the manifold goals set for the spiritual rebirth of this globe. For many decades pioneers—a veritable army—have gone to far-away lands, leaving homes, families and interests, not with the mirage of glory or notoriety or sudden wealth before them, and often without the essentials even of a modest, simple way of life, because they have been set on fire by the love of God and want to bring comfort, solace and joy to all with whom they come in contact. Some of the places to which these pioneers have gone were not shown on the usual maps, but it seems that as soon as they appeared on Shoghi Effendi's map they suddenly flared into public news as regions needing the attention of the world.

As harbingers of a new social pattern these pioneers travelled to thousands of localities, forgetful of themselves, willing to

* *The Bahá'í Faith, 1844–1963: Information Statistical and Comparative.*

contribute with heart, soul and body to the redemption of their fellow men suffering under political and social structures erected centuries ago, when men had little understanding of the ways and will of the Creator. For many centuries missionaries have gone into the wilderness to bring relief from sorcery, disease and ignorance, but their sacrifices—as proved by recent events in both Asia and Africa—have been vitiated to a large degree by the sectarianism of their denominations, by their intervention in political affairs and by their involvement in factional struggles.

Bahá'í pioneers, since the dawn of this new Revelation, and as deployed by Shoghi Effendi, have trodden every continent and island, to bring the light of unity among the children of man, by helping to tear down artificial and unnatural barriers erected by superstitions and prejudices and by reaching out friendly hands to the untouchable, the downtrodden, the afflicted, the illiterate, and to those discriminated against by reason of creed, race and colour. The Bahá'í pioneers are helping to raise these people to a new level of human dignity and are opening to them vast areas of better and enduring human relations.

Little did men know of, much less realize, the necessity envisaged by Shoghi Effendi, and indicated by him in his maps, to place ambassadors of goodwill wherever possible, as bearers of the divine Message of human sublimation! In the most recent years the United States of America, in creating the 'Peace Corps', has walked in the footsteps of the forerunner of universal solidarity, Shoghi Effendi. He knew that he had to reach the people of the world quickly, during the span of a few decades, and he himself set the example, because he dearly loved not only the followers of Bahá'u'lláh but all the members of the human family. He exposed himself to overwork, fatigue and hardship, and shortened his natural life-span to obtain for them what his heart had adopted as the goal of their happiness.

Most of the Bahá'ís never met Shoghi Effendi, but they knew he loved them more than he loved his own life. Many were inspired by his contagious enthusiasm and the sublimity of the objectives he set for those fleeting decades, scattered over the highways and by-ways of the world, to kindle anew the love for

God as reflected upon man. Over and over again he demonstrated that he was living on faith, and faith alone. And after he placed on his last map the spiritual victories won during the last five years of his tormented and laborious earthly life, his noble heart was stilled forever in that hotel room in London.

The original maps, and other maps which Shoghi Effendi had drawn but never released to the Bahá'í world, were bound in a cover of linen cloth by a skilful bookbinder and are now in Haifa, in the International Bahá'í Archives, for safekeeping. They remind us, as well as future generations of Bahá'ís, of the spirit of enterprise and ingenuity and devotion of our beloved Guardian, Shoghi Effendi.

PART II

The World Centre of the Faith of Bahá'u'lláh

V

Birth and Development of the World Centre

ALMOST one year before the end of the First World War, the Balfour Declaration,* made in the name of the British government, favoured a national home for the Jewish people in Palestine. Since the conquest of that land by the Caliph 'Umar—twelve years after the Hijra (A.D. 622, the first year of the Muslim era)—a succession of Islamic dynasties had ruled over the entire Middle East, until the fall of the Ottoman Empire in 1922, an Empire that had extended from Turkey and the Balkans to Morocco on the Atlantic Ocean. Thus it had been impossible for the Jewish population, dispersed throughout the Old World, to return to their promised land. The Balfour Declaration brought a ray of hope that their 'diaspora' might end, although the Mandate, which was given to the British government by the League of Nations at the end of the First World War and which lasted until May 1948, could not favour or encourage the return of the Jews to Palestine. It had to maintain the *status quo*, because of the prevailing Muslim population in the whole territory.

When Bahá'u'lláh, His family and followers were exiled to 'Akká in 1868, Palestine was a stronghold of Sunní Islám. To understand how terrifying were the forces of opposition against any Faith, other than Sunní Islám, it suffices to recall the intermittent sufferings and persecutions inflicted upon Bahá'u'lláh† and those exiled with Him, from 1867 until 1908. It was the revolution of the Young Turks that finally brought an end to the era of tyranny and oppression. Nevertheless, the Omnipotent had already decreed such far-reaching changes that their realization has been a true source of wonder. The construction under the

* Arthur James Balfour, First Earl of Balfour (1848–1930), English philosopher and statesman.
† Bahá'u'lláh died in 1892.

most adverse conditions of the Báb's Sepulchre, on the site blessed and chosen by Bahá'u'lláh on Mt. Carmel, established the Spiritual Centre of the Bahá'í Faith on that holy mountain in the most dramatic and unassailable manner. Moreover, two decades earlier, Sulṭán 'Abdu'l-Ḥamíd, in person, by assenting to the request to inter the sacred remains of Bahá'u'lláh within the precincts of the Mansion of Bahjí, had suddenly and miraculously sanctioned the way to implant in the soil of the Holy Land a new, eternal Qiblih, a point of adoration for countless generations of followers of a regenerating, dynamic and universal Faith. Thus the 'twin cities' of 'Akká and Haifa potentially became the solid spiritual foundations of the evolving World Order of Bahá'u'lláh.

Much has happened since those days, and the splendour and beauty now surrounding the two Holy Places are the fruits of the vision and skill of Shoghi Effendi.

There is no doubt that he must have been seriously concerned about the political future of Palestine. In some of his messages mentioning the possibility of another world conflict, he expresses anxiety for events which might involve the World Centre of the Faith. I well remember that one evening, at table, Shoghi Effendi related the information imparted by 'Abdu'l-Bahá concerning the erection of a befitting sepulchre for the Báb that would be worthy of a Prophet of God. Shoghi Effendi therefore felt that it fell upon him, the Guardian of the Cause of God, to carry out these instructions when conditions would permit and the political situation would warrant undertaking such a permanent and costly project.

When the devouring flames of the Second World War enveloped the whole earth, the situation in the Middle East became fraught with danger, threatening the very core of the Spiritual Centre of Bahá'u'lláh's Faith. But again, God's plan operated to protect men and possessions, bringing a solution which even today, at thirty years' distance, can only be considered the result of an intervention of Divine Providence. Palestine and all the Middle East were spared the scourge and destruction of war, thus permitting the planning of new developments at the World Centre of the Faith of Bahá'u'lláh.*

* See Appendix V for details.

In the forefront of Shoghi Effendi's greatest goals and accomplishments in the Faith must be considered the enhancement and beautification of the Holy Places connected with the lives of the Central Figures of the Bahá'í Faith. The setting is Mt. Carmel. No doubt those followers of past religions who came to this holy mountain were fascinated by its great beauty, made interesting by rugged rocks spread over its face like flocks of reposing sheep; by the myriads of wild flowers of incomparable grace and variety, and by its crystal clear skies and the blue Mediterranean Sea. This holy mountain, in a land that for millennia has influenced man's evolution and thinking, was destined to become anew the centre of miraculous developments leading to the regeneration of all mankind.

Bahá'u'lláh was brought to Palestine in 1868 as a prisoner of the rulers of the Persian and Turkish governments. During the long years of His sufferings and bondage it was not timely to provide an appropriate and dignified resting-place for the remains of the martyred Herald of His Revelation, the Báb, nor even to prepare an adequate place for this purpose in the Holy Land. During the last years of His life, however, He visited Haifa and pitched His tent on the slopes of Mt. Carmel. On one such occasion He expressed to His eldest son, 'Abdu'l-Bahá, the wish that a worthy memorial and resting-place be erected on the spot designated by Him, near a cluster of cypress trees.[5] These trees are still standing today, in great beauty and dignity, on the upper level of the ground south of the Shrine of the Báb, now part of the enchanting gardens surrounding that Holy Edifice.

The eagerness of 'Abdu'l-Bahá to comply with Bahá'u'lláh's instructions brought to Him, in His turn, additional and untold suffering, which He summarized in the following remark: 'Every stone of that building, every stone of the road leading to it, I have with infinite tears and at tremendous cost, raised and placed in position.'[6] In God Passes By, Shoghi Effendi enumerates some of the problems that beset 'Abdu'l-Bahá in His efforts to erect the Báb's Sepulchre, a strong building of Palestinian stone, of simple architecture, necessarily reinforced by buttresses—this prompted His enemies to accuse Him of building a fortress and a store for ammunition—and provided with heavy, majestic iron doors and multiple windows.

To describe the situation existing in Palestine during the last decades of the nineteenth and the first of the twentieth centuries is beyond the purpose of these recollections, but I wish to mention briefly what I learned from Shoghi Effendi himself. In his childhood and youth he witnessed the end of an era in a land overrun by tyranny, plagued by corrupt government, epidemics and poverty.

'There were no opportunities available in those years,' he once stated, 'because the collapse of the military, cultural and political structure of the Ottoman Empire was at hand, and the signs of the imminent disintegration of the last vestige of an ancient glory were evident even to my young eyes.'

These were the trying conditions under which the beloved Master, 'Abdu'l-Bahá, had to fulfil His mission, single-handed, opposed by a relentless foe, and with all His fortitude and strength undermined by forty years of privation and discomfort.

The Báb's remains arrived in 'Akká at the beginning of the year 1899, after almost fifty years of removal from hiding-place to hiding-place. The ascension of Bahá'u'lláh had taken place seven years earlier; during His lifetime He had arranged for several transfers of the remains to ensure their safety. But it was left to 'Abdu'l-Bahá personally to gather the precious dust of the Martyr-Prophet, and place it with His own hands in the Mausoleum He had erected for that purpose on the slope of Mt. Carmel, at the spot designated by Bahá'u'lláh Himself. Interment of the Báb's remains took place on the evening of the Feast of Naw-Rúz, 1909, one year after 'Abdu'l-Bahá's release from imprisonment and bondage.

Shoghi Effendi, as a youth of thirteen, had been an eye-witness of this historical and moving event. He related to me the whole episode of the placing of the Báb's luminous remains in the alabaster sarcophagus that had been donated and sent by the Bahá'ís of Rangoon, Burma. They were placed in the crypt in the now central room of the Mausoleum, which today consists of nine rooms, but at that time had only six rooms in two parallel rows, the crypt

EDITH MCKAY DE BONS AT THE WELL
of 'Abdu'l-Bahá's house, Haifa, *circa* 1915

CYPRESS TREES ON MT. CARMEL
where Bahá'u'lláh stood

THE CHAR-À-BANC OF 'ABDU'L-BAHÁ

VIEWS AT BAHJÍ IN THE EARLY YEARS OF THIS CENTURY
(*above*) The Shrine of Bahá'u'lláh and surrounding buildings
(*below*) The pine grove with the sea beyond

THE SHRINE OF BAHÁ'U'LLÁH AT BAHJÍ

(*above*) In the time of 'Abdu'l-Bahá
(*below*) After Shoghi Effendi developed the Ḥaram-i-Aqdas

THE SHRINE OF THE BÁB ON MT. CARMEL
(*above*) When 'Abdu'l-Bahá was directing its construction, *circa* 1904
(*below*) After Shoghi Effendi began to create the gardens, *circa* 1945

being then in the centre room of the row facing south. The heart-rending events that took place that night in that hallowed shelter, dimly illumined by candle light, were unfolded in precise and dramatic words which gave me a true vision of that long-awaited ceremony, the first stage in the unfoldment of many events to come, leading to the establishment of the World Centre of the Faith around that Sacred Spot.*

Transported by Shoghi Effendi's eloquent narrative I well understood the eagerness and urgency with which he had undertaken the construction of the outer Shrine of the Báb, which now graces the holy mountain. The hand of destiny made me his co-worker in securing the carved marble for that Holy Sepulchre in my native Italy, a privilege and honour that has blessed my mature years. That particular night, although I had already started on the work of obtaining and shipping the carved marble to Haifa, I realized more than ever how Shoghi Effendi had the ability to surmount any obstacle that came his way, shedding his inspiration and loving guidance in all directions. During the nine years (1948–57) that I assisted him in securing the material for the Báb's Shrine and the International Archives, I became more and more aware of the power emanating from his spiritual dynamism, which assisted me in overcoming serious difficulties threatening, at the time, the continuance and completion of the work.†

That same evening Shoghi Effendi related how, on 25 December 1939, thirty years after the interment of the Báb's remains and following a well-conceived plan, he had entrusted to the sacred soil of Mt. Carmel, not far from the Báb's Shrine, the bodies of the Purest Branch and the mother of 'Abdu'l-Bahá. Their burial-places are also near those of 'Abdu'l-Bahá's sister and His wife, thus establishing the focal point of the Bahá'í administrative institutions of the World Centre of the Faith. While Shoghi Effendi was relating these vital episodes in the historical

---

* See Shoghi Effendi's letter of 29 March 1951, entitled 'Spiritual Conquest of the Planet', for an explanation of the significance of the World Centre and the Shrine of the Báb. (*Citadel of Faith*, pp. 91–8.)
† See 'An Account of the Preparatory Work in Italy', *The Bahá'í World*, vol. XII, pp. 240–6.

E

development of the Faith in the Holy Land, I could strongly feel his anticipation of great things to come.

His enthusiasm, always an element of his eloquence, lent a deep tone of certainty to the exposition of his plans for the future, not only at the World Centre but also throughout the whole globe. As on previous occasions when I was privileged to listen to his enumeration of far-reaching plans for the expansion of the Faith he so much loved, my soul was filled with awe and gratitude, for he was indeed the master-builder of the World Order of Bahá'u'lláh.

As my recollections return on the wings of memory, I feel again that sense of joyfulness and elation which was with me whenever I was near him, a mysterious, unbreakable bond that influenced and guided me in all the manifold activities he called upon me to perform. It was not personal magnetism, but the influence of the spiritual force that constantly emanated from him, a power made up of inspiration, insight, understanding, acquiescence, faith, vision and, above all, of full reliance upon the divine assistance of the Omnipotent.

The task of erecting the outer building surrounding the Shrine of the Báb was not a simple one, under the conditions prevailing at the conclusion of the Arab-Israel conflict in 1948. Shoghi Effendi was fully aware of the almost insurmountable obstacles he had to face in order to carry out the diligently prepared architectural project in which time had to play the most important role.

Very little has been written concerning Shoghi Effendi's plans, inaugurated well before the erection of the outer Shrine of the Báb, except for his mention in God Passes By (p. 411): 'The dome, the final unit which, as anticipated by 'Abdu'l-Bahá, is to crown the Sepulchre of the Báb, is as yet unreared.' It is quite evident, however, from the vast and extremely beautiful grounds now gracing the environs of the Shrine, that the development of the gardens and of other buildings in its immediate vicinity was a continuous process in his mind, dating from the early days of his Guardianship when, in messages addressed to the Bahá'ís in the Western Hemisphere, he stressed the importance of donations of funds to enable him to purchase additional land around the Shrine. The manner in which he developed the gardens, leaving spacious areas on which other buildings could be erected, is definite proof that he was carrying out a well-envisioned plan for development and establishment of the spiritual and administrative seats of the World Centre of the Faith.

It is a saga of joy and dismay, of victories and delays, of hope, persistence and vision which if fully narrated would soften and conquer every heart. In the centuries to come, it will be seen that this enterprise, as embodied in this glorious and almost impossible task, was accomplished only by the will and determination of Shoghi Effendi. His boundless foresight and his indefatigable labours were the Pole star of his existence, by which he surmounted the difficulties and obstacles that very often opposed and threatened his plans during all the years of his stewardship.

In the months I spent in the Holy Land during the spring and early summer of 1952, when construction of the outer building surrounding the original Shrine was progressing with considerable difficulty—entailed by the illness and subsequent death of its architect, William Sutherland Maxwell, and by the serious illness of the building's contractor who was never able to return to the work—I learnt from Shoghi Effendi's own lips the magnitude of his vision and determination to create on Mt. Carmel the Spiritual Capital of the very first universal Faith. He often cited passages from the Tablet of Carmel,* and I became aware that each word of the text of this Tablet was ever present in his mind, as the inspiration guiding him in the vast and magnificent development of that area which, alas, was not to be completed by himself. A glimpse of the glory to come is given in his message dated 27 November 1954.†

His oft-repeated, rather critical references to the present neglected condition of the spiritual centres of both Christianity and Islám revealed his determination to enhance, in contrast, the ultimate beauty and future prestige of the World Centre of the

---

* See *Gleanings from the Writings of Bahá'u'lláh*, Sec. XI, for his translation of this Tablet.
† See *Messages to the Bahá'í World*, pp. 74–5.

Faith, which he so earnestly and lovingly had evolved in his mind and was eagerly trying to bring into reality on Mt. Carmel.

If the Master, 'Abdu'l-Bahá, had met with infinite difficulties in the erection of the inner building of the Báb's Shrine, it is certain that Shoghi Effendi had to face and carry on under an equal if not greater share of obstacles, anxiety, material and financial problems. Only his patience, courage and unfailing faith enabled him to overcome them. With a grieved heart he refers to some of these 'recurrent crises' in that historic message to the believers in the United States and Canada dated 25 December 1938,* when racial animosity, strife and terrorism were interfering with the project initiated to preserve and extend the area surrounding the Sacred Spots on Mt. Carmel and with the flow of pilgrims, whom he considered the 'life-blood' of the heart and nerve centre of the world-embracing Faith of Bahá'u'lláh.

For every difficulty he conquered, his compensation in the joy of achievement was boundless. Day by day, with regular visits, he observed the erection of the superstructure. As the carved marble and granite were placed in position, piece by piece, block by block, his vision took form. The project became a living reality in all its beauty—beyond all expectation. His happiness could not be contained.

How well I remember the light of elation that radiated from his handsome face when we gathered at his table for the evening meal, during those days and months after the quadrangular colonnade had been completed in all its majesty and work had begun on the octagon with its slender minarets, like immense white fingers reaching into space as if supplicating the infinity of God's love. It was an unforgettable period of Shoghi Effendi's life: appointment of the Hands of the Cause of God; creation of the International Council, the forerunner of the Universal House of Justice; the projected birth of the twelfth National Spiritual Assembly (Italy–Switzerland); preparation for launching the Ten Year Global Crusade and the very first Intercontinental Conferences in four continents of the world; acquisition of land at Bahjí around the Shrine of Bahá'u'lláh and beautification of that land;

* See *The Advent of Divine Justice*, p. 4.

anticipation of completing the Báb's Shrine to coincide with the centenary of Bahá'u'lláh's first intimation of His Prophethood revealed to Him in the 'Black Pit' (or prison) of Ṭihrán; drafting by his own hand the cleverly devised map showing all the goals of the Crusade—these were like golden threads which he adroitly manipulated to weave a world-wide pattern of enterprises involving the ingenuity, interest and efforts of every follower of Bahá'u'lláh. All these activities were for him the source of an intense happiness and intimate satisfaction that spurred him forward in the practical execution of God's plan for mankind.

I beg the reader to pause for a moment and consider how the erection of the outer structure of the Báb's Shrine was an integral part of Shoghi Effendi's universal conception of the expansion of the Faith and of the consolidation of its institutions at its World Centre, so that the mighty 'Ark' of God would sail on the slopes of Mt. Carmel and bring thereon the 'people of Bahá'.*

On that particular evening to which I have referred, when Shoghi Effendi spoke to me alone, he expressed his deep sorrow that even the immediate members of his family had never understood his persistent efforts to beautify the grounds around the Shrine of the Báb, in anticipation of the day when the Great Shrine, desired by Bahá'u'lláh, would come into existence in all its regal splendour and beauty and be surrounded by gardens of loveliness and perfection, gardens already being laid out during the long years of patient waiting. 'Never,' he said, 'in the religious history of mankind has a Prophet of God been so highly honoured within a century of His Mission, by almost His own generation, and with so much love and world-wide concurrence.' Again, the flame of eager enthusiasm was lighting his face as he spoke.

I could then fully share with him the vision of the New Jerusalem, the new City of God, the Abode of Peace, and understand his labours around that Sacred Spot, urged on by the impelling necessity of preparing the haven in which the Ark of Salvation would sail.† To it the world would turn for spiritual guidance,

---

* See Appendix VI for a discussion of the Tablet of Carmel, which is the Charter of the World Spiritual and Administrative Centres of the Bahá'í Faith.

† See 'The Unfoldment of World Civilization', included in *The World Order of Bahá'u'lláh*, p. 194.

as the source of inspiration, of sincerity, of divine justice and illumination.

In retrospect we can see how much was accomplished in that brief period of years and why Shoghi Effendi seemed to be ever aware of the shortness of time in which so much had to be made ready. Of all the great qualities that adorned his character, zeal and eagerness were outstanding. These two virtues acted as spearheads for all his manifold and burdensome activities, keeping him abreast of events and material limitations, inspiring all who understood his plight and dedicated themselves, mind and body, to lighten his burden and help him bring into reality his long-range plans. So great was his appreciation that many times, grateful for the modest assistance I could render him, he would look at me with loving eyes and, smiling, would say, 'I wish there were one more believer like you.'

As the Faith expanded and its institutions multiplied under his far-sighted guidance, it was imperative that the Shrine and its environs—the fountain-head of inspiration—should evolve with great power, prestige and dynamic impulse. This is the reason that Shoghi Effendi could not spare any effort, or hesitate, or brook any delay. For him it was like racing through space toward a luminous star, when speed and skill were of supreme importance, with no turning back or change of heart. The Faith of God was in the balance, and the propelling power was coming from the Almighty Creator.

The golden threads, spreading and weaving through all continents, oceans and islands of the world—sustained and strengthened by that celestial power that he, the Guardian of the Cause of God, knew how to tap—were slowly but surely enmeshing the earth, each strand carrying with it the vibrations of understanding, compassion and love, issuing forth from the mystic heart of the Guardianship.

VI

The Queen of Carmel

ELEMENTS of wonder have all along dominated the establishment and embellishment of the World Centre of the
Faith of God. Reference has already been made to many of
the difficulties encountered by 'Abdu'l-Bahá and the Guardian in
the erection of the Tomb of the Báb during the first five decades
of this, the twentieth century. During this period the Spiritual
Centre of the Faith evolved from its embryonic stage—a dream-
like plan seconded by courage and perseverance—to the completion, in 1953, of the superb Shrine that now graces the slope of
Mt. Carmel. The plan of God conveyed to man through His
Messenger Bahá'u'lláh has taken shape and is unfolding in a
manner made possible only through the indisputable intervention
of a superhuman power, even as the forces of opposition and the
frailty of other human elements resisted, step by step, the realization of this heavenly project.

Not long after Shoghi Effendi assumed his stewardship as
Guardian, it was possible for him, through the munificent assistance of a dedicated 'Iráqí Bahá'í, Ḥájí Maḥmúd Qaṣṣábchí,* to
carry out the arduous task, already referred to, of adding three
rooms along the south side of the Báb's Sepulchre as originally
erected under the guidance of 'Abdu'l-Bahá in the early years of
the century. Thus the shape of the building was changed from an
oblong edifice to one perfectly square, which would better lend
itself, in time, to embellishment by addition of an outer structure
embodying the graceful, yet majestic and lofty features desired
by 'Abdu'l-Bahá to honour the resting-place of the Martyr-
Prophet who heralded the advent of Bahá'u'lláh.

The beloved Guardian personally supervised this work, which
required excavation of the mountain-side to make sufficient space
for the additional rooms; a work accomplished by the use of

* See his photograph, facing p. 87.

61

simple tools and man-power, a toilsome and risky enterprise without the help of modern, specialized machinery.

In these rooms Shoghi Effendi established the first International Bahá'í Archives, in which were lovingly gathered and displayed in orderly arrangements, by his own hands, the Writings, the relics, the personal objects, photographs and portraits associated with the Central Figures of the Faith. His keen concern in preserving for posterity such priceless treasures—marks of great prestige in the history of the Faith—inspired him to announce in 1952 plans for the construction of a yet larger and more suitable edifice to house, without limitation of space, the contents crowded into the enlarged Shrine of the Báb. As we shall see later, transfer of the precious objects to the new International Archives was done after his passing, for the building was completed just before his journey in the summer of 1957, from which he was never to return to Haifa.

The circumstances that brought Mr. William S. Maxwell to Haifa in 1941, after the passing of his beloved wife May,* fitted in well with the plans formulated by the Guardian. Considering the age and now the enforced loneliness of his illustrious father-in-law, Shoghi Effendi invited him to come to the Holy Land as soon as he could settle his affairs and depart from his native Canada. My wife and I were then living in New York City and, having known Mr. and Mrs. Maxwell for some time, we offered to assist him when he passed through, to depart on an Italian ship for Naples and then proceed by another vessel to Haifa. We spent some precious hours in our home with him, before accompanying him to the pier and on to the steamer to recommend him to the staff, to ensure that special attention would be extended to him during his voyage. It was a blessing that he could leave when he did, because some months later, after the Pearl Harbour attack, the world was plunged into another global war, and communication with Haifa became difficult for nearly five years.

William Sutherland Maxwell† was born in Canada, of Scottish

---

* Mrs. Maxwell died in Buenos Aires on 1 March 1940; the Guardian accorded her the station of a martyr.
† See memorial article in *The Bahá'í World*, vol. XII, p. 657–62.

ancestry. His keen interest in design, painting and architecture, in which he excelled when still very young, added greatly to his distinguished and gracious personality. Tall, vigorous but gentle, he emanated an air of assurance and trustworthiness, which must have moved Shoghi Effendi. With the arrival of Mr. Maxwell and his presence in Haifa, the problem of choosing an architect to transform the long-cherished wishes of Bahá'u'lláh and 'Abdu'l-Bahá into design was solved, through the bounty of God. Mr. Maxwell was a deeply devoted believer, a well-trained architect with forty years of experience both at home and abroad, a fine artist whose pen and brush could render, in lines and colours, the expression of an inspiration with much beauty.

When I beheld the design of the Báb's Shrine it seemed to me that here all architectural canons of East and West were blended into an original, yet classic style suggestive of the lineage of the Báb, the expectation of Islám for the coming of the Qá'im, the prophecies of the Qur'án, the masterly standards of Greek, Roman and Christian decorative arts, all blossoming into a structure demonstrating the pure spirit of unity of the Báb's own dramatic Ministry, His piety, His innocence and His martyrdom.

Many times after I first saw Mr. Maxwell's designs, during the execution of the work and after beholding the completed Shrine in all its majesty and loveliness, I have asked myself if it could have been possible to find another such sensitive architect, capable of equalling or even rivalling Mr. Maxwell's project in conception or execution. His whole-hearted collaboration with Shoghi Effendi's views, his sympathetic interpretation of the Guardian's wishes and counsel, the tender love originating at their first meeting many years before, all had now deepened into a feeling of true veneration and respect, which Shoghi Effendi reciprocated with his usual warmth and kindness.

After Mr. Maxwell passed away in March 1952, whenever Shoghi Effendi spoke of him one could easily detect a sense of deep sorrow and genuine affection for his valiant collaborator who had shared with him perhaps the most difficult period of his life. Mr. Maxwell's poise and good humour, his inventiveness, his dexterity, his profound love for beauty and harmony of forms

63

and figures alleviated Shoghi Effendi's problems, for the Guardian was also doing his utmost to complete the gardens around the Sepulchre of the Báb and the Monument gardens initiated a few years before, with greatly limited means, material and manpower at his disposal.

Little by little Shoghi Effendi entrusted Mr. Maxwell with many details for beautification of the grounds. Mr. Maxwell, in his turn, produced some of the most outstanding decorative structures, such as the carved stone and wrought-iron main gate to the Shrine gardens, the lesser gates of the Monument gardens, the stone and marble bases of ornamental amphorae, vases and eagles, the sets of marble steps connecting the different levels within the grounds, the iron lamp-posts and an infinite number of other embellishments that add to the atmosphere of rare beauty characteristic of all the Bahá'í Holy Places, in Haifa and 'Akká.

The chief and most important task assigned to Mr. Maxwell, however, was the drawing up of architectural plans for the outer structure of the Shrine of the Báb. After his arrival in Haifa, he set up a studio in one of the smaller rooms of the Western Pilgrim House at 10 Persian Street, and equipped it with his drawing-table and board, his instruments and other paraphernalia needed to give substance to the creative power animated by his unfettered imagination. When I saw this *atelier* some years later, I was greatly impressed by the magnitude of work accomplished in such a small space, to which the varied collection of drawings, sketches, plans and water-colour paintings testified. Mr. Maxwell had a genius for detail; there was not even the most minute particular of his project that did not become the object of special care, illustrated with skill and precision, to show how it would look in actuality. There was at that time such an abundance and variety of sketches and studies as would have graced the collection of an art lover. To conclude this appraisal of his ability and reputation, I will only add that when contracts were assigned in Italy for production of the carved marble for the Shrine of the Báb, and the plans and designs made by Mr. Maxwell were submitted to the contractors, exclamations of admiration and praise were uttered by the members of the architectural staff, which included some college and university professors, and by the sculptors who were to carve the marble.

Shoghi Effendi, in his eagerness, was always ahead of everyone else, and even as he truly envisioned future developments in the Cause of God, so he also was anxious to see for himself the actual reality of material things, such as buildings, construction, art work and the like. Whenever, in Haifa, I asked his approval of something that had to be done, he would say: 'Show me how it is going to look.' He was accustomed to seeing, well in advance, how something would look because of the rare ability of Mr. Maxwell's 'magic brush'.

Although restricted by the war raging in many parts of the globe, the Shrine project continued to develop during the three years between the arrival of Mr. Maxwell at the World Centre and the world-wide celebrations of the first centenary of the Declaration of the Báb. A succession of intensive studies, proposals, outlines, plans and sketches, with a myriad of details, were submitted to and discussed with the Guardian, in order to carry out faithfully the directives given by 'Abdu'l-Bahá. I wish I could convey to the reader a comprehension of the magnitude of the labours involved to create this monumental gem of rare beauty. The graceful structure, interspersed with delicate ornamentation, called to mind the glories of the Roman and Islamic schools of architecture combined into one harmonious conception.

On 22 May 1944, when the Bahá'ís of the Holy Land gathered together in the precincts of the Holy Sepulchre of the Báb, to celebrate the hundredth anniversary of His Declaration, the completed model of the project was unveiled, amid the great rejoicing of the beloved Guardian and all those present. It was a tangible embodiment of years of dreams, aspirations and labour, a precursor of the day when the 'noble and imposing structures' anticipated by Bahá'u'lláh in His Tablets, to be raised 'throughout the length and breadth' of the Holy Land, could be built.[5] This Centenary was an historic milestone, a 'turning point', which, in the Guardian's words addressed to the All-America Convention held at this time, was 'to commemorate alike the Anniversary of the founding of the Faith of Bahá'u'lláh and the Birth of 'Abdu'l-

Bahá, the [fiftieth] Anniversary of its establishment in the Occident. . .'.⁷

Mr. Maxwell had made two valuable artistic contributions at this time. The first was a 'rendition' (painting) in colour of the proposed structure, showing the landscaping of the immediate vicinity.* Copies of it were distributed by Shoghi Effendi to all National Spiritual Assemblies and were later graciously donated by him to pilgrims when the doors of pilgrimage were again opened, at the end of 1951.

Mr. Maxwell's second artistic contribution was the aforementioned model. It stood about two feet high and was a work representing great patience and ingenuity. Mr. Maxwell had to rely fully on his inventiveness in the use of paper to resemble marble and other materials to give a very real illusion of the actual building. When Mr. Maxwell came to Rome in 1948, he brought with him a photograph of this model. It served as the most effective argument to convince the contracting firm to undertake the execution of the work, because they readily understood that completion of this original and graceful structure would confer on them great prestige and secure for them other work throughout the world. I personally was so intrigued by the photograph that I was able to start a publicity campaign for the Faith in the Italian press by its use, as also later in the Netherlands. Thus years before the completion of the Sepulchre, it was possible to make the public aware of the Faith and of the existence of such an architectural gem in the Middle East. The model is now preserved, in the main hall of the Bahjí Mansion, to bear witness, for many years to come, to the resourcefulness and ingenuity of the valiant and beloved architect, William Sutherland Maxwell.

'Queen of Carmel enthroned (on) God's Mountain, crowned (in) glowing gold, robed (in) shimmering white, girdled (in) emerald green, enchanting every eye from air, sea, plain (and) hill.'⁸ With these words the Guardian described the completed Sepulchre of the Báb, in his joyous cablegram to the Fourth Intercontinental Teaching Conference in New Delhi, October 1953. Of all the renowned domes of classic architecture, Shoghi

* This appeared as a frontispiece in vol. IX (1940–1944) of *The Bahá'í World*.

66

Effendi most admired those of St. Peter's in Rome by Michelangelo, and of St. Paul's in London by Sir Christopher Wren. His guidance to Mr. Maxwell inspired the creation of a happy combination of the two, embodying the characteristic of regality.

The reader who has not yet visited the Holy Land and seen the Sepulchre of the Báb can readily discern the genius of such a conception by viewing photographs available in innumerable publications. Pilgrims who came to Haifa during the erection of the outer shell of the Shrine and those who came after its completion and until May 1957, often heard the beloved Guardian speak of it with delight and admiration. His frequent references to the Shrine, using words of exultation and infinite joy, in his various messages between 1948 and October 1953, when the Shrine was completed, give the impression that they are sung from his heart, much as a mountain climber on reaching the summit of a peak might break out into a song of glorification and thanksgiving for divine assistance received in accomplishing the impossible.

Similarly, expressions of gratitude and praise for the painstaking labours of Mr. Maxwell were broadcast by Shoghi Effendi to the Bahá'í world, so that all the friends might join with him in honouring the illustrious architect of the Sepulchre of the Báb.

VII

The Superstructure of the Shrine
of the Báb

EARLY in 1948, as soon as it was evident that a new State of Israel would emerge from the Palestinian territory then under a League of Nations Mandate to Great Britain, Shoghi Effendi decided that the proper moment had arrived to fulfil the long-delayed plan of erecting the final majestic Mausoleum as wished and longed for by Bahá'u'lláh. The Guardian, in his wisdom and far-sightedness, had been preparing for such a moment for many years.

Shoghi Effendi had given serious consideration to the possibility of using local Palestinian stone and Palestinian labour. Palestinian and Egyptian stone-cutters and carvers were truly skilled at continuing the ancient tradition which, in the past, had made them the best builders in the Middle East. They had also served well in preparing the stone for the Báb's Tomb erected by 'Abdu'l-Bahá, and for the gates that now grace UNO Avenue at the main entrance to the gardens surrounding the Shrine. The conflict, however, that flared up with cessation of the British Mandate provoked a mass exodus of nearly all artisans, and they had not returned. Under these circumstances, Italy was the next best choice, for there the tradition of stone quarrying and carving had been carried on for centuries. Mr. Maxwell, whom the Hand of Providence had placed in the unique position of being the one chosen to carry out the designs, was therefore sent by the Guardian to Rome to search both for material and for proficient craftsmanship.

Uncertainty of travel conditions made the time of his arrival rather indefinite, but one early forenoon in April 1948, after several fruitless journeys to Rome's Ciampino airport, I saw him come down the ramp from a Norwegian aircraft and greeted him with a welcoming embrace. With him was Mr. Ben D. Weeden, a Bahá'í from the United States then residing in the Holy Land, whose wife, Gladys, was also serving the Guardian. Mr. Maxwell's blue eyes were smiling as he said to me:

'You were the last to bid me farewell when I left for Europe in 1941, and you are the first to bid me welcome on European soil.'

Mr. Maxwell's stay in Rome was a great joy for my wife Angeline and me. We were living at that time in the Hotel Savoia, as no apartments were available at any price in the city still occupied by Allied forces. Mr. Maxwell, therefore, came to live in the same hotel. His grace and humour, the breath from the Holy Shrines he brought with him, and his unbounded love for the Guardian showered us with an abundant measure of reward and courage. He was our link with the Guardianship, not only because of the great honour bestowed on him through the Guardian's marriage to his own daughter, and because of the crown of martyrdom won by his beloved wife May, but also because of his appointment by the Guardian as the architect of the arcade and superstructure of the Báb's Sepulchre, an honour now reflecting upon my humble person in the association with him in execution of the project. I felt that an act of Providence had placed me in Italy, my former homeland, at this time of need.

Some time earlier, Mr. Maxwell had wisely written to his former associates in Canada to secure the addresses of some reliable marble dealers in Italy, and on receipt of the information he had written to a few firms hoping to receive some favourable answers.

The entire Italian nation, however, was then still suffering from the great destruction brought by the conflict on its soil. Public services were almost non-existent. All railroads had been severely damaged and the rolling-stock destroyed or confiscated. Shipping was at a standstill. Several millions of its population were still prisoners of war in nearly every continent of the globe. Food, electricity and water were rationed and practically unavailable. A pall of despair clouded the life of the entire country, with little hope of relief to assist in restoring the shattered economy and open the way for spiritual revitalization of its people. What was left of the nation's industrial power was mobilized to produce goods for reparations and for reconstruction of the country.

Because of these conditions only one answer to his inquiries was received by Mr. Maxwell, and even that was uncertain, as we learned later, for practically no marble quarries in the region of the Apuan Mountains of Tuscany, where the best statuary and finest marble is extracted, were open, and any skilled, specialized labour had been dispersed during the war.

Shoghi Effendi had instructed Mr. Maxwell to seek a marble or stone that would be durable over a period of five hundred years. Therefore we went to the Museum of Geology of the University of Rome, to examine in detail dozens of specimens of granite and marble, to select the ones most suited for the work under consideration. Great was our disappointment when, in the next few days, we learned that the quarries containing the marble samples selected could not be exploited, because their accesses had been blown up by mines placed by the retreating enemy. It would be many months and require large capital investments before the quarries could operate again.

Time, meanwhile, was a precious element. The Guardian had sent me verbal instructions to carry out the work as quickly as possible, as soon as a decision had been reached concerning the material and workmanship, and to ship the finished material at the earliest possible date to the Holy Land. These were standing instructions that remained in force throughout the five years needed to complete the Shrine. As time went by, the note of urgency was increased, and production was speeded up to an almost unbelievable, even miraculous, rate.

The only firm from which Mr. Maxwell had received a reply was that of Messrs. Guido M. Fabbricotti,* of Carrara, the marble capital of the world. How this firm came to send a reply is related in the following episode and is yet another illustration of the element of wonder that pervaded every stage of activity connected with the conception, planning and execution of this lofty project.

Mr. Fabbricotti himself, who had carried on the tradition of

* See Appendix VII.

the firm established a century before, had passed away a few years earlier, and its affairs were being conducted by his two sons-in-law, Colonel Bufalini and Dr. Orlando. A technical adviser and consultant was Professor Andrea Rocca who had graduated at the beginning of this century from the Academy of Beaux Arts (*Accademia delle Belle Arti*), of Carrara, and was a brilliant architect. His knowledge of granite, marble and other building materials, not only in Italy but also in many other parts of the world, could hardly be matched anywhere. He was born of a long line of marble craftsmen who, as he used to say, went back to the days of ancient Rome. During the lean post-war years, when there was practically no marble business, he called almost every morning on the various firms in Carrara, in the hope of finding something to do. One morning, in the early spring of 1948, he entered the Fabbricotti office as one of the two partners was crumpling in his hand what appeared to be a letter. As he threw it into the waste-basket, Professor Rocca asked:

'What is that you are throwing away?'

'Oh, it is only a preposterous request for information that sounds like a fable,' the partner answered; 'something about a grandiose mausoleum to be erected in the Holy Land! But who can build such a costly structure at this time? Let us forget about it.'

Architect Rocca bent forward and lifted the crumpled letter out of the waste-basket.

'Let us read this again, together,' he said.

As soon as he became aware of its contents, he felt it provided the opportunity of a lifetime. After some resistance he induced the officers of the firm to answer it, and to offer their services in whatever capacity needed. From that moment on, Architect Rocca became the enthusiastic and indefatigable supporter of the project. Some weeks later, Mr. Maxwell met him in Rome and felt immediately that the project could be accomplished with speed and with the least element of error by a skilled staff under Professor Rocca's supervision. Architect Rocca's devotion to the whole work became his second nature; his competence and knowledge were astounding. He and I made a team of travelling

71

surveyors to the quarries to select the perfect marble and to the *ateliers* where it was cut and carved with the highest degree of skill. After erection of the Shrine of the Báb was completed we teamed up again for the production of the marble needed to build the International Archives on Mt. Carmel. My association with him lasted well over ten years and taught me to appreciate and admire his great talent and versatility in doing things with marble. Through our association he learned much about the Revelation of Bahá'u'lláh, and his respect for the Cause and his love for Shoghi Effendi, in time, knew no bounds. When he passed away on 4 November 1967,* Italy lost one of its best architects of the old school.

Some days after Mr. Maxwell arrived in Italy, he decided to invite the principals of the Fabbricotti firm to meet with him, to learn to what extent they could be of service. This was the beginning of another chapter in the extraordinary and memorable enterprise devoted to the erection of the Shrine of the Báb.

THE ARCADE

From my conversations with Mr. Maxwell I understood that Shoghi Effendi had decided to build the outer structure of the Báb's Sepulchre in different stages, owing to the limited funds available at the time and to the political situation. Mr. Maxwell had been charged by the Guardian, therefore, to contract only for construction of the arcade that would completely surround the original edifice erected by 'Abdu'l-Bahá, to which the Guardian had added rooms to make a quadrilateral polygon, such as would lend itself to be encircled by a colonnade protecting the four sides of the Shrine. The arcade has also the purpose of creating an ambulatory or covered way, for circumambulation of that Holy Place. Furthermore, the arcade made it possible to extend the base of the original Shrine to support the superstructure proportional to the whole design.

In Hellenistic and Roman periods of architecture, colonnades were widely used in shrines and temples, particularly after the invention of the Roman arch. The colonnade was adopted in both

* Exactly ten years to the day after the passing of Shoghi Effendi.

72

Christianity and Islám for religious structures; for example, in the cloisters of Christian orders and the great mosques of Islám. When Mr. Maxwell arrived in Italy, our first search for marble and granite, therefore, was limited to the needs of the arcade, and our first consultations with the Fabbricotti firm were directed to ensuring that there would be enough material to complete the first stage of the construction. After the negative results of our inquiries concerning suitable material in the Carrara area, Professor Rocca brought us a ray of hope when he suggested the possible use of Chiampo marble which comes from the region of Venice and, strangely enough, from the geologic point of view, is very similar to the Palestinian stone available in the Holy Land. The Chiampo quarries are between Verona and Vicenza, the former well known as the locale of Shakespeare's tragedy *Romeo and Juliet* and the latter as the birthplace and theatre of action of the great architect, Andrea Palladio (1518–80).* Some millions of years ago this region was a sea atoll; it is still possible to find fish fossils embedded in stones now located at high elevation above sea level. A large quantity of marble, of various colours and structure, is now quarried there. In the arcade of the Shrine, Chiampo marble is used for the arches, capitals, walls, corners and balustrade.

The quarry for the beautiful granite needed for the columns, pilasters and bases—called Rose Baveno granite—is located high in the north-west Italian Alps, near the borders of Switzerland and France. Mr. Maxwell's design called for twenty-four columns and eight pilasters (for the corners), all monolithic as requested by Shoghi Effendi. Because this quarry was outside the war zone, difficulties encountered were only mechanical ones, which were solved by ingenuity and perseverance.

Architect Rocca was dispatched to the two quarries, and his expert opinion brought us much joy: granite and marble of the finest quality could be had, within a relatively short time. As is customary in the marble trade, the Fabbricotti firm wanted to celebrate the occasion by giving a dinner for Mr. Maxwell in one of the famous Roman hostelries where rare wines and inebriating spirits are part of the ritual. It was a surprise, and perhaps a relief,

* See Appendix X.

73

to them when the invitation was graciously declined and the reason explained. Our relationships then became better founded, as there was much appreciation on their part of the habit of temperance which, over the many years of collaboration, proved the basis of much respect for the Cause and admiration of its followers.

The days that followed were busy indeed, particularly for me. Drawings and plans were discussed in detail, and every word of the discussion had to be translated from English into Italian and vice versa, with absolute accuracy, in order to eliminate any misunderstanding or error. During the ensuing years until completion of the Shrine, all correspondence to or from the World Centre had to be translated precisely, with the myriad of technical details and terms upon which the success of the enterprise rested. The slightest oversight or error would have been fatal and costly. Several days were spent by the contracting firm in making calculations, so as to quote inclusive rates for the material needed, for the best workmanship possible in its preparation, and for its delivery in wooden packing cases on board ships leaving Italian ports for Haifa.

Several cablegrams had been sent to Shoghi Effendi to keep him informed of the negotiations, and when quotations for the first contract were sent and received his approval, the way was open for drafting this document. It was signed by Mr. Maxwell for the Guardian of the Faith, on 29 April 1948.* At the Guardian's request, a further contract was discussed, approved by him, prepared and signed on 5 May. Thus, both contracts were made even before the State of Israel was proclaimed.

These two contracts set in motion an army of specialists anxiously waiting for work. I must note that never again could we have found such a team of the most skilled, competent and artistic workers, had the construction of the Shrine been delayed by one or two years. Again Providence had made it possible to make use of special craftsmen who were idle because of lack of work!

In Pietrasanta, for example, we had the great fortune to secure the services of a yard well equipped to transform the blocks of raw

* This event is described in my article in *The Bahá'í World*, vol. XII, p. 240.

Chiampo marble into the ornamental components of the Shrine. This small city, in the pre-Apennine hills of the Apuan chain of mountains, has been the throbbing heart of the marble industry of Tuscany for a millennium, in its strategic position between the quarries and a railroad spur that comes to within a few hundred yards. Before the railroad spur was in existence, one of the Roman consular roads, the Aurelia, passed nearby, leading from Rome along the coast to Genoa. Michelangelo, when procuring huge blocks of marble for some of his masterpieces, had passed much time in Pietrasanta, and it seems that the spirit of artistry in shaping stones into beautiful forms has remained with the people of that area; they have, for generations, maintained the primacy and prestige of this noble art.

In this small city, then, a team of sixty men, chosen from a hundred or more firms engaged in marble work in that region, set to work on the Chiampo marble for the arcade. Many of these men were graduates of the best art schools of Italy; others were sculptors, of established reputation, who undertook the modelling in clay of all the ornamental parts, including the capitals of the columns and pilasters, the panels of the façade and the finials of the balustrade. Draftsmen enlarged to natural size the thousands of drawings of every block or stone or decoration, from Mr. Maxwell's designs, to enable the stone-cutters and carvers to reproduce every detail with absolute perfection.

The working-yard for the huge blocks of Rose Baveno granite was at the foot of the mountain where the quarry was located. Each block of granite, about four times the size of the beautifully shaped, gleaming column to be extracted from it, had to be taken down the mountain to the yard, with great difficulty.

The consultations that followed the signing of the first two arcade contracts prepared the way for a close collaboration between Mr. Maxwell, acting for the Guardian, and the contracting firm with its architects and technical experts. My role was to act as personal representative of the Guardian for selection of material, supervision of its artistic carving, for the packing and shipment of the finished work, for its insurance, and as the clearing agency for the voluminous mail and exchange of technical data.

75

On 15 May 1948, Mr. Maxwell and Ben Weeden flew back to the Holy Land, taking with them to Shoghi Effendi the assurance that at last, notwithstanding the apparent difficulties prevailing in Italy, the erection of the long-awaited Sepulchre of the Báb was a certainty. Immediately after their arrival, reports came that the Guardian was overjoyed and had started work to prepare the ground for the foundation of the arcade with further excavation of the mountain-side, as the new structure would expand the base of the edifice to a size practically double that of the existing Tomb. Shoghi Effendi took it upon himself to direct this difficult and arduous task. As in 1928–9, when the three rooms had been added on the south side of the original edifice, so now the mountain had to be hollowed out still more to accommodate the arcade, again without the proper excavating equipment. The cut-away mountain-side had to be reinforced by an almost vertical wall; tons and tons of rock had to be carted away; trees had to be removed with care to be replanted as soon as the new construction would permit; and innumerable marble tiles paving the walk around the Shrine, as well as huge vases and pedestals, floral plants and hedges, had to be removed and temporarily stored, later to be reinstalled. Shoghi Effendi's drive to finish this work anticipated the moment when the site he was so lovingly preparing would be filled, as if by magic, with the towering architectural gem he had seen depicted in Mr. Maxwell's model and colour rendition.

At the very beginning of the work in Italy, the Guardian had instructed me to send him photographs of all clay and plaster models of the intricate decorative parts, for his approval, before starting their execution in marble. Communication with the Holy Land was difficult; messages, photographs and construction plans had to be sent by unscheduled aeroplanes in parcels taken to the Rome airport, and called for at the airport in Haifa. There was a constant element of uncertainty. Fortunately, however, telegrams and cablegrams, accepted at the sender's risk, went through with some speed, and were only very exceptionally delayed. Thus, the fluidity of contact with the World Centre was maintained.

When Mr. Maxwell returned to the Holy Land he prepared, with the assistance of the engineer of the project, Dr. H. Neumann, a professor at Haifa's Technion, the structural plans for laying the foundation and erecting the first elements of the colonnade. After some weeks the Guardian authorized me to sign some new contracts to provide for the marble façades up to and including the balustrade, and he left to my judgement the approval of the clay and plaster models for all the decorative parts of this stage of the construction.

Carved marble and granite columns, however, were not the only constituent parts needed to construct the arcade. As the political situation crystallized with proclamation of the State of Israel, it became evident that the economy of the new nation would undergo great changes from the systems hitherto in effect there, requiring radical adjustment of its industrial enterprises and its labour situation. It became imperative, therefore, to procure from outside the country, at least for the time being, all the necessary materials for proceeding with the construction of the Shrine. Attempts had been made locally in the new State, but with insignificant results. The influx, in large numbers, of refugees to the 'promised land', with the consequent need for dwellings, placed a great strain and priority on all building material. But again, Shoghi Effendi's judgement and decision proved to be essentially timely and wise, and the obtaining and shipping of the much needed material was referred to me.

The situation in Italy, however, as already pointed out, was perhaps even more critical than that in Israel. Demand for building material for reconstruction of the nation made it practically impossible to obtain any such items, especially for export. Every item of building material was controlled by licence issued by the Ministry of Industry and Commerce, which was granted only after a lengthy procedure. If the request was for export, further permission was required from the Ministry of Foreign Trade, with the approval of yet another Ministry, that of Finance, which controlled the Customs of the whole country.

Cement and structural steel were, of course, at the top of the list, both for frequency and quantity needed. Hundreds of tons were in constant demand from Haifa, and as the work progressed and the need increased, the supply from the overburdened Italian industry became scarcer and scarcer. Other needed materials included lumber for scaffolding and shuttering, nails, iron wire, wrought-iron gates and fences, iron posts, electric wiring and cable, insulators, iron and zinc pipe, chain lifts, various types of tools, anti-rust varnish, paint and, in due time, lamp-posts, lamp-holders, switches, metal chains, mouldings, marble pedestals, marble steps and tiles (other than Chiampo), door and window frames, plain and stained-glass window panes, marble adhesive, electric globes and lamps, as well as a variety of additional items essential to the construction work and too numerous to mention. I must say that only the intervention of divine assistance made it possible to comply with the construction demands, which at times were in quantities almost impossible to obtain. Yet not once was I forced to inform the Guardian that a request could not be fulfilled.

Many years have since passed and even today I still wonder how it was possible to obtain all that was needed and in such large quantities. I can only say that I was wholly confident in the power that emanated from the World Centre of the Faith; I knew that if the Guardian asked for something, nine-tenths of the problem had been solved. His daily prayers and supplications at the Shrines would solicit the intervention of heavenly assistance that would remove every difficulty, near or remote. I never informed him of the obstacles, the labour and the heartaches involved to obtain licences, nor of the many hours of work required each day, month after month for nearly five years. I had had to move fast from Ministry to Ministry, from committees to individual officials, all scattered in different parts of Rome, waiting long hours in ante-chambers, filling out forms, even paying dues in advance so that the applications could be considered. I am sure the Guardian knew well my anxiety and cares and pains, because in the rarefied world of the spirit in which he lived, he was open to perception and awareness far beyond the usual human limitations.

The answer and the reward came to me that first night I was in his presence, part of which I have described earlier in these recollections. Turning to the friends seated at his table for dinner, he said, among other things:

'We are very glad to have such a Bahá'í friend, to whom the whole world is indebted.'

Then, addressing me, he added:

'The service you have rendered is not sufficiently appreciated today, but it will be fully appreciated in the future... You see, you worked for so long all alone; and no one appreciates this more than I, myself. When you are alone, you have such a big weight to carry. Single-handed, you have rendered an historic service to the Cause... This evening when I went to the Shrine, I remembered you, and I have come to the decision that we shall have a "Giachery" door for the Shrine—one of the doors.'

After explaining some details concerning 'Abdu'l-Bahá's purchase of land for the Shrine, His sufferings in order to build it, and the difficulties caused by Jamál Páshá, he turned again to me and said:

'You are one of the three—Sutherland,* myself and you. Sutherland rendered services in connection with the Shrine which are most meritorious—more meritorious than anything I have done—more meritorious than anything Ugo has done.'

No more touching statement could have been said to compensate me for whatever efforts I had made to help carry on the work started by the Master, 'Abdu'l-Bahá!

Shoghi Effendi, as I have mentioned, had the rare capacity to visualize things as a whole after a plan had been conceived by him. When the possibility of erecting the superstructure of the Báb's Sepulchre seemed about to materialize, Shoghi Effendi intensified the landscaping of the surrounding grounds. Much inventiveness and imagination were required to adapt to the irregular nature of the ground the superb and graceful landscaping he planned, to make a befitting framework for the majestic structure of the Shrine when it would be completed. Therefore from the inner recesses of his refinement and good taste and from the natural resources at hand, with his usual enthusiasm, he drew the arrangements of colours, plants, flowers, trees and shrubs that make up

* Referring to William Sutherland Maxwell, F.R.I.B.A., architect of the Shrine and Hand of the Cause. This conversation took place on the evening of 4 March 1952, exactly twenty-one days before Mr. Maxwell's passing away, in his native Canada.

the beautiful gardens on Mt. Carmel. I saw him intensely at work, directing a few men to trace lines, stretch strings, place a plant here and there, or a pedestal or an ornament, to lay out, from the first moment, what would be stable and permanent. I cannot remember having heard him once say, 'Take that away', or 'remove' this or that. There was always an air of contentment and gratification radiating from his dear face, so that one longed to follow him to the end of the world. The vision of things to come, arrayed in beauty, was surely always before his eyes, and he followed this vision as a navigator charting his course from the stars in the dark sky of night, undisturbed by any turbulent elements raging around him. From reports I received from time to time on the progress made with the foundation, with excavation of the mountain-side, and with extension of the terrace to east and west in front of the Shrine, it was evident that Shoghi Effendi was eager to see, at last, the burgeoning forth into reality of the long-awaited Mausoleum for the Prophet of God to Whom he himself was related.

After about six months most of the material needed to start construction of the arcade, such as threshold stones, bases and socles of the columns and pilasters, all beautifully finished, was ready to be crated and shipped. Never shall I forget the astounding impression I received when, in the marble working-yard, I beheld the Rose Baveno columns, twenty-four of them, lined up like giant soldiers on parade, glimmering in the sunlight of a clear autumn morning in the Italian Alps! Only a few months before, I had seen the huge rough blocks of granite extracted from the bosom of the mountain, and a few men shaping them manually with sledge hammers. Now, like well-cut precious gems carved out from shapeless stones, the slender, towering shafts were proclaiming the perfection of their form and brilliancy to my incredulous eyes. An upsurge of joy filled my whole being, as I thought to myself how, erected *in situ*, this same sight would bring untold happiness to the heart of Shoghi Effendi and to the innumerable succession of pilgrims who, over the centuries to come, will visit that Holy Spot. I had seen the drawings of the arcade and of the individual columns many times, but the beauty of the conception unfolded itself fully only when I lifted my eyes to view the complete height of the shafts. I saw that they embodied the graceful Vignola conformation, adding great distinction to the whole project.*

Approval was enthusiastically given and provision made for packing all the material for shipment in mammoth, sturdy wooden boxes, and for conveying the 'giants' to a Tyrrhenian seaport from which they would be shipped to Haifa.

The long-awaited hour had come. Some kind of magic had to intervene now to start the spectacular task of moving a building of a very special nature and significance, piece by piece, from one continent to another.

On 1 October 1948, the following cablegram was received from Shoghi Effendi:

'Delighted splendid progress increasingly admire your indefatigable labours. Owing international situation urge start shipment material completed. Cable date shipment. Deepest love. Shoghi Rabbani.'

The prospect was challenging. Only a very few ships would venture into mined waters unsafe for normal navigation; moreover, space was lacking, almost unavailable. We had to do much praying, because every avenue seemed blocked. Shipping agents were seeking any possibility but without immediate success. Only faith could have removed the difficulties. If frustration or despair had taken hold of me, even for one brief instant, this whole chain of prodigious events would have been interrupted. Under the most distressing circumstances we never doubted, feeling confident that a propitious solution would soon be at hand. This was the lesson I had learned in working with Shoghi Effendi. A few years later, when I met him in person, I immediately knew the reason why, as I have explained.

A few days later another cablegram came, requesting the name of the steamer. The next day a ship was found and a telegraphic reply was sent to him, informing him that the first shipment would sail on the S.S. *Norte*, due to arrive in Haifa on 23 November 1948—a record of incredible speed in accomplishing the work

* See Appendix VIII.

81

since the April day when Mr. Maxwell had signed the first contract! Over one hundred and fifty tons of cut, carved and polished
marble and granite were shipped at this time, including the load
of a second ship, the S.S. *Campidoglio*, which sailed almost in the
wake of the first one. The *Norte* finally reached the port of Haifa
on 28 November, with the *Campidoglio* following a few days
later, as a true co-partner and escort in such a prodigious event.

From my own happiness in those days, I could evaluate the
extent of Shoghi Effendi's delight and gratification. Later I was
told that the arrival of the ship was anticipated and watched with
great elation, and when the precious loads had been landed and
carted with extreme hardship and many difficulties to the immediate vicinity of the Báb's Shrine, the joy of the beloved
Guardian knew no bounds.

It does not lie within the purpose of these recollections to give
a detailed schedule of the many contracts signed on the Guardian's
behalf for all the material needed to erect the outer shell of the
Báb's Sepulchre, over the period of five years, nor to list the names
and dates of departure of all the ships needed to convey the
material from Europe to the Holy Land. The reader should, however, pause to ponder on the thousands of details involved in such
an enterprise, which had to be executed with absolute thorough-
ness and great speed, notwithstanding the many obstacles arising
out of the political situation of post-war Europe, particularly in
Italy, plus the uncertainty of circumstances prevailing on land and
sea owing to the conflict in the Middle East.*

In reviewing retrospectively the efforts, the aspirations, the
hopes and the predicaments with which the beloved Guardian
had to contend, and at times struggle, all alone—as only a very
few around him were able to give effective assistance—plus the
limitation of funds that was a constant restraint to his enthusiasm
and desire to accomplish many other things, we cannot but
marvel at what, single-handed, he was able to achieve in those
nine fleeting years (1948–57) during which he raised to the highest
possible degree the prestige, nobility and significance of the

* See reports by Dr. Giachery and by Mr. Ben D. Weeden in *The Bahá'í World*,
vol. XII, pp. 240–6 and pp. 246–52.

Cause he was so lovingly and devotedly championing, establishing all the Institutions envisaged by the Founder of the Faith on a permanent and invulnerable foundation.

We shall temporarily leave the chronology of the building activities and devote some pages to the architectural conception of the structure and the analysis of its component parts in their relation to the birth and flowering of the Báb's Dispensation.

During my first visit to the Holy Land in 1952, Shoghi Effendi related to me that when 'Abdu'l-Bahá undertook construction of the original Shrine of the Báb in 1900–8, He wanted to have eight doors, but He could not achieve more than five. The Master's wish was finally fulfilled in 1929, when Shoghi Effendi added three rooms. Since the beginning of Shoghi Effendi's noble enterprise, when Mr. Maxwell brought to Rome his drawings of the superstructure and the photograph of the Shrine's model, I had observed that the number eight had a predominant part in the whole project. Without my asking the significance of that number in the structure and the surrounding grounds, Shoghi Effendi one day made reference to a verse of the Qur'án, which he first recited in Arabic and then in English: '. . . on that day eight shall bear up the throne of thy Lord'.* He then explained the sublime station of the Báb,† and how he guided Mr. Maxwell to incorporate the spiritual meaning of this Islamic prophecy in the project, to testify to His exalted station, to honour eternally the Martyr-Prophet enshrined in the Sepulchre, and to emphasize how closely the Báb's Revelation was connected with the expectations of the Islamic world. Shoghi Effendi further mentioned that 'Abdu'l-Bahá, on completing the initial six rooms, had named each of the five doors after one of the followers of the Faith, including those who had been associated with the construction of the Shrine, and that He always referred to the Shrine as the 'Throne of the Lord', and to the Casket of the Báb also as the 'Throne'. Even the Holy Dust was called by Him the 'Throne'.

---

* Sura LXIX, 'The Inevitable', verse 17, of Rodwell's translation. For Arberry's translation, see footnote p. 96.
† Rabb-i-A'lá, literally: Lord the Most High.

Shoghi Effendi also mentioned the names of the recipients of this great honour; he himself had named one of the doors of the three additional rooms, early in his ministry, and was naming the remaining two doors after Mr. Maxwell and Ugo Giachery.*

'The Master', he continued, 'had designed the inner Shrine so there could be eight doors, and you are one of the eight who have been singled out, and whose name will forever be associated with the eight doors of the Báb's Shrine. Also the Báb is the eighth Manifestation of those religions whose followers still exist. When Sutherland [Mr. Maxwell] designed the Shrine, I told him, "You must have eight columns on each side." '

The predominance of the number eight is evident in many other details of the Sepulchre and the grounds around it. The visitor, if he is observant, will see that the ornamental flower-beds are shaped like eight-pointed stars, outstanding decorative motives in the midst of the green lawns of English grass, so dear to the Guardian.

As the columns of Rose Baveno granite proclaim the glory of classic Roman architecture, the majestic ogee arches, seven on each side, bring the flavour of the Orient, reminder of the birth-place of the Martyr-Prophet and the splendour of Islám which flourished for over a millennium along the shores of the Mediterranean. This harmony of epochs and styles, perpetuating the artistic aspects of two spiritual forces that had been at variance through the centuries, is one of the inspired creations of the architect, who enhanced the uniqueness of his design by placing a composite Corinthian capital between each shaft and the base of the arch. Shoghi Effendi, who had guided the architect in the use of Western and Eastern styles, and left to him the artistic details, was delighted with the whole result, as it fulfilled an historical necessity by symbolizing a basic unity, so well expressed in forms more eloquent than words.

The acanthus is a plant which grows all along the temperate shores of the Mediterranean Sea. Ancient Greece adopted the leaf of this prickly plant as an ornamental motive in architecture and particularly in the Corinthian order of capitals. Later the Romans

* See Appendix IX for the names of the doors.

used the same pattern, adding something in the way of efflorescence. Thus the composite style was born. Mr. Maxwell, a master in the art of ornamental design, created for the columns and the pilasters a graceful and stunning capital in which the foliation, the volutes and the florets are vividly portrayed. The acanthus leaf was used again in the small panels on the masonry, between two arches, and generously in the four concave corners of the arcade which will be described later. The small panels, octagonal in shape, give the impression to the casual observer of being an arabesque design, in tune with the ogee arches, but they are actually in the same order and style as the capitals.

In recent years, before his passing, I happened to visit Architect Rocca, in his home in Marina di Carrara. When I reached the house I was greatly surprised to notice that right above the main door of the building was a white marble replica of the Maxwell panel. He must have noticed my bewilderment, for before I could utter a word he said: 'I could not resist; it is so originally beautiful that I had to place one in my home as a memorial to Mr. Maxwell and as a memento of my association with the work on the Shrine of the Báb'. This episode, I thought then, will bear witness, outside the Bahá'í world, to the ingenuity of the architect of the Báb's Sepulchre. Now that Mr. Rocca has entered the unseen world of God, I feel that the panel must have been the cause of great happiness to him, and that, whenever he entered his home, his pride in the significance of being selected by the hand of Providence as one of the side actors of a great drama must have overwhelmed him.

Much could be said of the many exquisite details of the various carvings which ornament the four façades of the arcade, particularly around the arches from base to finial, and in the carved mouldings (as torus, congé and cavetto), where the carvings follow the line of the arches, always terminating with a floral motive, like a jewel clasp for a necklace of precious stones.

The colonnade just described is an equilateral quadrangle in which the corners, instead of meeting at a ninety-degree angle, join in four ample concave recesses, each of which is surmounted by the symbol of the ring-stone 'Greatest Name', placed on an elaborate oval shield. The vivid imagination of Shoghi Effendi has provided at each corner recess a large panel framed by a carved floral festoon. Selections from the Writings of the beloved Báb are to be engraved in these curved corner panels to attest for centuries to come His readiness to sacrifice His life for the redemption of mankind. One evening Shoghi Effendi spoke of the plans he had made to have engraved in these corners 'the passage in Arabic, quoted by Bahá'u'lláh in the *Kitáb-i-Íqán:* "O Thou Remnant of God! I have sacrificed myself. . .".'[9] Then, turning to me, he asked me to get samples of different types of scripts, Kufic and other calligraphy, such as would be harmonious with the 'Greatest Name' in the panel above, and to inquire about the possibility of having an expert in this art of writing come from Egypt to carve inscriptions in the corners, when the way would be open. With the assistance of an Egyptian Bahá'í the books were secured and sent to the Guardian. Each of the four concave corners is flanked at each side by two pilasters of Chiampo, with bases and Corinthian capitals.

A substantial cornice surmounts the colonnade and the corners, delimiting the arcade below from the stone balustrade above it. Shoghi Effendi, in making reference to this balustrade, always called it the 'first crown of the Shrine'. It is a parapet composed of twenty-seven rectangular panels, seven on each side of the Shrine superstructure, except on the north side. Flanking each panel is a stone post with finials, twenty-eight in all; each post is the height of a man. The panels are monolithic and of flawless marble; each weighs nearly one ton and is framed in bas-relief of green glass mosaic inlaid with scarlet blossoms. Shoghi Effendi explained: 'Green denotes the lineage of the Holy Báb, and scarlet signifies the colour of the blood shed by His martyrdom.' Shoghi Effendi further explained that these panels, interspersed in the crown, would bear passages from the Writings of the Báb in Arabic. (By crown, as already stated, he meant the whole parapet.) In the days when the Shrine was being erected, plastic material was making headway in the building industry in Italy and the contractor wanted to make use of this material because it was so widely used in making mosaics. But because glass mosaic, made by one of the best firms in Venice, had proved its durability in other buildings

THE ARCADE OF THE SHRINE OF THE BÁB

(*left*) Erecting the first pilaster
(*below*) The colonnade with its
      Rose Baveno columns

CLAY MODELS OF SOME OF THE MOTIFS DESIGNED
BY MR. MAXWELL FOR THE SHRINE OF THE BÁB

(*above*) A Corinthian capital for the columns of the arcade
(*below, left*) A capital for the pilasters
(*below, right*) One of the star panels of the arcade

THE CENTRAL PANEL OF THE BALUSTRADE SURMOUNTING
THE ARCADE OF THE SHRINE OF THE BÁB
(*above*) Detail of marble carving and mosaic. (*below*) The north façade
facing 'Akká, with bronze gilt 'Greatest Name'

Ḥájí Maḥmúd Qaṣṣábchí

William Sutherland Maxwell

Leroy C. Ioas

Ugo Giachery

THOSE FOR WHOM DOORS OF THE SHRINE OF THE BÁB
WERE NAMED BY SHOGHI EFFENDI

and was used for all mosaic work in other parts of the Shrine superstructure, I insisted on its use in the balustrade panels. The large central panel on the north side of the parapet, facing the sea, is the twenty-eighth panel of the whole series. It is a masterpiece of beauty, craftsmanship and intricate design. When the entire balustrade was completed, Shoghi Effendi announced this to the Bahá'í world, and referred to that central panel as 'adorned with green mosaic with gilded Greatest Name, the fairest gem set in crown of arcade of Shrine . . .'.[10] And it is indeed a gem!

The central part of this panel is a large disk like a shining midday sun, with white and golden rays, holding within a nine-pointed star of green marble a bronze fire-gilded 'Greatest Name' in Arabic in bas-relief, visible from near and far. At the two extremities of this panel, on the left and right of the disk, there is a letter 'в', with carved foliage and flowers interspersed, reminder of the acanthus motive, and each facing the other thus: 'я в'.

Because of the delicacy of the carving, and the possible fragility of the mosaics, the shipment of these panels presented a special problem. Generally, all the carved marble was shipped from Italy to Haifa in sturdy wooden boxes of local alpine fir. When I went to Pietrasanta to approve this shipment of panels, I felt that the average packing would not be sufficient and that a second outer box would be necessary. This required an added expense which I submitted by cable to the Guardian for his approval. When the affirmative answer came, arrangements were made to purchase the additional lumber required, and in a few days the whole two hundred tons of marble were shipped. The ship which took the marble cargo stopped on the way at another port to load bags of black soot, used to make paints, a load which was unwisely placed on top of our wooden cases of marble. The sea journey to Haifa was rough, and the cargo must have shifted so that when the ship reached Haifa it was found that the majority of the bags had split open, the soot spreading all over the wooden cases. The extra packing had saved the marble from any damage, although the black dust had, in many instances, penetrated the outer boxes. The shipment, of course, was covered by insurance against this and other types of damage, but the delay in beginning again the reproduction of all

87

the damaged marble would not have permitted completion of the arcade in time, as so ardently wished by Shoghi Effendi, for the one hundredth anniversary of the Martyrdom of the beloved Báb. This episode is one other of the many elements of wonder connected with the erection of the Shrine.

To complete the description of the parapet of the arcade, I shall here add some details concerning the crowning panels of the four concave corners.

Immediately above the cornice on which the balustrade rests, the oval corner shield, wreathed by a garland of laurel leaves, is surmounted by sun-rays and additional floral carvings tapering to a sharp point, and rising over nine feet above the cornice. In the centre of the shield there is an oval panel of green marble called 'Ugo Vert'—from the name of the owner of the quarry, Count Ugo d'Ivrea of Gressoney*—on which is set, in special fire-gilded bronze, the symbol of the 'Greatest Name' used in the Bahá'í ringstone. This symbol was used by the Guardian on his own personal stationery, and is also frescoed on one wall of the room occupied by Bahá'u'lláh in the Bahjí Mansion, in the corner where He usually sat.

The ensemble of panel and pointed shield is dramatic and dignified, sustained by two large plain panels, one at each side, and held together by carved large acanthus leaves which give the impression of wings lifting the whole into that infinity of beauty and glory which surrounds the Holy Shrine.

The contract for the marble needed for this part of the structure had been signed in Rome on 7 September 1949, almost one year after the beginning of the erection of the arcade. This first unit of the Shrine, the arcade with its balustrade, was completed by the end of May 1950.

As the ninth of July approached—the first centenary of the Báb's Martyrdom—the Guardian, overwhelmed by the Shrine's magnificence and exquisite beauty, was filled with infinite joy. His message to the Bahá'í world[11] reflected his joy at this achievement, and announced the timeliness of erecting the octagonal unit of the superstructure of the Sepulchre, leading to the com-

* In Piedmont, Italy.

pletion of the domed embellishment of the precious Shrine erected by 'Abdu'l-Bahá. On that historic occasion, G. A. Borgese of Italy, then Professor of Italian Literature at the University of Chicago, a warm friend and admirer of the Bahá'í Faith, was invited to deliver an address at the public meeting held in the Temple Foundation Hall, to an audience of some five hundred persons.[12]

Reference has been made, in the preceding text, to 'fire-gilded bronze'. This is a time-honoured method of covering copper, bronze or silver with a layer of gold. A durable gilding was required for the Arabic lettering of the 'Greatest Name' symbols, and it was therefore decided to use this method still practised by some skilled goldsmiths in Florence, because it is much more lasting than any other process in use today.

THE OCTAGON

Shoghi Effendi's original plan was to build only the arcade of the Shrine, waiting then for better conditions—both political and economic—to continue the erection of the whole Shrine at a later date. This view had been communicated to me by Mr. Maxwell during his visit to Rome, in 1948. It was for this reason that the contract for construction of the whole edifice was not stipulated at the very beginning of the undertaking. This was confirmed to me by the Guardian himself when I met him in Haifa early in 1952. However, as the work for the erection of the arcade progressed, and the beauty of the edifice unfolded—'far beyond belief', as he stated—the perennial and consuming flame of achievement which burned in his bosom moved him to reconsider his earlier plan, and, trusting fully in divine assistance, he decided to undertake there and then the construction of the remaining superstructure, leading to the final erection of the gilded dome.

Those who were close to Shoghi Effendi in that period well remember how much concerned he was with securing the necessary funds to carry on the construction work. Appeals were made to the friends, particularly to those of the United States of America. Because of favourable developments in the new State of Israel he was able to announce, on 21 March 1951, that they 'impel me to take the major step in the development of the swiftly progressing, irresistibly advancing enterprise transcending in sacredness any collective undertaking launched in the course of the history of the hundred-year-old Faith'. And he renewed his 'fervent plea' for financial support, 'however great the sacrifice involved, however heavy the burdens, however distracting the successive crises of the present critical hour'.[13]

In some instances the friends provided financial loans that would ensure the continuity of the work, and which were later repaid.

At that time Italy was starting to recover from a disastrous war economy; the burden of reparation indemnities to be paid by that nation to the Allied Powers was staggering, and any activity that would bring ready foreign currency to the Italian treasury was not only welcome, but courted. As Shoghi Effendi agreed to make all payments in U.S. dollars, we had a strong bargaining advantage on our side. Although teaching the Faith was not allowed in Italy, and the believers—including myself and my wife—were regularly and systematically harassed by the police, the procurement of the marble and all other building material for export to Haifa was highly coveted, even though scarcity of the materials, as already explained, raised many difficulties at every turn. Shoghi Effendi during his ministry had to take many decisions, some of vital and supreme importance, and in my judgement one of the most remarkable was his decision to continue the Shrine's construction when he did. Labour in Italy was obtainable then at a very reasonable cost; the eagerness of the people to recoup their personal and national economy transformed them into eager, willing and persevering workers. A delay of even one year in the completion of the building would have increased considerably its cost, and the workmanship would not have been of the same excellent and high quality that it was then.

Clear proof of this became evident four years later, when I was called upon again by the Guardian to secure the marble and the material for erection of the International Archives on Mt. Carmel, concerning which an account will be given later on.

In an article which I wrote for *The Bahá'í World*, volume XII,* I stated in detail the great engineering work needed to raise the superstructure of the Shrine without touching or endangering the original edifice built by 'Abdu'l-Bahá. Right above the roof of that original building, supported by eight huge piers cast in steel-reinforced concrete reaching to bedrock of the mountain below the foundation of the Shrine, an eight-pointed star, also of steel-reinforced concrete, was cast in one day to make the solid foundation on which the superstructure rests. Heavy steel pipes, eight in number, resting on the meeting-points of the two superimposed quadrangles which form the star, sustain the clerestory above the octagon, and the dome. The casting of the star, two metres deep and half a metre wide, had to be done in one day—an almost impossible feat because of the lack of proper machinery and the limitation of labour—in order to have the huge polygon dry evenly and prevent future cracks in the mass of the concrete. It is to be understood that the cyclopean steel structure had been carefully prepared over a number of weeks, but the execution and completion of the concrete-pouring in one day, under the then prevailing condition and the many difficulties arising constantly, was a feat that will remain outstanding in the annals of engineering in the Near East.

The octagon, as the name denotes, is the eight-sided part of the Shrine which rises immediately above the arcade, and is located in the centre of the large platform which resulted from the casting of the concrete star already mentioned. The number eight has a new significance in this construction, which has to support at every corner a pinnacle, very much like a minaret. The pinnacles function also as anchors for the wrought-iron railing that rises above the roof of the octagon. This whole structure is of classic simplicity, with the motive of bas-relief pilasters on each side of the corners, rising slender and stately to the top of the walls, and joining with a large band of carved floral decoration that terminates in a gracefully moulded cornice. Each side of the octagon has three windows, a large one at the centre, with a smaller one at each side. Again the oriental motive embodied in the

* Pp. 240–6. See also photographs of construction, pp. 46–7.

arches of the colonnade is repeated in the ogee shape of the windows and in the ornamental moulding which runs along the contour of each. The iron frames for each window are divided in panels, twelve for the large windows, and three for the small ones, holding stained glass. This touch adds to the mysterious beauty of the sacred edifice.

The side of the octagon situated on the south of the building, instead of having a large window, has a door (with a grill and a glass panel), and provides the only access to the inside of the superstructure of the Shrine. Shoghi Effendi named this door after the late Hand of the Cause, Mr. Leroy Ioas, for his valuable assistance in the erection of the holy edifice from the time of his arrival in Haifa in the spring of 1952.*

Shoghi Effendi felt it was irreverent for anyone to walk above the tomb of the Báb, and only for technical reasons was it tolerated during the actual construction; but he warned us many times that the hallowed nature of the edifice would never permit one to perambulate over the sacred remains of a Prophet of God. And yet, of course, it has been and will be necessary at times to reach other sections of the superstructure for maintenance and needed repairs. For a long time after the completion of the Shrine, a small wooden bridge was left between the south side of the terrace around the octagon and the mountain; now I believe the connection from the outside is achieved with a very tall ladder.

Mr. Maxwell, when working on the project of the Shrine, had made provision for a staircase to be built in the south-east corner room. Nothing was done about the stairs during the construction of the arcade or of the other sections of the Shrine, because the three rooms added by Shoghi Effendi were being used to house the relics which formed part of the archives started by him. It was not until 1955 that the erection of the new International Archives building was commenced, and it was barely completed at the time of the Guardian's passing in November 1957. Another two years were needed for the completion of innumerable details, before the precious contents could be moved from the old archives quarters to the new building. I saw the plan for the staircase

* See memorial article, *The Bahá'í World*, vol. XIV.

several times during and after the visit of Mr. Maxwell to Italy, but no action could have been taken during the construction of the superstructure, because all precedence had to be given to the completion of the arcade within the dates of the centenaries of the Martyrdom of the Báb, in July 1950, and the Birth of the Mission of Bahá'u'lláh, in 1953.

The whole edifice displays a great variety of architectural and artistic gems, products of the inventiveness and refined taste of Mr. Maxwell; Shoghi Effendi highly valued and admired every expression of such taste, which manifested itself in the ornamental details abounding throughout the edifice. Nearly every stone shows the gracefulness of the Maxwell artistic talent; in some instances the delicacy of the design is like a beautiful piece of embroidery or hand-made jewelry. It would require much space and time to enter into the details of all the motifs which beautify every frieze, festoon, moulding, garland, arabesque, finial, leaf, flower, rosette and chaplet, with which the appearance of every component piece of marble, or granite, or iron-work, or glass, is enriched. In my judgement, one of the very best pieces of ornamentation in the entire project is the iron-wrought balustrade which rises above the octagon and encircles the clerestory, on each side of the octagonal terrace, between the eight pinnacles or 'minarets' whose architectural ornamentation is embodied also in the design of the balustrade itself. Before deciding on the final design, Mr. Maxwell had made many sketches to develop the main motif, each of which is a little gem of artistry in tempera, revealing over and over his boundless love for beauty and precision.

The balustrade railing is of wrought-iron, executed mostly by hand, its decorative elements all made by skilled artists who shaped the red-hot iron with a hammer. Every section, of which there are eight, is supported by heavy iron rods at either end, and is divided into nine parts, each supported by strong horizontal iron bars and the railing. Each terminal vertical rod is encrusted with acanthus leaves and terminates in a similar single leaf bent backwards, and a volute inwards, holding at its centre a six-petal rosette, all being connected with the railing. Each part is almost square and contains the enlarged contour of a flower, suggestive of a lotus blossom opening and, of course, also of the East. The whole design is so original and artistic in conception that one marvels at the perfect blending of styles of the Orient and the Occident.

While the balustrade railing was being made, I went several times to visit the blacksmith shop where the work was done, in a small township between Spezia and Carrara, not too far from the place where the marble was being worked. The owner, a dedicated and skilful man who loved his trade, had many workers under him, but among them was an artisan who seemed to be especially gifted. By taking a piece of red-hot iron, with a few hammer strokes he would produce an artistic object, a leaf or a flower. I became very fond of this man who, alone, did all the decorative iron-work for the Shrine of the Báb, as well as the lamp-posts, and some of the gates for both Mt. Carmel and Bahjí. He had a tenacity and endurance without equal, coupled with keen intelligence and the skill to produce beauty. His interpretation of Mr. Maxwell's designs is an example of the gift this man possessed.

Every piece of iron-work which came from that shop was required first to be covered with two layers of anti-rust paint, applied either by brush or by dipping, and then with a layer of special graphite-black varnish. Shoghi Effendi was very eager to see the balustrade finished, and when the huge wooden cases, each one with two sections inside, arrived in Haifa towards the end of February 1952, he had them immediately opened and the contents placed in view on the terrace before the custodian's house, near the Eastern Pilgrim House. I happened to arrive in Haifa two or three days later, and the Guardian spoke of the ornamental iron balustrade with admiration, praising the workmanship with much satisfaction and joy. To him, the arrival of new material for the construction of the Shrine was a cause of deep pleasure, because he was able to see the things he had long before visualized in his mind. He then gave instructions that the balustrade should be painted a dark green, and that its sections should be set up at the earliest possible moment in their places on the Shrine structure.

Shoghi Effendi had already experimented with the gilding of certain parts of the main gate to the Shrine gardens and the gates of the Monument gardens, and in his mind he had decided to have most of the decorative elements on the balustrade, such as leaves and flowers, also gilded. There was at the time in the city of Haifa a very skilled gilder, Mr. Klophatz, who had already done some of the work I have just mentioned, under the directives of Mr. Maxwell. He was called by the Guardian and they spent some hours selecting to advantage all the parts which were to be gilded.

This same artist first painted the particular spots to be gilded with a deep yellow varnish so that Shoghi Effendi could see the effect and how the iron would look after the gold leaf had been applied. By so doing, elements of error were practically eliminated. The Guardian asked me to check the progress of the work and to use my judgement in choosing additional parts to be gilded, in order to enrich its appearance. This was the system used by Shoghi Effendi for all the iron-work distributed on Mt. Carmel and at Bahjí, for the gates, large and small, and the lamp-posts. This artist, who had come many years before to the Promised Land from Germany, possessed a good education and much talent. He deeply admired the Teachings, some of which he had read, and he greatly enjoyed working under Shoghi Effendi's direction. His respect for him was touching, as no other man would have worked so long, in such trying conditions for only the compensation he received, but he had become devoted to Shoghi Effendi and admired what he represented. The process of gilding must be done where there is not the slightest air current. The artist therefore worked on location under a heavy tent, closed in (for many hours) on all sides, with the sun raising the inside temperature mercilessly. All eight sections of the balustrade were gilded in this fashion, from a scaffolding and within a tent which enclosed a whole length of balustrade, from pinnacle to pinnacle. It took many weeks. When the work was finished, and placed on view, the pride and happiness of the Guardian could not be described. It was a memorable day when the first balustrade railing, weighing nearly a ton, was raised by hand to be set in position. A dozen sturdy men were required to handle this assignment. The beauty of the handwork, the strength of its structure and the imposing part it played in the appearance of the Shrine, had electrified these men. I was present on that occasion, and can well remember the feeling of elation and satisfaction of the whole crew when the first balustrade was properly placed. Great happiness, many congratulations and much laughter accompanied the completion of this task. The other seven sections followed with the same spirit of collaboration and rejoicing.

The eight pinnacles, one at each corner of the octagon, which support the iron balustrades, are indeed original in conception. If we consider some of the famous mosques of the Islamic world, we can readily understand their decorative function and the character these pinnacles bring to the Shrine. The Báb was a Siyyid, entitled to be remembered in the same manner as the Prophet Muḥammad and the Imáms. Speaking one evening of the importance of the minarets in Islamic architecture, Shoghi Effendi said: 'The mosque of Medina has seven minarets, the one of Sulṭán Aḥmad in Constantinople has six, but the Qur'án mentions eight.' Furthermore, the eight slender minaret-like spires symbolize the bearers of the 'throne of God'.*

There are three component elements in each pinnacle. The lower part, based on the roof of the octagon, is one-half of the total height of the pinnacle, and is formed by the graved ensemble of fourteen acanthus leaves—seven on each side of the central point which coincides with the corner of the octagon. This part rises, its leaves at different levels, to the tip which bends outward. The two central leaves, the tallest of all, support a carved cluster of flowers, reminiscent of the motif at each of the four concave corners of the arcade. The next section is a fluted cylinder ending in a slightly wider circular platform, on which rests the cone-shaped finial. The lower and the middle sections consist of one solid block of marble, the cone terminal being a separate piece, connected with the middle section by a sturdy copper dowel. The middle section and the cone represent together the

* In the Qur'án, Sura LXIX, 'The Inevitable', verse 17, it is said: 'And the angels shall be on its sides, and over them on that day eight shall bear up the throne of thy Lord.' From Rodwell's translation. Arberry translates this verse: '...and the angels shall stand upon its borders, and upon that day eight shall carry above them the throne of thy Lord.'

upper half of the pinnacle's height. The reader would be interested to know that all abutting elements of the building, such as bases, columns, capitals and finials, are conjoined by copper dowel-pins, an ancient method widely used by the Romans in the erection of their majestic buildings and temples.

When the first pinnacle was in place, Shoghi Effendi instructed that the very tip of it be gilded, and this was done for all eight of them. When the sun shines, or the night reflectors cast their powerful light on them, they look like mighty candles alight— an eternal homage to the Báb, the Torch-bearer of Bahá'u'- lláh's Dispensation.

THE DRUM OR CLERESTORY

The most impressive part of the history of the Báb's drama is manifested in this portion of the Shrine. In it are permanently embodied the memories of His meteoric Dispensation. The graceful drum rises eleven metres from the level of the octagon's roof. It is built upon a circular steel-reinforced concrete ring, supported by eight mighty steel pipes which rest on the great concrete star, already mentioned. To procure these Manesmann pipes was not a simple matter. No steel factory in Italy was making them; yet to obtain them from another steel-producing country was also out of the question, as both England and Germany were occupied with their own reconstruction after the war and would have taken possibly a year or more to supply them. On the other hand, the sudden cabled request from Shoghi Effendi implied urgent need; any delay in finding and shipping the pipes would have considerably retarded construction. I well remember the days of feverish search in many directions and quarters; but faith and prayers helped us again. Somehow, in a neglected collection of building material in Milan, we found eight pipes—no more and no less—which had been ordered from Germany before the war for a certain project and never used; the length and diameter were exactly what we needed! Other difficulties, including obtaining the necessary export licence, left us breathless and weary, but we were filled with joy when we learned of the relief and happiness brought to the beloved Guardian.

The clerestory is a perfect cylinder, intersected by eighteen lancet windows which rise vertically for almost the entire height of the stonework. At the base of each window, there is a large block of carved marble jutting out from the surface of the cylinder. A similar arrangement is carried out for the top of the window, where the headstone, similarly carved, joins with the large decorative fascia of superimposed ogee finials which reach the brim of the dome.

The eighteen lancet windows represent and memorialize the Báb's Letters of the Living. In a cablegram sent in July 1950, and already mentioned,* the Guardian made an appeal to 'repay part of the infinite debt of gratitude owed its martyrs . . .'.[14] Although the Shrine is dedicated to the Báb, these windows offer a memorial to His heroic disciples, most of whom won the martyr's crown. The windows rise majestically in their simplicity and beauty. They were erected during September 1952. I was in Haifa at the time with Professor Rocca, the architect for the marble work in Italy, and we both marvelled at the unfoldment of this exquisite conception of the architect of the Shrine.

The head-mason and his crew were enchanted; they handled the heavy blocks of marble as if they were precious gems to be set in a necklace. Theirs was a deep pride at being connected with the execution of this great plan. One could sense the humility and awe which held these workers spellbound while they busied themselves with their tasks.

Daily and for long, I contemplated the blossoming of the windows and could not help thinking back to the days when those saintly souls, the Letters of the Living, were in this world, ready to give their lives for the Holy Báb's Cause, setting an example for thousands of other human beings, who, intoxicated with the love of God, would later march singing to their own martyrdom. I tried to remember their names, but that of Ṭáhirih, the Lady from Qazvín, came first to my mind. The pure, the beautiful advocate of womanhood, the serene poetess, whose oratory moved so deeply all to whom she spoke, a chosen Letter of the Báb, the courageous champion of Badasht! Now a window

* See p. 88.

will recall to the whole world her courage as the first woman apostle of any Dispensation.

It was Shoghi Effendi's idea to incorporate in the Shrine of the Martyr-Prophet these memorials to His apostles: windows, the perennial bearers of light, gateways from darkness to luminous glory, eyes from the realm of the spirit open upon the world of existence. Speaking one evening of these windows, Shoghi Effendi said: 'The Letters of the Living are the channels through which the light passes.' This similitude was to me highly convincing and deeply moving.

It was also his wish, nobly carried out by Mr. Maxwell, that the windows should have iron frames, divided into ten squares and two semicircular panels, each one bearing stained glass with floral decoration in brilliant colours, chiefly red, green and violet. In the mornings and afternoons, when the sunlight comes from the east or from the west, it strikes some of the windows on one side, and its beams travel across the drum to the windows on the opposite side, illuminating in all their glory the beauty and grace of the flower garlands. In recent years arrangements have been made to illumine at night the windows from inside, and when the whole Sepulchre is aglow with the light from powerful reflectors, the windows shine in their colourful splendour.

This is true also of the octagon windows, the glass of which bears a sober but at the same time highly decorative, geometrical pattern which tones with the simplicity of the marble architecture. The stained glass was produced by a firm in Turin, Italy, after other firms in Florence, in Spain and Belgium had been investigated. The Guardian wished to have a first-class *atelier* do the work, one which was capable of interpreting in its execution the delicacy and perfection of Mr. Maxwell's drawing. When the Turin firm was finally chosen, samples of coloured glass were sent to Shoghi Effendi to select the exact colours. At the same time the original Maxwell design was enlarged to the correct size by Professor Angelo Monti, a Florentine artist who specialized in stained glass. The owner of the firm, Signor Cristiano Jörger, a well-known and expert glass-maker, then executed the work with much skill and great artistic ability. By the end of 1952 the drum was completed, leaving only the dome to be erected to finish the Shrine.

THE CROWN AND THE DOME

The evenings spent at table with the Guardian can never be forgotten. The memories of the hours filled with the joy of his presence and with his enlightening and captivating conversation, which covered a variety of subjects, are the most precious possession of my mature years. How often now, as in a dream, I go back to review in my mind every detail of his discourses and compare his views and predictions with the realities of present-day events.

At that particular time, the erection of the Shrine of the Báb was of paramount importance in his mind; it was a subject which he favoured most and he expressed his ideas with deep conviction and much expectation. It was the early spring of 1952. The octagon had been completed, the ornamental iron railing placed in position, and the drum begun. His favourite conversation was then the crown and the dome, for which the architectural plans had been so beautifully made by Mr. Maxwell, incorporating some details suggested by Shoghi Effendi, and to which Mr. Maxwell attached much significance. Unfortunately, at the end of March, Mr. Maxwell left this world, and his guiding hand in the technical field came to an abrupt end. It was a very great sorrow for Shoghi Effendi, as he had lost not only his prized architect but a father, a friend and a counsellor as well. From then on, the Guardian alone had to reach many decisions of a technical nature, even though the engineering details were looked after by Professor Neumann of the Haifa Technion.

The reader may remember the 'rendition' in colour of the Shrine of the Báb made by Mr. Maxwell,* and presented at the celebration of the first centenary of the Báb's Declaration. It was published some four years before the beginning of the Shrine's construction, as the Guardian wanted to make the believers the world over aware of the imminent realization of this plan so long overdue.

* See page 66.

Now that the erection of the Shrine was a reality, the urgency of completing it at the earliest possible moment, in the perfect likeness of Mr. Maxwell's projected design, fired Shoghi Effendi's imagination and enthusiasm. The placing of the dome was for him the culmination of that glorious enterprise. Erection of the third crown, which surrounds the dome, was the visible expression of the regality of the 'Queen of Carmel'. I have said the third crown, because Shoghi Effendi considered this one the last of a series of crowns, embodied in tiers in the whole structure, just as in a mitre. The first, the balustrade of the arcade; the second, the pinnacles and the iron parapet of the octagon; the third and final one, the regal crown, the emblem of celestial sovereignty. Around the base of the dome there is a wide brim of marble, which meets the upper part of the drum. Immediately above the brim is an encircling garland with uprights in two alternating dimensions, the tallest being over two metres high, and the whole comprising thirty-six beautifully carved stalks with foliage and full blooms. The brim itself, so original in conception because it is not horizontal but bends down at about a thirty-five degree angle, represented a real challenge for both the marble workers and the builders. It is not made by solid blocks of marble carved to shape. That would have been too heavy for the nature of the structure. Instead, it consists of two slabs of stone, upper and lower, anchored together and to the drum by reinforced concrete—a marvel of engineering, considering the complete lack of the proper mechanical contrivances available at that time.

The construction of the dome itself was indeed a great challenge, because no heavy blocks of stone could be used such as those in the cupolas of the Pantheon and the Basilica of St. Peter, in Rome—two structures erected by the same method fifteen hundred years apart! As stated before, the entire superstructure of the Báb's Shrine is based not on the granitic depth of Mt. Carmel, but on reinforced concrete stilts capable of supporting only a limited weight. When Mr. Maxwell designed the dome, he was well aware that such weight limitations had to play an important part in carrying out the structural work. Well before the erection of the octagon began, the dome and its covering were two of the most important problems to be solved. There was the architectural drawing of the dome, but no indication of the material to be used in its construction, and for its covering Shoghi Effendi desired an integument of a gilded material.

At the very beginning of the project, when Mr. Maxwell came to Rome in 1948, the Guardian sent verbal instructions to begin the search for a suitable and lasting material for the outer finish of the dome. Many possibilities were then examined, and after Mr. Maxwell's departure the opinion of experts was secured to crystallize the choice upon materials which were available and offered the durability required. One by one, after some consideration, such materials as gilded copper laminae, mosaic, and vitreous coating were rejected, leaving the possibility of using faience or terracotta tiles. The latter seemed the more appropriate because imbrication* for the dome's covering was an essential requirement on the part of the architect, and could be carried out only by using tiles of a shape which could be properly manufactured and manipulated. When it was definitely agreed, with Shoghi Effendi's approval, to use tiles, the difficult part of the task began, as until then the whole matter had remained in the domain of theoretic investigation.

Italy is a country where throughout the centuries the erection of domed chapels, churches, and cathedrals had been of primary importance. Consequently a subsidiary industry had developed for the fabrication of tiles specially designed to supply the everincreasing demand. Before the Second World War, the centre of production of such tiles was in the Campania region, on the Tyrrhenian Sea, between Naples and Salerno, and particularly around Vietri. During the Salerno landing, which devastated that region with all its fury, these tile factories were destroyed. When, in the late months of 1948, the investigation for the Shrine started, it was impossible to locate one factory in operation capable of undertaking the work. The few factories which had started production, including some in other regions of Italy, were manufacturing rough tiles of red clay, and were unwilling or perhaps

---

* A method of placing tiles with overlapping edges to prevent infiltration of moisture from rain or snow.

unable to undertake such highly skilled work. Searches were also made in the island of Sicily, and in Spain and Portugal during the two ensuing years, with the same negative results. But the hand of Providence unexpectedly opened the way for realization of the important goal. Early in September 1951, the Fourth European Teaching Conference and the Second European Summer School took place in Scheveningen, in the Netherlands. There I had the opportunity to look for a factory capable of producing the type of tiles needed, for Holland is well known throughout the world for its faience work. After securing a list of the best known and most reliable factories, I spent two days visiting each firm. The affair proved to be disheartening because our inquiries were either received with incredulity or were declined for technical reasons. In the afternoon of the second day, however, after having already travelled throughout the Netherlands, I reached a small factory, the last one named on the list, which was located on the outskirts of the city of Utrecht, south of the Ijssel Sea, on a canal which later proved to be of some assistance. A preliminary conversation with one employee was continued with the director of the plant, who proved to be a well-spoken, competent, responsive and eager person. He was a chemical engineer by profession, a member of the nobility, and had taken on the management of this modest factory at the end of the war, and he was struggling to make it successful. His name was Junker Robert de Brauw. After my two days of wandering around the Netherlands and receiving only negative answers, it was like finding a ray of light on a dark sea of uncertainty. From the very beginning of our conversation he won my confidence and trust, and relieved me of all my anxiety. His statement: 'We have only made flat gilded tiles for a vertical suspension'—and he named a project just completed in another country—'but we are willing to try', was the most decisive point in his favour. The trust placed in him and his firm was repaid by skill, eagerness and whole-hearted collaboration. That night I returned to Scheveningen with my heart singing with praise and gratitude to the Almighty, and shared this joy with my dear wife who was the only person who knew of this mission. Next morning, another visit to Junker de Brauw consolidated our

H

understanding and opened the way to start the meticulous and lengthy researches and preparatory work. The approval of Shoghi Effendi soon came, with his blessing. Thus began another chapter of this wondrous story.

That Mr. de Brauw had been trained as a chemist was a great asset to our project, because three of the four problems in the production of the Shrine's tiles were of a chemical nature: namely, the composition of the tiles, the golden coating, and the glazing. The fourth issue consisted of several material aspects which physics and engineering were to solve and in which Mr. de Brauw was also very proficient. At no expense to the Faith, six months of research work were spent choosing the proper ingredients for composition of the tiles. Various samples were sent from time to time to Haifa to be tested at the Technion by Professor Neumann, for resistance to high solar and to frigid temperatures, moisture, air salinity, expansion and shrinkage, desert winds, and sand blasting, until the proper and most durable combination was found. Another object of a lengthy study was the size and shape of the tiles, but of this we shall speak later on.

Professor Neumann was to develop all the engineering details of the dome itself, which had to be light in weight but strong enough to bear the load of the tiles, the marble carvings which are the decorative and integumental parts of the dome itself, and the lantern which tops the whole structure of the Shrine.

When Dr. Neumann stopped in Rome, after a visit to northern Europe, I had the opportunity to discuss with him the plans he had devised to build a cupola that would be light and strong. He spoke then of a recent method of spraying cement mixed with fine sand and water upon a mould—sometimes consisting of an inflated balloon—which was used in Europe in its rapid reconstruction of buildings ravaged by the war. The process is called 'guniting'. He said, 'It will be as light and strong as an eggshell, and capable of holding tiles and stones, with a margin of weight capacity to spare.' The problem, however, was to decide upon the size and shape of the tiles to cover the dome, which did not yet exist. We did have theoretical measurements from the architect's drawings—according to which all the marble work was being prepared in Pietrasanta—but a risky decision was needed to determine the thickness of the tiles and the mortar to be applied upon the rough surface of the 'gunited' dome-shell. After many trials, Junker de Brauw acceded to my suggestion to build in the factory yard a replica of one-eighteenth of the dome out of wood, that all tests and experiments could be carried out as if the dome actually existed. This was a great help, and hastened the initiation of tile production. Having finally established every detail—with samples on hand approved by the engineer—a contract was signed in Utrecht in September 1952, for production of the twelve thousand tiles needed to cover the two hundred and fifty square metres of the dome's surface. Once more I wish to render a tribute of gratitude to Junker de Brauw, and his collaborators, who spared no effort or expense during the preliminary experimental period, to choose the proper ingredients such as Rhine kaolin and sand, and patiently to design and produce many samples of the fifty and more sizes and shapes of the tiles. They also undertook the production, packing and shipment of the whole supply with keen interest and enthusiasm. My personal relationship with Junker de Brauw became one of warm friendship, and his wise and skilful personal intervention in solving many of the technical problems in the manufacture and production of the tiles was evidence of the reverence and respect he had acquired for the purposes and aims of the Bahá'í Faith.

To the casual observer of the dome as it is now, all tiles look the same in shape and size, but the form of the dome—as designed by the architect—actually combines a cylinder, a sphere and a cone, thus presenting changes of the curved surface from the lower part by the brim to the base of the lantern at the top. This conception required, as already mentioned, more than fifty sizes and shapes of tiles which, during the experimenting, were individually designed, and by repeated trial and error were produced in clay, until perfection was achieved. Looking back, I can see clearly only what a great role the prayers of Shoghi Effendi had in this accomplishment and how the divine assistance flowed abundantly to remove every difficulty.

Junker de Brauw, because of his high connection with the

government, was able to secure the pure gold needed to cover, by a chemical reduction process, each tile with a thin layer of gold.

A system of packing in paper and double cardboard boxes, which was tested against breakage by throwing sample boxes from the height of a third floor, resulted in the delivery of the tiles at the port of Haifa without one tile either broken or damaged. Moreover, loading and shipping costs were considerably reduced because the factory was on the canal.

When, in early May 1953, the time came to cast the concrete cupola, a circular wooden shuttering—some forty-five feet in diameter—was erected inside the upper opening of the clerestory or drum; then reinforced steel was woven onto it and sprayed with concrete, which dried in eight days. By 11 May, the cement dome had been completed. This was the cause of much rejoicing for Shoghi Effendi as, after five years of labour, the completion of the Holy Edifice was near at hand. A few days earlier, on 29 April, the beloved Guardian, followed by Mr. Leroy Ioas, Hand of the Cause of God, and Dr. Luṭfu'lláh Ḥakím, member of the International Council,* climbed the scaffolding up to the base of the dome, and reverently placed a small silver box, containing a fragment of plaster from the ceiling of the Báb's prison cell in the Castle of Máh-Kú, beneath one of the gilded tiles in the first row.†
Those who were present related to me later that it was a deeply moving experience to see the Guardian mounting the ladder straight up to the dome, standing there with a luminous joyful countenance while performing that pious and historic act. He then walked around the base of the dome, came down the ladder, circumambulated the roof of the arcade, walked around the gardens for some time and then entered the Shrine for prayer and praise.

Completion of the dome followed in two months with feverish speed: the placing of the eighteen marble ribs and of the floral ornamentations between the ribs; the erection of the base of the lantern with its columns of Rose Baveno granite; the fixing of

* Later, he became a member of the first Universal House of Justice.
† These few tiles were affixed at the base of the dome for the celebration of the Ninth Day of Riḍván (29 April), prior to the casting of the cupola.

the 'bell' of the lantern and finial—the latter of Chiampo marble; and finally the placement of all the golden tiles. All this truly set a record in ability and swiftness, under the guiding hand of Mr. Leroy Ioas, who had supervised the construction since spring 1952, including both clerestory and dome.

In a cablegram addressed to the National Spiritual Assemblies of the Bahá'í world on 19 August 1953, Shoghi Effendi announced the end of all the structural work on the Shrine, including the placing of the gilded tiles; and he foresaw the completion of the Holy Edifice in the following month, to coincide with the New Delhi Intercontinental Teaching Conference which concluded the 'world-wide festivities of the Holy Year commemorating the centenary of the birth of the Mission of Bahá'u'lláh'.[15] At this Conference, 7–15 October 1953, a message from Shoghi Effendi confirmed the consummation of that noble enterprise initiated over sixty years before, and requested that a 'befitting memorial gathering pay tribute' to the Shrine's immortal architect, Mr. William Sutherland Maxwell. Shoghi Effendi honoured also, by mentioning their names, this writer and Mr. Leroy Ioas, for their parts in the construction of the Shrine.[16] The same message contained the most beautiful and poetic description of the Holy Shrine, expressing Shoghi Effendi's pride and marvel in the following words:

> . . .Queen of Carmel enthroned
> on God's Mountain, crowned
> in glowing gold, robed in
> shimmering white, girdled in
> emerald green, enchanting every
> eye from air, sea, plain and hill.

In February 1954, a personal memento from Shoghi Effendi was brought to me in Rome by an American pilgrim, Mr. Frank Baker, the husband of the late Hand of the Cause, Mrs. Dorothy Beecher Baker, who had lost her life in an aeroplane disaster in the skies over Italy, one month before. This memento, an invaluable recompense for the efforts made to assist him in the completion of this epic enterprise, consisted of a large sepia-coloured photograph of the Shrine of the Báb, taken from the west—the first photo of the kind I had ever seen since the completion of the building. On the back, penned by the loving hand of Shoghi Effendi, was written:

To dear Ugo in loving appreciation of his historic services to the Shrine of the Báb

Shoghi

VIII

The Gardens Surrounding the Shrine
of the Báb

MENTION has already been made of Shoghi Effendi's
great love for beauty in the world of nature, love
which was reflected in his eagerness to landscape most
of the ground around the Shrine of the Báb, and extend the gardens on the mountain-side, below and above the Holy Edifice.
Since assuming the Guardianship, his efforts, displaying originality, talent and good taste, were directed at beautifying the whole
area. His keen observance of nature and love of gardens greatly
assisted him in this work. When I first met him, I was astonished
at the encyclopaedic knowledge he possessed on this subject,
which, combined with a practical ability, made him the most outstanding landscapist in all Palestine. I vividly remember the exchange of views on gardening—as in my youth I had learned quite
a lot from the gardeners on my family's estate in Sicily, where
climate and flora are very similar to those of the Holy Land—
and Shoghi Effendi's surprise in finding out how much I shared
the enjoyment of his avocation although with a lesser degree of
competence. On my part, having greatly admired the work already accomplished by him up to 1952, I was utterly fascinated
with the versatility of his original mind.*

A few days later, on the evening after my first visit to the
Shrine of Bahá'u'lláh and the Mansion of Bahjí, the Guardian
asked me what I had first noticed on entering the Mansion. He
was looking at me intently, with an expression of expectation on
his dear face, and when I replied that on the wall at the top of the
staircase I had seen the framed photograph of an interesting man's
head, possibly of a Persian, his face became aglow with an inner
feeling of pleasure and gratification. 'Oh, I am glad you did see

---

* See Appendix I, p. 191, for a similar statement by Dr. Alaine Locke.

it,' he said smiling; 'how observant you are. I placed that picture there myself for everyone to see. It is our remarkable and celebrated gardener Abu'l-Qásim, whose services to the Master and myself will never be forgotten.' I had heard before of Abu'l-Qásim,* and of his great competence and dedicated activities, but I had not seen his photograph, now so much honoured as to welcome every visitor who enters the Mansion of Bahá'u'lláh.

Some months later, when I visited one of the farms previously belonging to the Master, purchased by Him on the east shore of the Sea of Galilee, in commenting upon the perfection of the agricultural developments visible all around, I was told by those who were then attending the farm: 'This is not all our merit; what we are now doing is what we learned from the Persian Bahá'ís who cultivated the place formerly.' That testimonial strengthened my conviction that the enterprising spirit displayed by Shoghi Effendi in beautifying the grounds around all the Holy Places of the Faith had deep roots in the traditions of Persia, so famous since ancient times for its celebrated ornamental gardens.

It is impossible for me adequately to relate the history of the development of the gardens around the Shrine of the Báb. The difficulties in purchasing the necessary land, since the days of 'Abdu'l-Bahá and through the stewardship of Shoghi Effendi, have elsewhere been mentioned,† and the reader can well imagine the Guardian's anxiety to acquire enough ground on that holy mountain to ensure the beautification of the environs and the privacy which would protect the sacredness of the Mausoleum, and to permit hosts of pilgrims and visitors to come from all over the world to enjoy the spiritual atmosphere of that hallowed spot without outside intrusion. The beloved Master, 'Abdu'l-Bahá, from the very beginning of His erection of the first six rooms of the Shrine, had arranged for a small flower garden compatible with the ground then available around the building. I remember having seen, years ago, a photograph taken possibly in 1907 that

* Ustád Abu'l-Qásim K̲h̲urásání, who in the eve of his life offered his priceless treasures—various relics and Tablets of 'Abdu'l-Bahá—to be preserved on his behalf in the National Archives of the Bahá'ís in America.[17]

† See *God Passes By*, page 275; Shoghi Effendi had also experienced many difficulties in land purchase.

showed the arrangement of some shrubs and flower plants in front (the north façade) of the Shrine. This garden extended a little to east and west of the building, and was protected by an iron fence of a simple design—perhaps four feet high—and a wood bower at one end, holding up climbing vines. Not much water was then available for the garden, other than that gathered from rain and stored in a cistern, adjacent to the Shrine. This cistern 'Abdu'l-Bahá had built well before the construction of the Shrine was initiated. I vividly recollect Shoghi Effendi speaking of this important step taken by 'Abdu'l-Bahá right after He had decided to erect that sacred building. The limitation of water prevented expanding the cultivated ground.

It was again the creative ability and eagerness of Shoghi Effendi that made it possible to bring more water to the mountain, thus permitting development of an extensive plan of beautification of the grounds. The result was a departure from the formality of English or Italian gardens, as he adapted his cultivated taste to the nature of the ground, the type of trees, of shrubs and flowers that would survive and thrive in the climate of that country, and to the general landscape of the whole region.

The rocky and impervious slopes of the mountain presented many difficulties to the habitual gardener, firstly because of limited accessibility, and secondly because of the erosive action of the winter and spring torrential rains which would wipe out any growing thing other than well-rooted trees.

The answer, as 'Abdu'l-Bahá had anticipated, was terraces that would retain the soil and provide level ground on which to plant flowers and shrubs. My impression, when I first beheld that part of Mt. Carmel on which the Shrine is located, was that of a huge stage set up for an epic drama. I find it difficult to convey in words the feeling that overcame me as I considered the details, so well thought out, of the delightful and harmonious landscape surrounding the focal point—the Shrine of the Báb. I recalled childhood memories of the crib of the infant Jesus, at Christmas time, surrounded by clay angels and awed figures of men and animals, trees and flowers and burning candles, and the music of a mechanical carillon, repeating a seraphic tune over and over again. Then, as that memory faded, I saw the Shrine in its true reality, half erected, emerging from a garden of enchantment, which like a precious mantle of green would enhance the beauty of the gold-crowned 'Queen of Carmel', the dramatic crèche of a New Revelation for a new world!

Immediately after starting his historic Guardianship, Shoghi Effendi devoted some of his precious and busy hours to laying out a general pattern of a garden which would surround the original Shrine erected by 'Abdu'l-Bahá, and to preparing a setting for embellishment of the Shrine.

In the early 1920's, the pattern started to unfold. The ground was levelled in front of the Shrine; the sharp pendency of the mountain was lessened in the rear and at the sides of the building, permitting hedges and flowers to be planted,* and paths, walks and steps to be laid out, much as we see them today.

'Men really know not what good water's worth.'†

Although in earlier times an aqueduct had been built to bring water from the Lebanese mountains to the city of Ptolemais ('Akká), it had been rendered ineffective by neglect. A real system of water distribution did not come into existence until after the creation of the State of Israel. Wells and cisterns—the latter to conserve rainfall—were generally used to provide water for domestic consumption. As mentioned at the beginning of this chapter, Shoghi Effendi solved the problem of watering the Shrine gardens with ingenious and practical technique. When the house of 'Abdu'l-Bahá, at 7 Persian Street, was built in the first decade of this century, a deep well, located on the south side of the building, had at the time an excellent supply of water, which was at first drawn up by the ancient method of a pulley, cord and pail, and subsequently by other methods, including a pump actioned by a windmill. The only way to secure the water needed for the Shrine gardens was to bring the water of that well up the mountain. The Guardian personally related to me what a challenging task it was to find so much iron pipe locally; pipes of

* A list of the plants used is given in Appendix XI.
† Byron in *Don Juan*, Canto ii, st. 84.

various diameters, assembled with the use of different junctures, had to be used, until the whole distance from the house of the Master to the Shrine of the Báb could be covered.

The reader should consider the technical elements that had to be overcome in negotiating both the distance and the difference of levels. The other problem to be solved was the high pressure needed to lift the water from the level of almost zero to over five hundred feet. The old windmill was unable to accomplish this task and was discarded for an electric piston pump which later was replaced by an electric high-pressure rotative pump, that increased the supply of water brought up the mountain to fulfil the needs of the ever-expanding gardens.

The steepness of the slopes was overcome by terraces made by filling retaining walls with earth. The first was the large terrace in front of the Shrine which extended on its east and west sides. Other terraces followed at the rear of the Shrine, in parallel, and of the same length as the first one. Some rather steep paths and a series of steps made it possible to circulate around the Shrine with some facility. Shoghi Effendi adopted the same system for the Monument gardens to the south, and later again when the International Archives garden was being laid. Once I asked him why some of the paths were so steep. He looked at me with a mild expression of surprise on his face, as if I should have known the answer, that the beauty of the gardens surpassed in importance the convenience of the ever-increasing number of visitors.

The terrace in front of the Shrine was considerably extended to the east during the spring of 1952. Most of the retaining walls had hitherto been built of dry stones, that is, without mortar or cement; this extension, however, and the two lower terraces towards the east, were supported by cut stone and steel-reinforced concrete.

The Municipality of Haifa was selling a large quantity of stones from buildings which had been torn down to make room for new constructions, and Shoghi Effendi contracted to buy as much as possible and cart it away with our own truck. The construction of the Shrine had reached the level of the pinnacles and he was extremely anxious to complete the extension of the garden at an early date. We had a crew of workers unloading the truck and bringing the stones to the masons; no matter how fast they worked, there was a constant excess of stones to be moved to make room for the successive arrival of a new load. I was not aware that sometime during the forenoon hours, the Guardian was following with powerful binoculars the work on the wall from one window of his home which looked directly towards the Shrine. One morning we were short of a workman, and to help expedite the work, I helped to move the stones, little knowing that I was being observed from a distance by Shoghi Effendi. That night at the table—perhaps I looked a bit fatigued by the unusual labour—Shoghi Effendi asked me what I had been doing during the day, and I answered that I had spent the forenoon at the terrace wall, and the afternoon at the Shrine. He looked at me intensely and then he said, 'I saw you this morning carrying stones; you must not do that; when you will see your Guardian carrying stones, then you shall be authorized to do the same.' There was such a tone of love and compassion in his voice that I could hardly contain my tears, but I keenly felt how much he had appreciated that humble action of devotion. This was Shoghi Effendi, the planner, the engineer, the essence of justice, the liberal and loving true brother!

By the time the huge wall was finished, and the great pit filled with stones and earth, there had been planted trees and hedges, flowers and grass. In two weeks the carpet of tender green new grass extended from one end to the other of this terrace, which enjoys one of the most beautiful views over the city of Haifa, the bay of 'Akká, and the endless Mediterranean Sea. Cypress trees were planted along the northern aspect of the terrace, new lamp-posts were ordered in Italy, and later erected, and iron fences, gates, urns, eagles and peacocks were placed on marble or stone bases, to enhance the grandeur and the mystic beauty of that blessed spot. Looking out from the north side of the terrace, one sees, immediately at the foot of the mountain, Carmel Avenue, a straight thoroughfare which passes through the midst of the German Templars' Colony and reaches the port of the city. All the land between the Shrine and the foot of the mountain, at the beginning of Carmel Avenue, which the Guardian had purchased in various lots over many years, was to be transformed into luxuriant gardens, thus completing the ornamental sylvan frame around that blessed focal point, the Shrine of the Báb. To Shoghi Effendi, the connection between the Shrine and Carmel Avenue was essential, for it had been planned by 'Abdu'l-Bahá a quarter of a century before with a series of nine terraces, and this plan was set in his mind. Technical difficulties arose which only his inventiveness and perseverance were able to overcome. My heart still pains at the thought of the arduous and Herculean efforts of the beloved Shoghi Effendi, who, single-handed and over-burdened by a magnitude of other activities and anxieties, planned and brought into existence the nine terraces, upon which 'the bare feet of the pilgrim kings of the world'—as he often repeated—'would tread the hallowed ground to reach and circumambulate the Shrine of the Báb in adoration.'

I was told that during the clearing of that ground, one small house stood in the way, which the Guardian wanted removed. He waited for days to have the work done by a crew of bungling men, until, unable to contain his disappointment, he went to the place and, seizing a heavy sledge-hammer, with unsuspected skill demonstrated to the workers, by well-aimed blows, how to deal with the matter. By evening the house had been torn down, and the stones were later utilized in terracing the ground. Because of the interference of some Covenant-breakers, the work which had been initiated in the late 'twenties was completed only in the early spring of 1951, when the last two terraces, closest to the Shrine, were finished to his joy and satisfaction. Palms and cypresses were planted and electric lights set all along both sides of the nine terraces, fulfilling what had been one of the cherished wishes of 'Abdu'l-Bahá.

When this writer reached Haifa in March 1952, at the request of the Guardian, he was informed of certain plans Shoghi Effendi had devised for the beautification of the lower end of the terraces at Carmel Avenue, the embellishment of the grounds around Bahjí, and the construction of a magnificent Shrine around the existing Tomb of Bahá'u'lláh. 'I have asked you to come here, to consult with you on these matters,' he said to me right after my arrival, 'and I shall want you to secure estimates of costs for such projects; do not think that your work will terminate with the completion of the Shrine of the Báb,' and in saying so he looked at me as if he wanted me to be at his service for a long time to come. It was a moment of great inner happiness for me, because I wished nothing more than to make his burden lighter on matters in which physical efforts and aptitude were essential.

Mr. Maxwell, at the request of the Guardian, had prepared architectural plans for a monumental gate to be built at the lower end of the terraces facing Carmel Avenue. It was a classic project, somewhat on the order of the gate at the entrance to the gardens on UNO Avenue, but on a wider front and more dramatic. It consisted of two posts of considerable height, and four smaller ones, all of marble, which would support a large iron-wrought gate of conventional baroque design, and four smaller iron panels. These smaller panels matched the same design, and would be placed two on each side of the central gate. The four smaller posts were to rest on a dressed marble wall about four feet high. The plan of Mr. Maxwell included also an artistic circular fountain which Shoghi Effendi at the time felt would not yet be feasible; the fountain was to be placed at a certain distance before the gate. The whole project was indeed handsome, and would have enhanced considerably the beauty of the whole area. Bids for this project were secured, approved and contracted for the work to be executed over a period of a few months. When the material—marble and iron-work—arrived in Haifa, I had already left the Holy Land, and could not explain why Shoghi Effendi, after seeing some of the finely executed parts of the gate, suddenly decided to use all that material in the beautification of the grounds at Bahjí.* In a later chapter I shall indicate where the many component parts of it are to be found.

To add some final words to the subject of the gardens, I would like to mention that one section of the grounds, in the proximity

---

* It seems that agreement to this plan could not then be reached with the Municipality of Haifa, which owned the road abutting on the terraces.

of the Eastern Pilgrim House on Mt. Carmel, almost in front of it, was transformed by the Guardian into an enchanting tropical oasis, with desert plants and many varieties of cacti, which lend to the spot a highly admired exotic appearance.

Among other things of interest is the varied colour of the paths; some are bright white, filled with pebbles from the Sea of Galilee, while others are ochre-red, covered with crushed roof tiles of French manufacture. During the last century, when the influence of France was strong in Syria, red roof tiles, made in Marseilles, little by little supplanted the crushed stone on arched ceilings used by the Arabs, according to the Roman method of making roofs. Nearly all homes, before the advent of reinforced concrete, had such roofs. Shoghi Effendi, whose talent for originality was immense, devised the idea of alternating paths of different colours in the gardens, and kept on buying discarded roof tiles—from demolished houses or other sources—and having them crushed into small fragments by an ingenious, hand-operated, small machine. In the late 'fifties, however, the supply of red tiles became scarcer and scarcer, and crushed bricks were used as a substitute.

I would like also to call the attention of the reader to the fact that it was Shoghi Effendi who, since the early days of his ministry, organized the outer illumination of the Shrine of the Báb and of the gardens. Long before the new superstructure of the Shrine was initiated, the building erected by 'Abdu'l-Bahá had been illuminated on the outside by small electric reflectors, the light of which became more and more powerful and luminous, as conditions permitted and better equipment was secured. I remember how often he would tell the visiting pilgrims that because a simple candle was denied the beloved Báb during His imprisonment in Máh-Kú, His resting-place was to be eternally a temple of light. This was also true inside His tomb, where there is a magnificent chandelier, with almost a hundred electric bulbs that, when lighted, turn the sombre dim light of the inner chamber into the full glory of brilliant sunshine. The adjacent tomb of 'Abdu'l-Bahá is also illuminated by another crystal chandelier, a splendour which can hardly repay the beloved Master for the glorious light of His exemplary life diffused over three continents of the world.*

One other outstanding and yet most attractive feature of the gardens is provided by decorative objects spread throughout the grounds, in positions where they produce an impressive effect. They include vases, obelisks, urns, fountains and birds, placed on pedestals of dressed local stone or of Carrara marble. Some urns are beautiful examples of Italian carving; others are reproductions of peacocks, eagles, or flowers—mostly tulips—made of pewter or other lead alloy, which Shoghi Effendi purchased from time to time in Europe. They are fine works of art endowed with graceful elegance which add considerably to the beauty and magnificence of the gardens surrounding the Shrine. I well remember the eagerness of Shoghi Effendi in placing such ornamentations as soon as the ground of the terrace was made ready. Often I was charged with the purchase in Italy of pedestals, marble blocks, columns, and bird-baths, and with making sure that such valuable ornamentations were securely fastened to their bases, to discourage souvenir hunters. Visitors or pilgrims would often ask the meaning of peacocks and eagles situated in the proximity of the Shrine, imagining that perhaps an esoteric or mystical significance was connected with the Bahá'í Revelation. The beloved Guardian, at times much amused, always infinitely patient, would explain how in ancient Persian literature the peacock was considered the symbol of eternal life, while the eagle he considered the symbol of victory. Therefore they were befitting ornaments to decorate the earth ennobled by the 'Dust' of the Martyr-Prophet, the Báb, Whose ancient roots stemmed from the land of Fárs (Persia).

---

* These two chandeliers were placed in the Shrine of the Báb in 1952; the one in the tomb of the Báb was made in Germany; the other, in Czechoslovakia. Both were gifts from two Bahá'í friends.

IX

The Garden Nurseries

REFERENCE has often been made to the limitation of financial means from which the Guardian suffered, a condition which now makes it almost impossible to understand how he could have done so much with the little he had. The prestige and decorum of the Faith were to him the true foundation upon which the fame of the Revelation of Bahá'u'lláh would spread throughout the world, and his inventiveness and ingenuity would plan things which could not be provided otherwise for lack of means. Therefore to make the gardens as beautiful as he envisaged, he had to overcome many difficulties by seeking from the beginning the elements necessary to give substance to his plans. The spartan life lived within the limitations imposed upon 'Abdu'l-Bahá and His family by a relentless foe had tempered the character of the young Shoghi Effendi who, in becoming accustomed to privations on the one hand, rejoiced in the satisfaction of self-imposed discipline on the other. This quality of thrift in non-essentials remained one of his sterling habits, which permitted him to demonstrate his generosity in all its nobility on matters which reflected upon the greatness of the Cause of God.

Under Turkish domination and under the British Mandate, the policies of both governments were to limit expenditures to strictly military and civil administration, with practically little or no outlay of funds for things considered unnecessary, such as beautification of the land, reforestation or experimental and botanical gardens. One of the things which attracted my attention on my first visit to the World Centre of the Faith was the existence of two nurseries which Shoghi Effendi had established, one in Haifa and one in Bahjí, to assure a constant supply of trees and plants for the expansion of the gardens. In Haifa, the nursery was located on the grounds north and east of the Pilgrim House,

I

near the Tomb of the Báb; that ground is now partly used as a parking space, and partly as a flower garden. In Bahjí, it was located not too far from the main entrance to the inner garden of the Mansion and is now part of the path that leads from the eastern terraces to the Master's Tea House. In both nurseries there were hundreds of clay pots of different sizes and depths, in which small trees, shrubs and flower plants were growing from seeds or cuttings. These were the product of the foresight of Shoghi Effendi, whose sagacity had envisioned the ideal beautification of the landscape around the Holy Places of the Faith. What chiefly caught my fancy were the cypress yearlings which stood upright like egret plumes waving in the breeze. While in the nurseries, with the roots imprisoned in small pots, they would not grow very fast but when transplanted into the fertile soil of that land, they would immediately increase from day to day in size and height. Shoghi Effendi spoke several times to me of his efforts to obtain trees and plants, and how he had to search in many directions to remedy a situation which was rather difficult to overcome. Many times since those days, and especially whenever I have visited the Holy Land, I have wondered what would have happened to the land around the sacred Tombs if Shoghi Effendi had not taken to his heart, in every minute detail, the destiny of its beauty and glorification.

In the early 'fifties, after the formation of the State of Israel, it became possible to secure from governmental nurseries some of the trees needed, particularly the cypresses which with their graceful stateliness have become the ornamental landmarks of the Bahá'í properties in the Holy Land.*

---

* This writer would like to remember an earlier gardener, who tried his very best to start and develop the Garden of Riḍván, near 'Akká, and was much esteemed by Bahá'u'lláh, for his loyalty and skill. His name was 'Abdu'ṣ-Ṣáliḥ, originally from Iṣfáhán, the son of earlier believers who had reached 'Akká in order to be of service to the Blessed Beauty. (See *Memorials of the Faithful*, pp. 26–8.)

X

Pilgrimage to the Shrine of Bahá'u'lláh

THE first time I beheld the Shrine of Bahá'u'lláh, I was overcome by deep emotion and, as I walked close to it, trepidation and excitement made it almost impossible for me to advance further. Years of expectation surged in my mind, and the desire to prostrate myself upon the Holy Tomb, for a long time the goal of my life which was now becoming reality, was at the same time urging and restraining me. Perplexity held me fastened to the ground, and if it had not been for the gentle calling of my escort, I should have remained in that state for quite a long time.

It is not possible to describe the feeling of exaltation and awe which overtook me upon entering the door of that Sacred Sepulchre! The world with all its immensity whirled away into nothingness with the rapidity of lightning. I was alone, relieved of cares and thoughts, free from all attachments, as if suspended between heaven and earth. I could only feel the fast beats of my heart and the humming of infinity. There was nothing but light all around me and a powerful fragrance never known before. As in a dream, transported by the attraction exercised by the mystery emanating from the most Blessed Spot in creation, I reached the portal leading to the inner chamber of the Tomb and fell on my knees and placed my forehead on that hallowed Threshold. I felt the need to conceal my face in the ground, as my whole being was gripped by a strong sensation of guilt—guilt for having arrived so late in my life. I could hear myself saying: Forgive, forgive, forgive ... for a long time, and then a great peace filled me. My whole past life came before me as an irrelevant episode of eternity, while the present and the vision of the future filled me with unprecedented joy and the lightness of freedom. Glory, immense glory, through a path which precluded any return; a complete sublimation in the transcendency of creation; the certainty of nearness to the 'Mighty Root' from which the greatness and the perfection of the whole universe had been brought to earth. Prayers of thanksgiving and praise came to my lips; streams of unending tears flowed from my eyes, while in my thought all those whom I loved, like a legion of luminous entities, headed by none other than Shoghi Effendi himself, passed rapidly, moving forward and rejoicing with me.

When I came back to the reality of this contingent world, I felt that something had happened to me; my heart was filled with contentment, stability, expectation and unfading certainty. All those I loved became closer to me than ever before. Shoghi Effendi was eternally linked to my soul, while the problems of everyday life disappeared as small clouds swept by a fresh wind.

That same night, at the dinner-table, upon inquiry by the Guardian as to my impression of the Shrine of Bahá'u'lláh, I tried to express the tumult of my feelings. Shoghi Effendi looked at me with tenderness and understanding, and explained the influence upon the human soul of the earthly remains of the Messengers of God. 'They are, no doubt, endowed with a tremendous spiritual influence and far-reaching power. . . in the sense that Their dust was the physical mirror of the greatness of God.'[18]

Some weeks later, as already mentioned,* it was my special bounty to be with the Guardian at the commemoration of the Ascension of Bahá'u'lláh in His Shrine. After the commemoration ended in the small hours of the night, Shoghi Effendi, accompanied by the President of the International Bahá'í Council, returned to Haifa; all the other guests remained in Bahjí spending the rest of the night in the Mansion.

* See page 23.

XI

The Gardens at Bahjí

FOR quite some time Shoghi Effendi had desired to acquire more land adjacent to the Sepulchre of Bahá'u'lláh and the Mansion, in order to beautify the grounds of the true Qiblih of the Faith—the most majestic and dignified centre for all the followers of Bahá'u'lláh, as he personally related to me—but this had been impossible because of the interference of some ill-willed meddlers, until the opportunity came again right after the creation of the new State of Israel. The reader may remember the difficulties experienced in his efforts to restore the Mansion to its original condition, after the utter neglect into which it had fallen after the ascension of Bahá'u'lláh, and to obtain from the Mandate authorities the custodianship of this historic building, which for many decades had been the stronghold of an ignoble band of the breakers of His Covenant, who were entrenched in the precincts of the Most Holy Shrine of the Bahá'í world. This situation had grieved 'Abdu'l-Bahá beyond any capacity of endurance. On that particular night, previously mentioned,* during which the beloved Guardian spoke to me alone for many hours, he related all the suffering and the anguish of so many years of evil plotting, first against 'Abdu'l-Bahá, and after His passing, against himself. He went into the details of the provocations, the fiendish machinations, the defiant and open hostility, backed at times by, and in alliance with, sworn external enemies of the Cause for the express purpose of destroying the Divine Covenant, a spiritual madness which had contaminated almost all the surviving members of the family of Bahá'u'lláh. Once the evacuation of the occupants of the Mansion and its restoration had been achieved, Shoghi Effendi immediately began to direct his efforts to beautification of the little land available and particularly of the small plot to the north and west of the Shrine, and of the strip enclosed between

* See page 17.

the wall of the Mansion's garden and the east side of the Shrine and the building used as an early pilgrim house. Araucaria and tangerine trees were first planted there, with a few cypress and orange trees in front of the Shrine. It was in this small garden that the commemoration I have mentioned in the previous chapter took place. The rest of the grounds, a few metres away and all around the building, was a sea of sand, in some places actually dunes, while at about one hundred and thirty metres' distance, opposite the door of the Sepulchre, there was a large deep pit, possibly excavated a long time before to obtain sand for building purposes. On the west side, and at the rear of the Shrine, there were some olive trees, a few eucalyptus trees, and some ancient pines, which at the time of Bahá'u'lláh's residence in the Mansion were the only source of shade and coolness, during the torrid heat of the long Palestinian summers. This was the condition of the grounds around that Blessed Spot when I first saw it.

On the occasion of my first pilgrimage, Shoghi Effendi spoke to me at length of the plans he had for expansion of the gardens and beautification of the Shrine—one of the goals he had already set for the Ten Year Crusade. He commissioned me to secure, on my return to Italy, drawings and estimates of costs. Of this I shall give more details later on.

Towards the end of 1950, Shoghi Effendi had initiated negotiations with the government of the State of Israel for the acquisition of additional land around the Shrine and the Mansion. The opportunity to obtain such land came when that government, having decided that no alien could reside in the vicinity of the borders of the new nation, became willing to exchange some farm land belonging to Bahá'ís of Persian nationality,* located near the border of Jordan, for the same acreage around the Qiblih of our Faith. When the door of pilgrimage was opened again at

---

* The two brothers Ḥasan and Faríd and their sister, children of Dhikru'lláh and grandchildren of Mírzá Muḥammad Qulí, the faithful half-brother of Bahá'u'lláh and His companion in exile, spontaneously offered their farms for the exchange, and the Guardian compensated them for their loss to enable them to purchase other workable land in another location. The brothers were expert agriculturists and enjoyed a great reputation in the Jordan Valley.

the end of 1951, one of the first Western pilgrims was an American believer from Wisconsin, Mr. Lawrence Hautz, who made himself useful in carrying on the preliminary negotiations for the exchange of this land. They were difficult and protracted negotiations which, when completed, had lasted two years. The efforts made by Mr. Hautz and by Mr. Leroy Ioas, who, in March 1952, had assumed the General Secretariat of the International Bahá'í Council and taken over the negotiations, were acknowledged publicly by Shoghi Effendi in a message sent to the Bahá'í world the following November, after signature of the agreement had taken place.[19] In the spring of that year definite assurance of the exchange had been given, with the perfecting of the legal instruments of ownership to follow, an intelligence which highly encouraged the Guardian to proceed with his plans.

At about the same time, a great victory over the Covenant-breakers, who had instituted legal proceedings against the Guardian to prevent him from starting his beautification programme, resulted with a decision by the Israeli Government, who granted to the Guardian, as the sole Custodian of the Bahá'í Holy Sites, authorization to demolish the dilapidated buildings cluttering the Sacred Precincts. On more than one occasion Shoghi Effendi had spoken to me of the condition into which the surroundings of the Shrine of Bahá'u'lláh had deteriorated for decades, even to the indignity of allowing a blacksmith shop near the entrance to the Shrine—an incredible effrontery to the sacredness of the Most Holy Shrine of the Bahá'í world. His words of condemnation, broken by the emotion of his repressed deep sorrow and contempt, are still ringing in my ears, as the desecration of the Holy of Holies, for such a long time, had filled his heart with an anguish that those who were close to him felt he could no longer bear. I was utterly disconsolate, particularly during the period of the above-mentioned legal proceedings against him, when he passed through one of the most desolate periods of his life, with his health considerably impaired by the heart-felt grief.

On the occasion of this legal trial, he had summoned me to Haifa to assist him as much as possible and I was therefore an eye-witness to the shameful behaviour of the Covenant-breakers, the agonizing sufferings of the Guardian, and the ultimate victory of the cause of justice.

After my arrival in Haifa, Shoghi Effendi had often spoken of another task he would entrust to me, a task which he defined as 'spiritual'. It concerned the erection of the Most Holy Shrine of the Bahá'í world: 'The Shrine of Bahá'u'lláh, the One Who had sent down the Prophets'.

Because of the enthusiasm and the vigour with which he spoke of this subject, there was no doubt that he had a tentative plan for the beautification of the precincts of the Holy Shrine. He had a unique manner of asking questions, that at times could appear unrelated, but the answers he received were in his brilliant mind put in the proper place and sequence, to construct by his power of visualization the reality of things to come. For several nights he inquired about types of statuary marble—his preference was white Carrara, about methods of producing columns of very large dimensions, about triumphal monuments erected in ancient and in modern times to honour individuals or which were dedicated to faiths, cults or the arts, and the possibility of having an architectural plan and then of the project itself being carried out in the shortest possible time.

These conversations took place a little more than five years before his passing, and although the idea of his death, even at some time in the distant future, never crossed my mind, I was constantly under the apprehension that there was an impelling force that urged him to accomplish as much as he could while he was on earth. His manifold and far-sighted plans, which embraced a multitude of activities at the World Centre and throughout all the continents of the globe, bore eloquent testimony to this.

Later on I shall give a brief description of his idea for the Shrine of Bahá'u'lláh, 'only an embellishment', he would say, 'as the great Shrine, of untold magnificence, would be erected in future decades.' After he verbally revealed to me the project he had in mind, and charged me with securing drawings and estimates of cost, the opportunity, for which he had long waited, to beautify the grounds around the existing Shrine, arrived in the late days of April 1952.

XII

Embellishments to the Shrine of
Bahá'u'lláh

ONE evening, Shoghi Effendi came to the dinner-table with an expression of inner joy and determination on his face. After the usual greetings and before we started our meal, he looked around and said: 'Early tomorrow morning we all shall go to Bahjí; I am asking every available man to be there, as we have some very important work to do.' This was the beginning of one week of intense labour which completely changed the nature and aspect of the grounds—already described as a 'sea of sand'—into a garden and paradise of incomparable beauty.

The reader can hardly imagine what took place in those blessed days. All able-bodied men were there at the appointed hour. Shoghi Effendi with his masterly skill, already demonstrated in his beautification of the surroundings of the Shrine of the Báb, followed a plan preconceived in his mind. Assisted by his chauffeur, who carried a ball of string and some wooden pickets, he traced all the paths, nine in number, which like a fan were to radiate from the Shrine of Bahá'u'lláh towards a semicircular line (130 degrees; that is, about one-third of an arc) one hundred and ten metres away.

Guided by the strings which marked the paths, some of the gardeners dug small trenches in which to plant hedges of thyme. The widest path was the one leading from the 'circle' to the door of the Shrine of Bahá'u'lláh. With a joyous expression on his face, Shoghi Effendi said: 'Finally we have a dignified way to reach the Shrine, the approach to which I shall further beautify.'

A group of small dilapidated buildings cluttering the south end of the space between the Mansion of Bahjí and the Shrine was in no time torn down and the stone used to build a level platform in front of the Mansion on the side of the main entrance. Everyone was working with alacrity and high spirits, as we were conscious of the process of purification of that holy ground —often blessed by the presence of God's Manifestation—and of the creation of the 'Ḥaram-i-Aqdas',* to surround forever that Most Sacred Spot. Each one was doing a chore; personally, I was helping Shoghi Effendi with the tracing of the paths and the star-shaped flower beds. I was so entranced with his speed and resolution in giving form to a life-long dream that I had no eyes for anything else but him.

The word magic cannot well define what was taking place at every moment. It was like a powerful and ever-present force of enchantment creating beauty in a hundred places at the same time. Shoghi Effendi was moving about directing, counselling, cautioning, encouraging, explaining, demonstrating how to do apparently impossible things, and rejoicing in the transformation of the land under our very eyes. In the afternoon a drizzle came down but he would not leave the grounds, determined to accomplish as much as was possible before sunset. Markers and trees placed by the previous owners, who had never permitted either the purchase of the land or extension of the gardens around the Shrine, were removed. Young trees were brought in and planted along the paths; the outer semicircular line was doubled to make a wide tree-bordered avenue. Iron gates, steps, stone decorations, flowering plants, top soil and grass seeds were brought from Haifa, from Mt. Carmel, the Riḍván Garden, and the Master's House to give consistency to the superb embellishment plan.

During the night Shoghi Effendi developed a cold but in the morning he returned to work, feverish and suffering from all the inconvenience brought by the rheum. For three additional days he did not give up; there was ground to level, trees and borders to plant, and a hundred other details, all well established and correlated in his mind, and which only he would be able to accomplish. The sand was disappearing; the stones from the demolished buildings were already covered with good soil; hedges, pedestals and flower-beds were in place, and the neglected

* The outer sanctuary of Bahá'u'lláh's Shrine.

area, which for over half a century had been a scourge to the sanctity of the Holy Tomb, was not only cleansed and purified but had acquired also the beauty and the fragrance of a true 'Holy Court', worthy of the 'Dust' of the Founder of God's Most Holy Faith!

By the end of the fourth day, the sacred precincts of the Qiblih of the Bahá'í world had taken on the appearance of a beauteous, entrancing garden, looking as if it had been there from ancient times, and much as we see it today. Our triumphal return to Haifa could be compared to the return of the Argonauts after securing the Golden Fleece.

In the days which followed, Shoghi Effendi made further plans for embellishment and arranged for the gate, which had been prepared for the foot of the terraces leading from the Shrine of the Báb to Carmel Avenue, to be erected at the end of one of the nine paths leading from the Shrine of Bahá'u'lláh to the circle. For this was the path that ran through the high trees, often used by the Blessed Beauty, to shade and cool Himself during the high temperatures of the summer months.

The wrought-iron panels meant for the sides of that gate were utilized, together with the proper masonry, to fence the western side of the new garden which had been built upon the rubble of the destroyed buildings. The stone used for the support of the gate and its accessories was durable Italian granite, called 'breccia of Brescia', the same material that was used in the construction of King Victor Emmanuel's memorial monument in Rome. Here I would like to add that the aqueduct which crosses the property was exposed before the beautification of the grounds began. It would have crossed the path where the Italian gate was erected, but was, with the consent of the Antiquities Department, covered over when the levelling of the ground took place. Italian marble came once more to the assistance of the embellishment plan, providing steps for the different levels, pedestals for ornaments, and some delicate columns with capitals, which are still in the outer and inner sanctuaries of the Shrine.

The magnificent Collins gate, entrance to the broad path leading to the door of the Shrine, was obtained by Shoghi Effendi in

England—a gift to him by the beloved Hand of the Cause and Vice-President of the International Bahá'í Council, Amelia E. Collins.* It was erected in the following months, together with the pyramidal-obelisks and the flower-urns of lead, which border the path on each side. It was Shoghi Effendi's ardent desire to pave this most important path, leading to the Holy of Holies, with white Carrara marble. He had spoken to me of this, but perhaps because of the high cost, or the exposure of the marble to the hot sun which would alter its structure, he abandoned the idea, I believe temporarily, until his complete plan could go into action. Instead, he resorted to the use of the small white pebbles from the Sea of Galilee, such as he had used on the path between the second and third gates leading to the Shrine of the Báb on Mt. Carmel, and at the house of 'Abdu'l-Bahá at 7 Persian Street.

These pebbles are almost white and perfectly shaped: a phenomenon which I have rarely observed on the shores of other oceans, seas, and banks of rivers. The first time I beheld them, I was entranced by their whiteness and the regularity of their shape and size, and the thought came to me that it could not have been otherwise, as provident nature had readied the most perfect ground to hold the feet of the Christ and His fishermen apostles.

The following year, when the spring rains came in deluge, lashing the grounds under a strong north-east wind, a good part of the new garden was flooded. This called for an immediate remedy and Shoghi Effendi had the answer ready. Why not build a sort of impediment in the form of an embankment which would prevent the rain water from settling in the gardens? This first embankment took the form of a mortarless terrace, which became an excellent point of observation. This so pleased the Guardian that he added a second one and made plans for the third, which was not completed until after his passing. Gates and steps were made available to allow visitors to climb to the very top, with three broad paths, one on each terrace, which were bordered with cypress trees and reached to the main gate at the south-west end of the huge rampart. In no time the side of the

* See memorial article, *The Bahá'í World*, vol. XIII, pp. 834–41.

terraces looking towards the Shrine were landscaped with row upon row of geraniums, making the earth appear as if on fire with their innumerable red-flaming blossoms. On admiring the beauty of the whole project, there came to my mind a description I had read some time before of the Sumerian terraces of ancient Babylonia, famed for their beauty and magnificence. This was another expression of the imagination of Shoghi Effendi which was manifested with practicality and brilliance.

The various smaller wrought-iron gates and the dozens and dozens of lamp-posts placed all around the newly expanded gardens were produced in Italy at the request and to the specifications of Shoghi Effendi himself. When I returned to the Holy Land two years later, and visited the Shrine of Bahá'u'lláh one day after sunset, I was overcome by the serene beauty of the whole garden, lit by the generous system of illumination that the Guardian had developed, which added an element of mystery and wonder. It is like fairyland, I was repeating to myself, overwhelmed by the bliss of silence and solitude—the true 'Celestial City', where the certainty of God's presence was filling my soul with rapture and joy.

Shortly after sunset on the very day of His ascension, 29 May 1892, the earthly remains of Bahá'u'lláh were laid to rest in the most northerly room of a series of three dwellings used by members of His family. The interment consecrated that humble dwelling as the most Holy Spot on earth for the followers of His Faith. This one-storey building, adjacent and to the west of the Mansion, was a very simple structure of local stone, built in the Arab manner resembling a cube with a flat roof, a rather modest and unpretentious sepulchre for a Divine Messenger, the universality of Whose Message would in due time attract pilgrims from the four corners of the globe.

On my first pilgrimage, when visiting the room used by 'Abdu'l-Bahá in the pilgrim house at Bahjí—the most southerly of the three dwellings—I was shown a large quantity of architectural drawings and other papers, contained in a wooden coffer, which, it seems, had been there untouched for half a century.

They were shown to me probably because the papers and drawings were written or illustrated in Italian. It was the project of a monumental tomb for Bahá'u'lláh, made by an Italian engineer and architect, Henry Edward Plantagenet, a descendant of the Royal Family which ruled England from 1154 to 1485. This gentleman, who was born and lived in Florence, Italy, had been engaged by the Ottoman government to build the Syrian railroad, and had spent some years in that country.

From the drawings it was evident that he had been requested by some other member of Bahá'u'lláh's family to prepare the project. Obviously, he was inspired by some Bábí conception, for the monument consisted of a large structure in the form of a five-pointed star, the same shape as the pentagram used by the Báb in some of His Tablets and Writings. I have said 'some other member of the family', because 'Abdu'l-Bahá had a different plan which He was able to carry out in part. To protect and embellish the exterior north and west walls of the inner Shrine, a façade was made of soft local stone carrying out prevalent motifs of Arab architecture—a skilful execution of stereotomy—which lends great dignity to the unadorned and informal original structure.

The handsomeness of the simple façades, topped by the pyramidal red-tiled roof, cannot escape the keen observer. When I approached that holy building for the first time, I was deeply touched by the simple beauty of its appearance; in that simplicity there was a greatness which expressed good taste, gracefulness and a symmetry conveying classic harmony. In my youth, in my native Sicily, I was given the opportunity to learn how to appreciate the beauty of the Islamic arts, particularly of architecture, which used cut sandstone to erect some of the jewel-like buildings still in existence.

That night, and later on, in discussing with Shoghi Effendi the details of his plan, I voiced my praise for the façades of the Shrine and I became intimately happy in learning how much he valued its simple beauty. This was the point of departure for the embellishment of Bahá'u'lláh's Sepulchre: 'The building as fortified by 'Abdu'l-Bahá will not be touched; it will remain as the core of the new structure to surround the whole area, an inestimable gem representing the focal point of adoration for all the present and future followers of Bahá'u'lláh.' Shoghi Effendi was considering ways and means by which this might be accomplished, and after considerable discussion of a number of possibilities he finally contemplated surrounding the Sepulchre with a colonnade which would dramatize it from far and near: a total of ninety-five monolithic columns of Carrara marble, of Doric design, with capitals inspired by the purest existing examples of that order; all the columns arrayed in pairs, two in depth, over a platform of the same marble, accessible by a series of five steps, the whole ensemble 'like arms stretching ready to embrace'.

On several evenings the Guardian spent some time explaining the concept he had in mind, in order that I might secure drawings and estimates of cost. Each of the ninety-five columns would be six metres tall, supporting a carved capital—the weight of which would come close to a half metric ton—and each shaft, with the base and the capital, would stand up in the air almost seven metres; that, added to the height of the platform, would make an awesome complex whose brilliant majesty would glorify and enshrine the precious and sacred Holy of Holies.

On the evening of 4 March 1952, at the dinner-table, Shoghi Effendi turned to me and said: 'When the dome [of the Báb's Shrine] is finished, your work is not finished. We cannot hope to build the Shrine of Bahá'u'lláh now—that is impossible—but we can do something intermediate. The Master added a wall around to reinforce the original room. We cannot leave it for an indefinite time in this manner.'

Then, turning to Larry Hautz, he added: 'If you succeed in getting this land around the Shrine—it is very extensive—it will be a great blow to the Covenant-breakers. You will not only have dealt them a terrible blow, but you will have paved the way for the construction of what is going to be the intermediate stage between the present structure of the Shrine of Bahá'u'lláh and the final building, which will be on a scale far greater than the Shrine of the Báb.' Towards the end of the evening, he returned to this subject and added:

'We expect to get fifty acres at Bahjí . . . [permitting] avenues one hundred metres long, all smooth paths converging; we shall keep on building it, we shall build around it: a semicircular, double colonnade with columns all of marble. Preferably ninety-five in number, white, with ornaments, flower-beds, lawns and hedges.'

A detailed request, embodying this preliminary concept of the Guardian, was sent to Italy for scale drawings and estimates. The drawings for the columns with related bases and the capitals, when completed, were sent to Shoghi Effendi with reasonable estimates of cost. The price asked at that time was most moderate compared with the mounting costs some five years later. In his message of 30 June 1952, the Guardian told the Bahá'ís of the world: 'The assistance required for the acquisition of extensive properties, comprising both lands and houses, in the immediate neighbourhood of the Most Holy Tomb in Bahjí, and for the embellishment of the approaches of that hallowed Shrine—the Qiblih of the Bahá'í world—as a necessary prelude to the ultimate erection of a befitting Mausoleum to enshrine the remains of God's Supreme Manifestation on earth, must be generously and systematically extended.'[20] I well remember how pleased he was when a generous and prompt contribution—perhaps the first to that project—was sent by a loving and dedicated Persian believer. Shoghi Effendi, however, later abandoned the project of constructing this colonnade and concentrated on the embellishment of the surroundings of the Sepulchre of Bahá'u'lláh, including new wrought-iron gates for the entrance to the Shrine on the south side and for the Ḥaram-i-Aqdas.

During this time Shoghi Effendi started to experiment with red bricks, produced in Israel, for the erection of some gate-posts and lower walls in the area around the Mansion of Bahjí—a substitute for costly marble brought from Italy. The use of bricks pleased him considerably, particularly because of the quaint aesthetic effect which blended well with the nature of the ground and the general landscape.

The Guardian's plan to extend the gardens to the east of the terraces, in the same semicircular pattern he developed on the west side, was one of his cherished wishes that he was not able to accomplish during his lifetime, as the long-protracted negotiations for acquisition of the land—which became available only a few months before his passing—did not permit him to see his dream come true in all its glory.

The entrance door to the Shrine—of hard wood, quite sturdy, with metal hinges and handmade lock—must have been placed there for many decades before Shoghi Effendi started his programme of embellishment. It was a rather strange door which did not hang perpendicularly and was difficult to operate because the hinges of each half-door were not perfectly aligned, thus giving to the whole door an inclination of several degrees. I believe this was originally done in order to let the lashing northern rains of the Palestinian winters drain away faster. That door was plain and unadorned, not really befitting the sublimity of the edifice to which it was attached, and therefore needed to be replaced. To shelter the entrance from the rain, the Guardian, some years before, had erected a protecting canopy of heavy wooden beams and planks, one end resting on the wall, the other on two slender columns of white marble, supported by two masonry posts. I had returned to Italy from my fourth visit, when I received from Shoghi Effendi a sketch for a new door and a request to secure a scale drawing and estimate of cost.

Tuscany, one of the central provinces of Italy, has been known for centuries for the skill of its artisans, heirs to the Renaissance artist-craftsmen working in the *ateliers* of the most renowned masters of that time. Metal, wood, marble, leather, silk and many objects attest the good taste and refinement of their makers. Tuscany became, therefore, the place where the door of the Shrine of Bahá'u'lláh would be executed, and the city of Pistoia—once famous for the most luxurious carriages produced there until the beginning of this century—was chosen.

After inquiring among architects and artists, it was possible to find a reliable carpenter and cabinet-maker. His name was Saiello Saielli, and he was a willing and intelligent craftsman who fulfilled to the letter Shoghi Effendi's expectation. Being an expert in wood, Mr. Saielli was helpful in selecting the proper kind of well-seasoned oak, possessing the best grain, free of any blemish or imperfection.*

Owing to the climate of the Holy Land, and particularly of 'Akká, the structural frame of the door was to be built with layers of wood placed so that they would compensate for any stress or pull caused by heat, cold or humidity, thus preventing the slightest warping. Before the door was started and during the months it was executed, I made many visits to Pistoia to consult and decide upon certain technical details, the decorative motives, and the finishing of the oak and the hardware, such as copper nails, a bronze lock and hinges. Each half-door was divided in four quadrangular panels in addition to the base plinth; and within the centre of each panel was carved a nine-petal rosette with turned-up edges, a reminder in its grace and design of the oriental lotus flower. To ensure that these floral panels would be perfectly equal, we arranged to have a sculptor make a model panel in its right measurements, first of clay and, after approval, of gypsum, so that the carver would have a perfect example to follow in every detail. The result was excellent as can be seen by all those who have the good fortune to visit the Qiblih of our Faith. The general decorative scheme was completed by semi-spheral knobs of wood, distributed symmetrically around the door frame, and by protective doornails in the plinth; rosettes, knobs and doornails were gilded by hand, thus enhancing the beauty of the polished oak. To prevent inconveniences that may develop in the use of either iron or bronze hinges, it was decided to use ball-bearing hinges; these were placed under and above the half-doors and will outlast the durability of the oak itself.

I was not in Haifa when the door arrived, but I soon learned that the beloved Guardian was overjoyed by its simplicity, perfect execution and highly decorative beauty, and he gave instruction to have it put up at once; a cable of appreciation came in the days following, bringing much cheer to my heart.

It is not possible to recollect in detail all the improvements and beautifications which Shoghi Effendi, himself, planned and exe-

* Mr. Saielli made also the wooden core of the bronze door and the balustrade of the International Archives. See page 161.

cuted, particularly with reference to the gardening and the addition of ornamental objects throughout the whole area. My heart is deeply moved whenever I walk around the gardens and see all the things he accomplished with so much love and such boundless eagerness: a living reminder of the happy days when he was on this earth.

A good many years ago, the believers of Rangoon, Burma, shipped an alabaster sarcophagus—as they had done for the remains of the beloved Báb*—to be used in the Shrine of Bahá'-u'lláh, to gather in it His mortal remains. It reached the shores of the Mediterranean, but because of the unsettled situation in the Near East area, it could never be brought to its destination. The beloved Guardian asked me at one time—in the late 'forties—to arrange for its transportation to the Holy Land, but the worsening political situation did not permit the consummation of the plan. The sarcophagus is now in good hands waiting for the opportunity to be sent to its rightful destination and thus fulfil another wish of the Guardian, as part of his plan to beautify that Holy Shrine.

In future, as the world Bahá'í membership increases and means become abundant, no doubt the erection of a magnificent mausoleum, as envisaged and desired by Shoghi Effendi, will be an impellent necessity accomplished by the enthusiastic support of every believer from every land of the globe. Then, the twin Spiritual Centres of the Faith, Haifa and 'Akká, will irradiate their resplendent glory with a potency that nothing on earth shall be able to surpass.

* See page 54.

XIII

The Mansion of Bahjí

Greetings and salutations rest upon this Mansion, which
increaseth in splendour through the passage of time.
Manifold wonders and marvels are found therein, and
pens are baffled in attempting to describe them.

1870

THESE verses are engraved in Arabic, on a marble tablet
placed immediately above the entrance door of the Bahjí
Mansion. This imposing structure, known then as the
palace of 'Údí Khammár, built in the plains of 'Akká for a
wealthy Syrian at great cost, was completed about two years
after the arrival of Bahá'u'lláh in that prison-city, when His tribu-
lations had reached new heights. It is almost incredible that the
builder, whoever he was and whatever his aims and vision, had
unknowingly disclosed a prophetic pattern of the events to come.
While the Blessed Beauty was suffering from the sudden, heart-
rending loss of His beloved son, Mírzá Mihdí, 'The Purest
Branch', the hand of destiny was preparing a dwelling-place
where His Majesty and Splendour would be asserted in their fullness. He, Himself, defined it as 'the lofty mansion', and as the spot
which 'God hath ordained as the most sublime vision of mankind'.[21]

Because of an outbreak of a contagious epidemic, the owner
and his family had fled from the palace, never to return. The
Mansion was first rented and later purchased for Bahá'u'lláh;
thus for almost twelve years after His confinement within the
walls of the prison-city of 'Akká—and following the two years
He spent in the Mansion of Mazra'ih—'the doors of majesty and
true sovereignty were flung wide open,'[22] as stated by the Master,
'Abdu'l-Bahá. It was in this Mansion that Professor Edward
Granville Browne, the orientalist from Cambridge University,
was granted, in April 1890, four successive interviews with

Bahá'u'lláh, so eloquently described by this distinguished professor in words known to every Bahá'í the world over.[23]

As already mentioned in these recollections, after the passing of Bahá'u'lláh the occupancy of the Mansion was taken over by the Covenant-breakers and their families. Shoghi Effendi spoke to me on several occasions of the situation which ensued thereafter. At the time of Bahá'u'lláh's passing, the Mansion was owned one-third by Badí'u'lláh* and two-thirds by 'Abdu'l-Bahá, but the former immediately sold his share to the Chief of Police in 'Akká. Years after this man's death, his family migrated to Damascus retaining the part-ownership for well over three decades, until the passing of 'Abdu'l-Bahá, when Shoghi Effendi took immediate steps to regain possession of the remaining one-third. Unbelievable developments created by the machinations of a Covenant-breaker, who was working at the time in the Land Registry Office of 'Akká, made it possible to thwart and impede Shoghi Effendi's efforts to purchase the share available.† Such situations made it impossible for the Guardian, for almost four decades, to regain full ownership of the Mansion for the Cause. It was only some months before his passing that the matter could be definitely settled. In the course of those decades, however, two things happened which permitted him to gain control, if not full ownership, of the Mansion. The first was the collapse of a large part of the roof of the edifice; the second was the arbitrary seizing by force of the key of the Shrine of Bahá'u'lláh from its custodian—the already mentioned faithful gardener Abu'l-Qásim—an event which precipitated the intervention of the Palestine Mandate authorities, who recognized officially Shoghi Effendi as the sole Custodian of the Bahá'í Holy Places.

The collapse of the roof was a matter which deeply troubled the beloved Guardian; that such a holy and historical building was falling into ruins gave him no peace of mind. When he approached the Mansion's occupant, 'the Arch-breaker of the Covenant', to induce him to make the necessary repairs, he was told that for

---

* An unfaithful half-brother of 'Abdu'l-Bahá.
† At that time it belonged to other Covenant-breakers, respectively uncle and father of the above-mentioned registrar, who also kept a share for himself.

lack of funds nothing could be done. Then Shoghi Effendi proposed to restore the building as befitted such a holy place, an offer which was readily accepted. After being vacated by its occupants, the Mansion was at long last completely restored at great cost, and exempted from taxation and, being classified as a Bahá'í Holy Place, it came fully under his custodianship. When the occupants vacated the premises, they left ruin everywhere, taking away whatever was transportable, with the exception of a single candlestick which was left behind in the room where Bahá'u'lláh passed away.

With all his enthusiasm and eagerness, Shoghi Effendi restored the building to its original state and furnished it as a place of visitation and pilgrimage, where the Bahá'ís visiting the Holy Places at the World Centre could sleep for two nights. He also personally looked after the most minute details, placing relics, decorations, paintings, and other pictures, books, tapestries, rugs, lamps, and chandeliers, practically with his own hands, in their present locations.

Some years ago I met a gentleman, author of some publication on archaeology and Palestinian architecture, who told me that 'without any doubt, the Mansion of Bahjí was considered the most beautiful building in the country'. I believe that so far nothing comparable to the classical beauty of this building has yet been erected. Shoghi Effendi did not spare any effort to bring the Mansion—a Holy Place by rights—to the distinguished rank of a veritable museum in which relics, mementoes, portraits and books are enshrined and displayed, to glorify the great destiny of the building as promised in the marble inscription mentioned at the beginning of this chapter. As was done in the Shrine of the Báb on Mt. Carmel, soon after the passing of 'Abdu'l-Bahá, electric illumination was installed by an American believer, through a small generator located in the garden close to the door of the west wall of the inner garden. On my first pilgrimage the generator was still there.

From the beginning of his Guardianship, Shoghi Effendi had nourished the idea of making the Mansion the physical focal centre of the memories of God's Manifestation on earth, something so greatly missed in the other Faiths of the world. It was also a great challenge to him to restore the fabric of the building as it had been in the days of Bahá'u'lláh. He mentioned to me his whole-hearted commitment to carry out this plan, the final and glorious stage of what was to become a sequence of blazing and permanent landmarks connected with the earthly life of Bahá'u'lláh: the home of His birth and the Síyáh-Chál in Ṭihrán, the Most Great House in Baghdád, the houses in Constantinople and Adrianople, and the Most Great Prison in 'Akká. As was his nature, he spoke with emphasis as if looking at something real, already existing, that he was describing, joyfully, anticipating the fullness of the accomplishment. For it was Shoghi Effendi who was the responsible animator, assisted by the believers of the world, for the acquisition and preservation of these holy sites.

It would not be within the spirit and purpose of these recollections to describe in detail the characteristics of the building; but in order to render honour to the noble efforts made by Shoghi Effendi, I shall briefly summarize what he accomplished with such marked success. The Mansion of Bahjí is composed of a ground floor with spacious rooms and high ceilings, surrounded on the north, west and south sides by a graceful arcade which confers an air of spaciousness and strength to the whole building. Around this floor there is a small enclosed garden of flowers and citrus trees. Each room on these sides opens on the colonnade, while on the east side, in addition to some doors of rooms, there is the main door leading by a staircase to the upper floor. This upper and only other floor was designed for comfortable and gracious living. On reaching that level the visitor enters, by a short corridor, a large hall paved with marble and flooded with light penetrating from a series of large windows opening into the roof, which is supported by eight marble columns, in the manner of an Islamic courtyard. This hall, with its majestic size and luminosity, lends itself perfectly to the plans devised by Shoghi Effendi, as the area of the floor and of the walls gave him the opportunity to display world-wide historical mementoes, and many visual representations of milestones in the development of the Faith. Over a number of years, whenever some remarkable happening took place, he found a way to remember it by a picture, a relic, a drawing, or some other object placed on the walls, while models of the Shrine of the Báb and of Bahá'í Temples, already built or to be built, were placed on small tables located in the centre of the floor right under the well of light. From this central hall, many large rooms branch out, some with windows opening on the small garden, others opening on to the broad balcony which runs above the arcade. All rooms have much importance in the purpose of the restoration and some are furnished to remind us of a few of the outstanding believers of the world. The one room in which Bahá'-u'lláh passed away remains as it was.

Each room is furnished with simplicity and in good taste, the general *décor* being characteristic of the land of Bahá'u'lláh's birth, transporting the visitor into a Persian atmosphere of many decades ago. Rugs, textiles, bronze ewers, fine glass and porcelain lamps, vases, bowls, mirrors, basins, and many other ornamental objects add to the air of mystery which pervades the Mansion.

Shoghi Effendi destined all the rooms, except that of Bahá'u'-lláh and the two adjoining ones, as lodgings for pilgrims, retaining one for the use of himself when in Bahjí; and to remind visitors of the creative power of the New Revelation, he placed in every room, except Bahá'u'lláh's, hundreds of Bahá'í books published in nearly all the major languages of the world. These books testify to the immensity of Bahá'u'lláh's Revelation which is permeating every land of the world. How eager the Guardian was to place the new publications that continually reached him on the shelves of the many chambers of the Mansion! A copy of every first edition was kept in the chamber he had destined for himself. How delighted I was to see copies of the first Italian translations of the Writings carefully placed among the hundreds of other publications he kept in his quarters. His insight had prompted him to establish a monumental record for all the generations of Bahá'ís to come. The Mansion is not an archive, a reliquary, a library or a shrine, but it is a combination of all four to satisfy the longing of the visitor's soul.

For the seeker whose fantasy and imagination are alive, the

experience of visiting this unique building is conducive to much intimate joy. My personal sensation was of indelible exaltation, second only to the feelings experienced in the Shrines of Bahá'u'-lláh and the Báb.

The focal point of the Mansion is the chamber occupied by Bahá'u'lláh; it is at the south-east corner of the edifice, provided on two sides with ample luminous windows, one side looking towards the plain, and the other to the terrace from which, at a fair distance, Mt. Carmel is plainly visible. Part of the terrace is screened with framed plate-glass panes in colour, a sort of shelter from the glaring sunlight from the south and west, especially in the late spring and summer months. A marble fountain, which at one time spouted fresh water, is at the back of the screen. It must have been of great relief and enjoyment to the Blessed Beauty, after the many decades of unbearable sufferings, to listen to the ripple of that water falling into the font. A door leading from His room to the terrace made it possible for the august Occupant to move outdoors at any time and with a great amount of privacy. This part of the terrace is covered, and the roof is sustained by slender marble columns which add their beauty to the landscape, as if one were looking at it through a precious frame. I have stood many times, mostly at nightfall, in that particular corner of the terrace, enjoying the unique view of Mt. Carmel in the flaming glow of sundown. It was to me a world of make-believe, to imagine that Bahá'u'lláh was standing there, a little ahead of me, beholding with His keen sight the Carmel blazing in its glory. I could see in the distance the white edifice and the golden dome of the Shrine of the Báb, just as the Blessed Beauty might have anticipated, as He Himself might have imagined it: a reality already decreed in God's ledger. That chamber is the true goal of every visitor to the Mansion; the description given by Professor Browne has fired the imagination of countless pilgrims and visitors who have succeeded one another for nearly a century.

When I reached the door of that room for the first time, my heart was pulsating with great trepidation; I removed my shoes and my eyes caught Professor Browne's immortal page of his interview with Bahá'u'lláh. Shoghi Effendi has placed this document, printed and framed, beside the door, for everyone to see and be reminded of the drama which took place in that chamber—the Mouthpiece of God telling the Western scholar what the destiny of mankind would be: the Light of the East shining upon the dimness of unbelief; the promise of a spiritual regeneration for the whole world.

'In the corner where the divan met the wall sat a wondrous and venerable figure... The face of him on whom I gazed I can never forget...'[24] These words were ringing in my mind when, putting the curtain of the door aside, I entered that sacred room. The light was quite dim, all windows being hermetically closed with the exception of two small circular ones high up on the wall which allowed some light to filter in. I prostrated myself on the floor, unable to raise my eyes in any direction, least of all towards the famous corner. Hope and awe kept me fixed to that floor, sobbing, aware of His presence, of His piercing eyes that would read my soul. Moments of supreme ecstasy gave me fleeting images of the life He had spent there, in His vital regality, with one imperative thought in His mind: the redemption of man. Much time passed thus, and when the reality of the surroundings became evident and I dared to look, I saw His fur coat, His táj, and the corner where the Wondrous Figure had sat. Many a visit I have made to that room over a number of years, and the process of sublimation and return has been as engaging and as powerful as that first time.

Again, it was my good fortune at one time to be in the Mansion and in that chamber with Shoghi Effendi. He was the talisman that brought to me, closer than ever, the majesty of the Blessed Beauty; his chanting, unique in tonality and emotion, made the heart throb with that quality of infinite love which surely belonged to the world of saints and angels.

The chamber that Shoghi Effendi had selected for himself is located on one corner of the main hall. It has the same dimensions as the one used by Bahá'u'lláh, and also opens on the terrace, close to the fountain. The iron bed which is in the room, in the same location where he had placed it, was used by him every time he went to Bahjí, and spent the night there.

The nearness to the Tomb of Bahá'u'lláh offered a rare and unique possibility of praying at the Tomb until late at night and early in the morning. Those of us who were allowed to stay some days in the Mansion, as pilgrims, can well remember the hours of true bliss, forgetful of the outer world, living intensely in a state of rapture and beatitude every instant spent within the Mansion and the Sacred Sepulchre. Awakening in the morning in one of the Mansion's chambers, refreshed and infinitely happy, I could hear the chanting of the Guardian who had already entered Bahá'-u'lláh's chamber, a music which would enkindle heart and limbs with a wondrous eagerness to do things. One day when I was allowed to enter his chamber, I noticed with amazement that, on the wall by the head of his bed, Shoghi Effendi had placed the photograph of the first Italian Local Assembly, that of Rome, to which both my wife Angeline and I belonged. When I mentioned this to him, he looked at me with overwhelming tenderness and said that nothing had pleased him more than the establishment of a Bahá'í administrative institution in the Christian capital of the world. On that occasion he added, 'There are three religious centres in the world with distinct functions: Rome, Mecca, and Cairo, where the Cause will register its greatest victories for the Faith in the future.' I am not able to comment further on the chamber chosen by Shoghi Effendi, but to the sensitive visitor it will appear, as it did to me, the distinguished retreat of a superior mind desirous of tranquillity—a retreat filled with living memories of the recent past, conducive to meditation and noble thoughts, and, above all, permeated by an air of purity and innocence, an aura Shoghi Effendi carried with him.

Another room of the Mansion, one of the smallest on the north side, was destined to receive all printed publicity on the Faith, over many years. In the centre of this room was an ever-growing pyramid of newspapers which the Guardian would deposit himself, one on top of the other, as they arrived from all parts of the world in many different languages.

Many other wonders are enshrined in the Mansion, but I would rather leave it to the ingenuity and the perspicacity of the visitor to discover them and utter cries of delight and astonishment.

When the Mansion was used for pilgrims, who usually remained in Bahjí for two days, the rooms of the ground and the first floors were used as sleeping quarters for them. Unforgettable days of supreme enchantment they were, when one became at once the ennobled dweller of the lofty Mansion, its proud defender, and the humble-hearted seeker of the mysteries of creation. Many nights I have spent in those hallowed chambers, with prayers on my lips, my heart filled with joy and contentment, hearing the echo of footsteps and voices of the past, sheltered in the certainty that God's Messenger had breathed there hopefulness and blessings for all men. Once I had this rare privilege when Shoghi Effendi was there, and my cup of joy overflowed.

The little garden, encircled by a stone wall which is a part of the Mansion, was at the time of my first pilgrimage a veritable little paradise; after many years of neglect, following the passing of Bahá'u'lláh, Shoghi Effendi had brought the garden back to its pristine charm, by planting trees, shrubs and flowers all around. On the east side, there were tangerine, orange and lemon trees; red blazing geraniums and roses on the north, and jasmine of several varieties on the west. It was early spring when I first visited the Mansion, and I could inhale the strong scent of jasmine and orange blossoms as I walked outside the dividing wall, towards the main door. Once I entered that door, the fragrance grew so strong that for a moment I felt inebriated, as though from a draught of heavenly nectar. At that time the land outside the wall surrounding the small garden was wild and abandoned; it belonged to absentee owners, and was cluttered around the eastern wall with dilapidated and shabby dwellings occupied by large families of nomads. All this made a strong contrast, and caused my mind to race back to the days, seven decades before, when the Blessed Beauty was able to enjoy the redolence of that little oasis and the shade of its trees, while outside, all around, the land was neglected and barren. Singing birds and turtle-doves were now nesting in the trees and shrubbery, well aware of the perfect safety from men or animals offered by that hallowed enclave. That day before leaving, I gathered some jasmine blossoms, and that night I put them in a small vase

146

which I placed in front of the Guardian at the dinner-table. There was no need for words on his part; he looked pleased and deeply moved. He searched my eyes with his luminous gaze, smiled, raised the flowers to his nostrils and with much delight breathed in the strong scent. Some time after, I heard that jasmine was his favoured perfume.

XIV

The International Archives

AS previously mentioned, the far-sightedness of Shoghi Effendi had prompted him to establish and develop an archive of the Faith in which relics and Writings would be gathered and preserved for posterity—for believers in general, historians and others—in order to assure authentic sources of information. Immediately after completion of the three additional rooms of the Shrine of the Báb in 1929, he started to assemble every available item that he could secure, concerning the Writings and the records of the lives of Bahá'u'lláh, the Báb and 'Abdu'l-Bahá, and displayed them as best he could at that time, in the newly-added rooms. As time passed, however, it became evident that the space was insufficient and only temporary, considering the fact that the Shrine was exclusively destined as a sepulchre, a place so sacred that he envisaged the time when visitors would be allowed only to circumambulate the edifice. Another small building, situated very close to the tomb of the Greatest Holy Leaf, in the Monument gardens near to UNO Avenue, was also utilized by the Guardian as part of the archives, and many objects and mementoes were guarded and displayed there. He usually made reference to that building as the 'Minor Archives'.

During my first two visits to the Holy Land, Shoghi Effendi spoke often of the importance of archives not only at the World Centre of the Faith but also for every national and local administrative body. Being well acquainted with the difficulties arising from the uncertainty of historical origins, facts and developments of some of the religions of the world, he encouraged individuals and institutions to develop, along well thought out plans, what would in time become the authoritative and genuine sources of the history of the Cause throughout the world, with an incredible variety of information reflecting the habits, culture, social and intellectual evolution of peoples, and the inception and development of the Faith, including its pioneers and early believers, in all continents of the globe. On such occasions, Shoghi Effendi spoke of the need for erecting a special building, somewhere on Mt. Carmel, in which to gather and preserve all the items already assembled, and all others yet to come.

Before proceeding to the momentous decision of building the new International Archives, I should like to mention an episode which further demonstrates the eager interest of Shoghi Effendi in collecting information and facts pertaining to the Sacred Writings and the history of the Cause. One evening, as I entered the dining-room, the Guardian was already seated at his place at the table, his face shining with an inner jubilation which he could neither control nor conceal. At his side, upon the table, stood a small bundle, an object wrapped in a coloured silk handkerchief, typical of the East and of Írán in particular. As soon as we were all seated and attentive, even before dinner was served, he said that a pilgrim had that day arrived from Ṭihrán, bringing with him one of the most precious documents to be placed in the archives. He untied the handkerchief and with great reverence lifted out a manuscript in book form, and, placing it in a position that every one could see, added that it contained two original Tablets in the handwriting of 'Abdu'l-Bahá. One was the *Íqán** and the other was a Tablet the name of which I do not now remember.

These manuscripts, Shoghi Effendi stated, were transcribed by 'Abdu'l-Bahá in His beautiful calligraphy, when He was about eighteen years old, and bore some additions in the Hand of Bahá'u'lláh, insertions which He had written on the margins of many pages in reviewing the manuscripts. Shoghi Effendi had never before seen the original of the *Íqán* and was deeply astonished to discover that the phrase he had chosen from this book and placed on the title page of his translation of Nabíl's Narrative, *The Dawn-Breakers*, was an after-reflection of Bahá'u'lláh's, written by Himself, on the margin of one page. The phrase in question is the one starting: 'I stand, life in hand, ready; that perchance. . .'[25]

* *Kitáb-i-Íqán* (The Book of Certitude).

The Guardian, that evening, was not only astonished but overjoyed as well, because he was conscious that through a mysterious process he had been inspired to adopt that phrase as an eternal testimonial to Bahá'u'lláh's yearning to sacrifice His life for the Báb, the Primal Point. All of us who were seated at the table were awed and profoundly stirred, and I, in particular, felt that the existence of a spiritual link between our Guardian and the invisible world of God was something that no one should ever doubt.

On other occasions he told us how the archives were being enriched with the 'sword of Mullá Ḥusayn', the 'rings of the beloved Báb', some of His garments, and many other relics which he had placed on exhibit accompanied by small inscriptions on cardboard written by his own hand. Shoghi Effendi was always eager to increase the knowledge of every one who came close to him, and did not spare any effort to reveal or explain episodes and facts that were part of his heritage and vast culture, particularly when they referred to the history and the development of the Cause.

On the subject of the archives, one evening he revealed how the Tablets of the Báb to the Letters of the Living were found. He started by saying, 'Where did the original Tablets come from, and how is it we have them all in the archives?'

'When the Master passed away,' he continued, 'we found the whole set of these Tablets, in the original, twenty in all. They must have been in the papers of the secretary of Bahá'u'lláh, Mírzá Áqá Ján, and must have been given to Bahá'u'lláh years ago. The Bahá'ís had no knowledge of them during the days of the Master. One Tablet is addressed to the Báb, Himself; the last one, written on blue paper, is addressed to Bahá'u'lláh, "Him Whom God has manifested and will manifest";* these last two bear three seals each.† In addition we found in the Master's papers Tablets of Bahá'u'lláh addressed to the Master.'

The reader can well understand the Guardian's decision to

---

* 'He Who is made manifest in the past and in the future' is another rendering of this inscription.
† See *The Dawn-Breakers* (U.S. ed.) for facsimiles of these Tablets.

assure a new and larger home for all the precious objects and manuscripts, as a part of the development of the World Administrative Centre of the Faith on Mt. Carmel.

THE PROJECT BEGINS

When one year later, in October 1953, I reached New Delhi for the last of the Intercontinental Conferences, I was given a message from Shoghi Effendi and a drawing, to be displayed at the Conference. It was a rough pen and ink drawing of the edifice to be built for the International Archives, and to be shown to the assembled believers to make them conscious, as the message suggested, of the immediate necessity of assisting the Guardian in carrying out his project. All the days of the Conference the drawing was placed at the front of the speakers' table. It represented, in a general manner, a Greek temple reminiscent of the Parthenon, and also of temples in Paestum near Salerno, Italy, and in Agrigento in Sicily. The style was Ionic and showed a monumental and spacious building. Shoghi Effendi's message instructed me to take the drawing to Italy and secure an approximate estimate of cost, an important element for the Guardian to know in order to reach a decision. Knowing well the eagerness of Shoghi Effendi, and being myself anxious to render to him some additional service, now that the Shrine of the Báb had been completed, I wrote an explanatory letter and dispatched it, together with the drawing, to a trusted friend in Italy to start some inquiries pending my arrival.

Because of a prolonged stop-over in Persia, I did not reach Rome before the end of December, and was then able to send the information requested by Shoghi Effendi immediately after the festivities of the New Year. A well-developed plan of the building, incorporating all the characteristics shown in the sketch, was dispatched to the Guardian together with an approximate estimate of cost, which had been secured from one firm only. Some changes in the approaches and the front of the building were suggested in return by Shoghi Effendi, and this process was repeated once more until the drawings prepared by Architect Rocca* were accepted by the Guardian with enthusiastic approval.

* See page 71-2.

The first tentative estimate had been encouraging to the point of inducing Shoghi Effendi to seek a definite and set cost that would guarantee the execution of the work within a certain time and without additional increase because of material or labour problems.

As with the Shrine of the Báb, there was indeed a divine intervention which permitted the Guardian to consummate his much longed for plan for the International Archives. With his approval, after the working drawings had been perfected and completed, I called for bids from four different firms to provide the marble carved and ready to be loaded on ships sailing from one of the main Italian ports. It was an interesting and challenging experience because although the firms in question seemed eager to secure the work, they must have committed some errors of judgement, as three of the bids were so far apart from the first estimate that it would have been almost impossible for the Guardian even to consider them. As the marble was to be the same 'Chiampo Paglierino', already used for the Shrine of the Báb, I felt it would be a considerable saving if the work could be done as close to the quarries as possible; it was our good fortune to receive the fourth bid from the firm which owned the quarries and had a well-equipped laboratory in the little town of Chiampo. Their bid was so reasonable that for a while I thought it to be a mistake, the difference from the other estimates received being quite considerable. All this work occupied a good part of the year, particularly because detailed plans had to be made to enable the engineering staff of the laboratory to become acquainted with and conscious of the work they would have to undertake. There was still another element which for some time delayed the Guardian's final decision; namely, the acquisition of a piece of land which belonged to an enemy of the Faith, and which was essential as it formed part of the plot on which it was decided to erect the Archives building. It took many months of difficult and involved negotiations, culminating with the intervention of the Israeli Government, before settlement was reached. On the eve of the thirty-third anniversary of 'Abdu'l-Bahá's ascension, the contract to secure the land was signed, with much relief and thankfulness on the part of Shoghi Effendi, who expressed his feelings in his historical message to the Bahá'í world of 27 November 1954. The way was now free to initiate what he defined as '. . .one of the foremost objectives of the Ten-Year Plan'.[26]

The whole year of 1954 had been one of great achievements, following the power released by the four Intercontinental Conferences which had spurred the Bahá'ís of all continents of the globe to accomplish magnificent, selfless deeds that brought encouragement and satisfaction to the beloved Guardian. His gratitude to the 'pioneers' who responded to his call—by him named the Knights of Bahá'u'lláh—was perpetuated in his creation of a Roll of Honour, for their activities added much prestige and strength to the process of the spiritualization of the masses. The acquisition of the site of the Síyáh-Chál, in Ṭihrán, and the evolution of the Institution of the Hands of the Cause of God, with the appointment of Auxiliary Boards throughout the Bahá'í world, were two other outstanding victories of that propitious year.

Indeed it was also an auspicious year for ourselves, because on 25 November we received a cable from Shoghi Effendi reading as follows: 'Permitted pilgrimage you and Angeline dearest love Shoghi.' Our elation could not be contained and we made immediate plans to leave Rome within a few days. But another cable came requesting us to postpone our pilgrimage by one week. Late in the evening of Saturday, 11 December, we left Rome's airport for Lydda where we arrived early the following morning. For Angeline, it was the greatest happening of her life, to be at the World Centre and meet Shoghi Effendi, as it had been for me some years earlier. At dinner-time, Shoghi Effendi received us most lovingly and asked Angeline to sit in the place of honour. He was extremely happy and spoke of the progress of the Faith in Africa, which seemed to be at the time his favourite subject. In the days that followed, he mentioned the work to be undertaken in Italy for the International Archives, and requested me to verify personally the delimitation of the area upon which the building would be erected—already tentatively made by himself—a difficult task to accomplish considering the roughness of the ground chosen on the slope of Mt. Carmel and the lack of surveyor's instruments. When I went to the site the following morning, I was amazed to see how well the marking had been done under his direction, with the assistance only of his chauffeur, using wooden pickets and white strings. The salient point—part of the whole plan for the establishment of the edifices of the Administrative Centre of the Faith—which was paramount in the mind of the Guardian, was the orientation of these structures towards the 'heart and Qiblih of the Bahá'í world'. To the countless pilgrims who have since then visited that blessed spot on the holy mountain, as well as to the endless stream of visitors who daily wander throughout the whole area, the beauty and perfect order may appear the result of skilled engineering calculations done over a number of years. Nothing could be farther from the real truth, as the credit beyond all praise goes to the talent, versatility and ingenuity of Shoghi Effendi alone.

The succession of days during that pilgrimage was filled with joy and delightful new experiences. The Guardian had already started to landscape the ground in the immediate vicinity of the chosen site, and I well remember his satisfaction and jubilation when on one of those evenings at table, turning to Angeline, he said: 'I have just finished planting eleven cypress trees along the future path leading to the Archives building.' Vision and unswerving determination! What an edifying lesson to all of us sitting at the table! As the days passed, Shoghi Effendi requested us to remain longer than the normal duration of the pilgrimage. As we were revelling in this added bounty and making plans to use the precious time to the best spiritual advantage, on 24 December at table, the Guardian, turning again to Angeline, said: 'I would very much like to keep you and Ugo here indefinitely, but Ugo must return to Italy and start immediately to work on the International Archives.'

Although we would have loved to remain near to him for a longer time, we rejoiced because here was the opportunity to render him another great service that would bring much solace and happiness to his heart. The following evening was parting time, and the impending departure next day cast a shadow of sadness upon us. Shoghi Effendi, conscious of the atmosphere brought by the occasion, spoke with a brilliancy surpassing in my memory that of any previous evening spent with him. Again, visions of the things to come were unveiled before our eyes as a certainty in the immediate future. The spiritual conquest of the various continents of the world and the multiplication of the institutions of the Faith were assured by his warm and melodious voice. We were not leaving his presence, but carrying away, to be with us forever, his dreams, his vision and the certainty of extraordinary things that were to happen.

As soon as conditions would permit, he said, he would instruct the election of new National Spiritual Assemblies, and he made reference to the day when the establishment of independent Italian and Swiss National Assemblies would come to pass.

'I have brought with me some gifts,' he said, 'that I wish you to take back to Europe; they are for the National Ḥaẓíratu'l-Quds of Rome and Berne, and they will become permanent property of the National Assemblies of the two countries, when these bodies come into existence.'

They were a large piece of brocade for Rome, which had lain for a long time upon the inner Shrine of Bahá'u'lláh, at Bahjí, and a 'Greatest Name' embroidered on silk, from the Tomb of 'Abdu'l-Bahá, for Berne, plus two photographs of the Bahá'í Temple in Wilmette, two lithographs of the 'Greatest Name', two copies of the seals of Bahá'u'lláh, to be equally divided between the two Communities, and a photograph of the Shrine of the Báb for Berne, and of the Shrine of Bahá'u'lláh for Rome. He then gave me instructions as to how these objects should be preserved, for all generations of believers to come.

When the time came to leave his presence, he arose from the table and, coming close to us, bade us farewell in a moving manner.

'You shall both return to see the Archives when completed,' he said, and embraced me tenderly, holding me in his arms for a long time; then taking Angeline's hand in his, he added: 'I want you to travel and see the friends.' Everyone was deeply moved.

Little did we know that this was the last time we would see our beloved Guardian on this earth! We left next morning for Lydda, but our plane was much delayed and did not depart from the Holy Land until the early evening of the following day, Monday, 27 December 1954. The next morning we reached Rome's Ciampino airport and, two hours later, we were home, filled with high hopes and joy; that same afternoon a cable from Shoghi Effendi reached us, bearing a message of love.

There was no time to spare; the work for the Archives had to take precedence over everything else, for in my ears were still ringing the Guardian's last instructions as to how to go about securing a favourable contract, and the importance of this new enterprise: '. . . a most valuable storehouse of information regarding all the aspects of the Faith . . . Future generations of believers surely will be in a better position than we are to appreciate truly and adequately the many advantages and facilities which the institution of the Archives offers to individual believers, and also to the community at large. . .' If the responsibility for this enterprise, resting on every believer (according to the Guardian), was definite and weighty, mine would be far greater and more vital. Therefore I decided to give absolute priority to the execution of this magnificent plan, the spiritual implications of which were to assist over a long range in time and space the prestige and greatness of the Cause of Bahá'u'lláh. It was with much regret that I had to suspend temporarily the translation into Italian of the Writings of the Faith, a work which had already produced many volumes of the Bahá'í Teachings in my native language.

The next immediate step was to get in touch with the firm which owned the Chiampo quarries and had made the lowest bid a few months earlier. The firm in question was the Industria dei Marmi Vicentini, situated in Chiampo and having also a representation in Rome. Two days after our return to the Eternal City, the negotiations started in good earnest, and once more Architect Rocca was to play a vital part in the execution of this project; his skill and competence, fully demonstrated during the construction of the Báb's Shrine, were to be relied upon once more and, with the Guardian's approval, he was engaged to supervise strictly the production, cutting and carving of all the marble needed for the building. His energetic and enthusiastic activity made him a precious collaborator, his full time being completely free and at the disposal of the Faith.

The time had now come to conclude the contract during a visit to the firm in Chiampo; once there, and after having met some of the officers of the firm, Professor Rocca was surprised to find that an old friend and school-mate, Architect Ercole Sanguinetti, was the commercial manager in charge of sales. This was an unexpected bounty as the mutual esteem and friendship between the two gentlemen opened many avenues of understanding and closer collaboration. The general manager, a former Italian naval officer, and the chief engineer of the plant at once became keenly interested in the project and were helpful and accommodating in many ways. Also the whole technical staff, from the miners in the quarries to the draughtsmen and the artisan carvers and sculptors, assumed an attitude of eager consideration, lending their ability and skill with sincere enthusiasm in whatever role they were called on to play in producing the marble required for the finished building. A firm and final estimate was secured and submitted to the Guardian. It was accepted by him by cable on 3 January 1955. Some days later the contract was signed in Rome, thus opening the way for the realization of yet another of Shoghi Effendi's happy expectations. When he was informed of this historical event, a cable, 'Delighted loving prayers accompanying you', came from him in the afternoon of 12 January, a date never to be forgotten!

Conditions in Italy had considerably changed since the days when the Shrine of the Báb had been started, with favourable situations in regard to labour, technical means and shipping. Again, a veritable army of draughtsmen, modellers, stone-cutters and sculptors was mobilized, while miners in the quarries of Zanconato and Nicolato in the territory of Chiampo were wresting from the bowels of the earth hundreds and hundreds of tons of marble in huge blocks—a difficult and meticulous work because only the most perfect marble was selected from the abundant yield of the quarries.

PLANS BECOME A REALITY

Before proceeding to other technical details, it would be useful to the reader who has not yet visited the World Centre of the Faith to have a general description of the building erected on the slopes of Mt. Carmel between the years 1955 and 1957. Shoghi Effendi had supervised and guided the execution of the drawing, which—as I have already mentioned—was exhibited for the first time at the Intercontinental Conference in New Delhi in 1953. It represented a building similar in appearance to the celebrated temple of Athena, in Greece, known the world over as the Parthenon. The substantial difference, however, consisted in the fact that the Parthenon was built in Doric style, while Shoghi Effendi had selected for the Archives the Ionic order. The latter distinguishes itself by the spiral volutes of the columns' capitals, well-known in the architectural world by those of the ancient temple of Athena Nike.

The approximate measurements of the building are one hundred feet in length, forty-five in width, and thirty-six in height.* It is an imposing structure formed by a central hall cella, built upon a podium and surrounded on all four sides by a majestic colonnade, consisting of eight fluted columns in the front and the rear of the building and of fifteen columns on each of its north and south sides. Each column is composed of three sections or drums, for a total height of nineteen feet, while the base and capital add three feet to the full height of the column.†

It would have been a great feat to have monolithic columns but, most wisely, Shoghi Effendi decided to have them composed of drums which, according to Greek architectural canon, must be of uneven number, the choice falling upon the number three. This brought about a considerable economy in cost of the whole structure and simplified greatly the problems of shipping and

* Respectively, thirty-two metres long, fourteen metres wide and twelve metres high.
† A total of seven metres.

erecting *in situ* huge one-piece columns without the proper engineering machinery. Each column is fluted with vertical grooves from base to capital, an amazing work of precision done by expert hands. I was completely fascinated watching those men execute such a difficult and delicate task with steady hands, without committing the slightest error, as even the smallest fault would have required starting the whole section of the column again.

When the first completed column was erected in my presence in the yard of the laboratory in Chiampo, I could not believe my eyes; its beauty and perfection were beyond any possible imagination! The men who had done the work stood around to see the expression on my face. For a moment I felt it was only a mirage, a sort of dream produced by my fantasy, but when I looked again on the faces of those humble workers, waiting for a word of praise and appreciation, I felt a great and intimate joy. As I shook their hands and warmly felicitated everyone, I thought with anticipation of the moment when Shoghi Effendi himself would behold a similar sight, and follow breathlessly the erection—one by one—as if by magic, of all forty-six columns.

A staircase, almost as wide as the building, ascends from the level of the ground to that of the podium. Fifteen comfortable steps lead to the front portico on which opens the imposing single door of the building.

On the opposite, or western, side of the building, there is a huge window, almost as large as the rear terminal wall, with coloured stained-glass panes, sustained by a sturdy hand-wrought iron frame. Besides shedding daylight inside the main hall, this window is so perfectly oriented towards the west that, during the hours when the sun starts its descent, its beams strike the whole window so that it becomes alive in a glory of consuming light. The window is composed of a sturdy iron grille which holds aloft sixty-five panels of stained glass in three colours, the centre of each a golden disk surrounded with ruby-red and blue panes alternating with clear glass. Many samples of coloured glass were gathered from different sources—Italy and other European countries—and sent to Shoghi Effendi, who made his choice of colours. The columns all around support the entablature composed of the trabeations which hold the ceilings of the front and back porticos, and of the corridors along the north and south sides.

On the north and south walls there are six simulated windows on each side—in accordance with the strictest Greek architectural tenet—but above each one of them there is one real window of smaller dimensions. These twelve windows, provided with iron frames and clear glass, permit the daylight to penetrate inside the main hall and, in particular, illumine the two balconies which run all along the upper level of the hall itself.

Under the podium and the whole cella there is a large basement which extends itself under the main staircase. Ventilation for this useful underground space is provided by spiracles opening on the north side of the wall towards the sea.

To terminate this summary description of the building, mention remains to be made of the east and west tympana which complete the façades outlining the shape of the roof. On the east tympanum, looking towards the Qiblih of the Faith, there is a large mosaic disk with the 'Greatest Name' in the centre. From it departs a cluster of long and short rays in the manner of a risen sun; the rays carved in the marble are gilded. The decorative design of this tympanum was chosen from many others, and it had been the original idea of Shoghi Effendi. He charged me to secure many suggestions from the leading architects in Rome, and I applied to the Dean of the School of Architecture of that University, who himself, after a few weeks, provided some drawings, several with arabesque ornamentations, and others with more unconventional motives. When the sun rises every morning in the east its beams strike this beautiful and original frieze, which, as if it possesses an inner power, comes alive in a blaze of light.

Returning now to some other details embodied in the building, I would like to say that the inner structure of the walls is made of *ytong* blocks, a Swedish invention of the post-war period, and is covered with thick slabs of Chiampo marble on the outside. The architraves, the columns, the bases and capitals, the tympana and other decorative parts such as the door corbels, the friezes, the antefixes, the acroteria and the entablature are all made of solid marble. The beams of the floor and of the ceiling, the podium and the staircase are made, instead, of reinforced concrete covered with heavy marble.

The door is a masterpiece of ingenuity. It was originally conceived by Shoghi Effendi, who chose this Greek style of door with rosettes from many different types, as the most beautiful and dignified for this position. The pattern consists of ten bas-relief rosettes arranged in two rows, each having nine petals and an unopened bud at the centre; the whole door, studded with knobs symmetrically placed, is finished at the base by a protective knobbed plinth. Before preparation of a model was started, I visited the Roman antiquities to study closely some of the most ancient doors still in existence and use, and came to the conclusion that the door of the Archives should be made of hard wood covered with a heavy bronze lamina, while all the decorative parts of the ten panels and the knobs should be in solid cast bronze. A reputable sculptor from Carrara made the model of one panel to exact proportions, from which a full-scale model of the door was made for the Guardian to approve. The photograph of this model was published in the United States *Bahá'í News* of June 1956, and after its approval it served as a guide to the carpenter and the foundry undertaking the execution of the door. The city of Pistoia in Italy—not far from Florence—has been famous for many centuries for the skill of its artisans in woodworking and decorative bronze casting. In this century the best railroad-cars are made there for the Italian State Railway. Therefore it was decided to seek out the most reliable foundry and woodworking firm to execute such an important element in the construction of the Archives. After some inquiries and preliminary consultations, the choice fell upon the firm of Renzo Michelucci, for the metal part, and Saiello Saielli,* for the wood-carpentry work. Great care was taken to choose well-seasoned and dry planks of oak-wood for the frame upon which the bronze plate would be placed. Similar care was taken to counterbalance the traction created by the grain of the wood in order to prevent any warping due to

---

* This firm has been mentioned on page 135 as the executant of the work for the wooden door to the Shrine of Bahá'u'lláh.

climate or other adverse conditions. Wooden pegs and copper nails were used to eliminate the possibility of damage produced by iron rust, with the wood being treated with special oil and wax. The door, quite a big one, measuring over eleven feet in height and six in width,* is divided into two sections. It presented a challenge to the craftsmen, who I believe had never made a door of such size and refinement. During the time the door was being made—it took six months to complete—I went many times to check on the progress of the work, including the bronze casting, the gilding of the rosettes, and the packing of the two half-sections of the door in a huge case for shipment to Haifa. Concerning the gilding of the bronze rosettes, we entrusted this particular and delicate job to the same Florentine gilder who had gilded the 'Greatest Name' monograms of the Báb's Shrine. He gave first a silver plating to the bronze, and then used the fire-gilding method previously described.

The door, being quite large and heavy, could not be attached to conventional hinges and we therefore ordered special ball-bearing hinges, made of the finest steel, which would permit opening and closing of the door with the least possible effort. When the door was completed, it was really magnificent, and when Shoghi Effendi saw it, he was truly overjoyed. It was placed in the building and was functioning before he left Haifa in the early summer of 1957, never to return again.

By then the building had been finished, and it was possible for him to see and appreciate many of the things made in Italy, which completed all the structural and subsidiary elements of the whole edifice. I shall mention a few briefly. First, there was the beautiful grilled inner vestibule door, the duplicate of an ancient Greco-Roman bronze door, the design of which Shoghi Effendi much admired, and which was in perfect harmony with the style of the building. The large window, which occupies a good part of the surface of the building's west side, was another result of Shoghi Effendi's personal decision, an innovation in the architectural style chosen† which, when completed, fully produced the effect

* Equivalent to 3.80 by 1.80 metres.
† Greek temple architecture had no windows.

162

he wanted. The iron frame for the window and the bronze grilled door of the vestibule were made in Sarzana, Italy, by the firm of Malatesta, the same firm that had produced all the lamp-posts and the various gates now visible on Mt. Carmel and in Bahjí. The firm of Jörger, in Turin, which had made the stained glass for the lancet windows of the Shrine of the Báb, had ceased to exist some two years before on account of the death of Mr. Jörger himself. A search was made in other localities, including Belgium, but without success, as although the task appeared to be quite easy, it required much skill because the colours chosen by the Guardian were different from those available in standard coloured-glass panes. Remembering that a small stained-glass factory at one time had existed in Palermo, Sicily, specializing in making church windows and panels, I made a journey to that island, and learned that the original owner had passed away but that his son, a professor at the local Accademia di Belle Arti, and an associate professor of the School of Architecture of Palermo University, was still engaged in making rare and highly artistic stained-glass panels for decorative purposes. A meeting with him revealed his willingness to undertake the work and thus the way was opened to carry out this unusual task. Some samples of the final colours were made and dispatched to Shoghi Effendi, together with a full-scale drawing of one panel, and the estimate of cost for all sixty-five panels. After acceptance of the colours and estimate, the work was initiated. Professor G. Gregorietti, the artist in question, had a modern and ample *atelier*, where he accomplished the work meticulously and alone, including the operation of the kilns and the soldering of the hundreds of yards of lead alloy binding. During the months required to finish everything, I went to Palermo several times to make sure of the quality of work and of packing when all was ready to ship. The final product was perfect and when placed in its permanent location was highly praised by the Guardian. After his passing, in reviewing some of the technical details of the Archives, the Hands of the Cause in the Holy Land felt that this large window was vulnerable from the outside, and it was decided to place in front of it, in the exact pattern of the original grille, an additional one of steel, which was produced immediately by a local ironmonger. Thus this side of the building was protected against any possible attempt at trespassing.

The interior of the Archives also possesses something in its structure which was the specific idea of Shoghi Effendi, namely, the two balconies which run along the south and north sides of the main hall. Access to the upper level is by two small staircases, connected at the top by a narrow corridor from the centre of which a complete view of the whole interior is obtained. The stair located on the north side is extended down to the basement. These balconies were decided upon by the Guardian in order to provide more space for exhibits; to the visitor the wisdom of this addition is immediately evident.

Here I wish to call the attention of the reader and the visitor to the wooden balustrades along the two balconies. The style and design of such a balcony were chosen by Shoghi Effendi; it is the replica of a famous balustrade designed by the great Palladio* for the Villa 'La Rotonda', in Vicenza. It seems that the Guardian became acquainted with this type of balustrade by perusing an architectural book, for it exists in Mereworth Castle, near Maidstone, Kent, which was built by a Scottish architect, Colen Campbell, who made a perfect replica of the Palladian villa mentioned. After receiving instructions from Shoghi Effendi that an accurate copy of the balustrade should be made, I went to Vicenza, accompanied by Professor Rocca, to study the original. Gaining access to 'La Rotonda', we were able to take careful measurements and make various drawings, which assisted greatly in drafting the final working plans for the artisan who was to carry out the work. Again, the choice fell upon Saiello Saielli, of Pistoia, who worked for many months with much enthusiasm and skill in the production of this highly decorative and outstanding crowning of the two balconies. The most perfect oak-wood was chosen, uniform in tint and texture, and a variety of ingenious details were incorporated during its manufacture to make the balustrade solid and extremely safe. When the complete work reached Haifa, and the balustrades were erected in the proper places, Shoghi Effendi was

* See Appendix X.

incredibly pleased and highly praised their beauty and workmanship.

Another important element in the completion of the building was the gabled roof and its covering. The ancient Greeks, and the Romans after them, used timber to make this type of roof and then covered it with heavy copper laminae. After exposure to nature's elements it assumed a sort of cobalt-green colour which, in temperate climates, sometimes blended with the colour of the sky. Shoghi Effendi wished to have the Archives covered by such a roof, but he would not consider the use of copper because of the danger that the marble might be stained by the metal's oxide during the sometimes torrential rains in the Holy Land. It was decided therefore to use fired clay tiles, glazed to the hue of ancient copper. The firm Westraven, of Utrecht, Holland, was again consulted, and experiments were made to prepare several samples of colour from which Shoghi Effendi could choose. The important point was that the tiles should be similar in size and shape to those used in ancient times. Nearness to the wealth of archaeologic antiquities in Italy made it possible for me to find the most authentic model. Drawings were then prepared to scale and the tile factory made a few samples for the Guardian's approval. When this was received, a contract was signed in Utrecht, on 6 June 1956, to produce 7,892 tiles sufficient to cover the five hundred square metres of roof.

The co-operation received from Junker R. de Brauw was once more the source of great satisfaction and relief, as it made possible the production of tiles which were perfect in measurement to fit the roof-space. As with the dome of the Shrine, a section of the roof was built in wood so that each tile produced could be tested on it for accuracy. A few necessary devices were incorporated to make the immobility of the tiles permanent, and, once placed *in situ*, it was amazing and highly rewarding that not even the slightest error of space was found; every tile—and there were nearly eight thousand of them—fitted perfectly in its place. As to their appearance, Shoghi Effendi was delighted; the colour selected by him blended with that of the sky on clear days. The majesty of the ensemble of front and rear tympana—each topped at its apex by a carved anthemion and connected by the *corniche*, above which rise 235 carved acroteria plus four additional anthemia at the four corners—gave to Shoghi Effendi the inspiration to call it yet another crown. The International Bahá'í Archives, he wrote, is the 'initial Edifice heralding the establishment of the Bahá'í World Administrative Centre on Mt. Carmel', contributing together with 'the stately, golden-crowned Mausoleum rising beyond it, to the unfolding glory of the central institutions of a World Faith nestling in the heart of God's holy mountain'.[27]

The other elements which enhance the greatness of this Edifice are the lighting system and the pavement of the main hall. Plans had been made by Shoghi Effendi to illuminate the interior of the Archives, supplementing the large rear and small side windows with powerful chandeliers hanging from the ceiling, and with wall brackets well distributed on the south and north walls. I was requested to secure a catalogue of crystal chandeliers, from which Shoghi Effendi selected a very beautiful one provided with sixty lights, and well decorated with prisms and pendants. Six were ordered from a Bohemian firm in Czechoslovakia, and they arrived during the summer months of 1957. These chandeliers were not seen by Shoghi Effendi, as the packing cases were opened only after his passing and the chandeliers placed in service early in 1958.

The original floor was made of green tiles of compressed cement, executed in Italy, but when they were set in place it was found that they did not match the beauty and refinement of the building. It was then decided to cover this layer with almond-green vinyl tiles made in England by Semtex Ltd, a subsidiary of Dunlop & Co. The whole surface to be covered was almost 450 square metres, and it represented a difficult and challenging task which required much endurance and skill. Marble was used instead in the vestibule and for the staircases.

During the summer and autumn of 1957, Shoghi Effendi had gone to London to complete the purchase of various furnishings and ornaments for the Archives; he had just completed his purchases, when a sudden illness took him from our midst. It thus became the responsibility of Rúḥíyyih Khánum, in the months

166

THE INTERNATIONAL ARCHIVES ON MT. CARMEL
Entrance as seen from the east

The door of Grecian style with bronze
gilt rosettes and knobs

Three Chiampo columns, with
Architect Rocca

Upper section and Ionic capital of
the first column

SOME ELEMENTS OF THE INTERNATIONAL ARCHIVES BUILDING

that followed, to transfer the material contained in the archive rooms of the Shrine of the Báb to the new building and to display everything in accordance with the Guardian's wishes as occasionally expressed to her. I am certain that Shoghi Effendi would have been extremely happy and pleased to behold the finished building, because during one of the months preceding his passing I received a cablegram from him, reading as follows:

'Congratulate you splendid historic highly meritorious achievement ensuring execution details structure Archives particularly Greatest Name. Present future generation believers including myself profoundly grateful. Shoghi.'

Here I would like to add that on each of the two side platforms of the main entrance staircase Shoghi Effendi wanted to place a large marble eagle, for which sketches and scale drawings were made and approved: the two eagles having semi-spread wings, ready to fly. One day a cablegram from him was received in which the plan for the eagles was abandoned. In their place there are now two beautiful wrought-iron torch holders, bought by Shoghi Effendi, which have been transformed into electric beacons—a luminous and friendly welcome to those who approach the Archives after sundown; the simulated glass flames were specially made in Murano, Venice, Italy.

The magnitude of the enterprise is perhaps best illustrated by some additional dates and statistics. It took seventeen ships to carry the total of one thousand tons of carved marble for the Archives building from Italy to Haifa. Other ships were used to transport structural steel, cement, floor and roof tiles, lumber, stained and clear glass, small and large iron window-frames, varnish and paint for the interior, chandeliers, electric and other wires, the main and the vestibule bronze doors, the oak balustrades and plinth for the balconies, lamp-posts and many other items, such as chain-lifts, nails, drain-pipes. The one-third section of every column weighed two tons; each capital and the six anthemia, one ton each. The roof tiles weighed forty tons and were packed in 7,200 cardboard boxes with the additional use of 25,000 metres of gummed paper in strips.

M

The first load of marble left from the port of Trieste on the S.S. *Nakhshon*, of the Zim Line, under the command of Captain Israel Auerbach, on 10 August 1955, barely seven months after the signing of the contract, and consisted of 169 cases brought to the ship-side in eight railroad cars. The first column was raised in December 1955, on the north-east corner of the podium, facing the Qiblih; all the others followed thereafter and the entire structure was completed by June 1957, under the supervision of Hand of the Cause Mr. Leroy C. Ioas.

As previously mentioned at the beginning of this chapter, Shoghi Effendi had started the landscaping of the grounds well in advance of the building operations and had traced a wide arched path, the 'arc', to which he had made reference in some of his messages to the Bahá'í world. During the summer of 1956 he bought in England a certain number of iron and bronze gates to be used both on Mt. Carmel and at Bahjí; these gates were received in Haifa during the early months of 1957. The 'arc' had no opening into UNO Avenue and, before departing for Europe that year, Shoghi Effendi had given instructions to cut in the rock wall a large opening to enable the placing there of a beautiful and stately wrought-iron gate, part of the above-mentioned shipments. The gate was to be suspended from two pilasters of Dover-stone, each surmounted by a decorative urn carved from the same stone, but it was not raised until the beginning of 1958. Following the passing of Shoghi Effendi, it was the source of deep joy for me to direct the execution of this opening—which had to be blasted with explosives—and the construction of the semicircular recess with its retaining walls, the set of steps leading to the 'arc', and the erection of the gate, a work that Shoghi Effendi would have loved to accomplish himself. On the first day of Riḍván, 1958, the gate was officially swung open, and became the entrance to the 'arc' leading to the International Archives, and to the future Edifices of the Central Institutions of the Faith.

The happy conclusion of Shoghi Effendi's efforts to initiate the series of buildings required for the full establishment of the Bahá'í World Administrative Centre offers to the believers the world over the opportunity to collaborate—in the years to come —with the realization of his cherished plan. Then the World Centre of our Faith will rise to such glory as cannot yet be fully understood. I was able to have a glimpse of it through the ideal conception of the whole plan so well expressed to me by the Guardian on more than one occasion during my presence in Haifa. Then his memory and his life of consecration shall be glorified to the fullness of his wisdom and his understanding of the plight of mankind.

XV

The First Ma<u>sh</u>riqu'l-A<u>dh</u>kár of the Holy Land

THE table conversations of Shoghi Effendi revolved mostly around the developments of the Faith, his far-sighted plans, and the glory of the events to come. The fascination of his manner of speaking with great conviction kept me spellbound every time I sat at his table. His assurance gave me the impression of an Argonaut who, navigating the seas in search of some rare treasure or unknown land, was always ahead of himself, seeing far beyond the power of human eyes. No one could entertain the slightest doubt that the Faith of Bahá'u'lláh would cover the earth, as he often stated, and that for the first time in the evolution of the religious thought of man, a Spiritual Centre of a conscious and universal Faith would be implanted in the heart of God's holy mountain.

In previous pages, I have tried to illustrate how much Shoghi Effendi laboured to initiate this magnificent plan and carry it to the tangible embodiment which he achieved. To him the spiritual trilogy was represented by the Most Holy Shrines of Bahá'u'lláh and of the Báb, and by the Ma<u>sh</u>riqu'l-A<u>dh</u>kár, which from the summit of Mt. Carmel would, as a silent teacher, proclaim the One Faith of Bahá'u'lláh. I happened to be in Haifa when Shoghi Effendi, fulfilling one of 'Abdu'l-Bahá's longings, was directing the preparation of the design for the Temple to be erected on the holy mountain. By the end of May 1952 the project had been fully accepted and approved by the Guardian. The drawing was taken to Florence, Italy, to be developed in detail by a professional man, after the completion of which a wooden model was made by a specialist in Rome.* This model was presented and placed on view at the Intercontinental Conference held in Chicago, in 1953,

* See *The Bahá'í World*, vol. XII, p. 548, for a photograph of this model.

where Amatu'l-Bahá Rúḥíyyih Khánum, accompanied by the Vice-President of the International Bahá'í Council, Hand of the Cause Mrs. Amelia Collins, represented the Guardian. The model is now in the main hall of the Mansion in Bahjí, awaiting the day when it will be erected on Mt. Carmel. At the time the design was completed, no land was yet available, although Shoghi Effendi had often expressed the need to secure it in a dominant position on the holy mountain, and had almost pinpointed the location he considered desirable and essential.

It was to be on the very top of the western end of Mt. Carmel, as close as possible to the site where the Blessed Beauty planted His tent on one of His visits to the holy mountain: an advantageous location that would permit the Temple to be seen from every point of approach, for it would tower above any other construction that could be erected at a future date upon that promontory. For centuries the land that Shoghi Effendi wanted was owned by a religious order which had built there a monastery in the twelfth century, but had left the rest of the land uncultivated and unused in any other manner.* Shoghi Effendi directed the Hand of the Cause and Secretary-General of the International Bahá'í Council, Mr. Leroy Ioas, to investigate the matter and conduct negotiations for the purchase of enough land to permit, at a future time, the erection of the Mashriqu'l-Adhkár and the landscaping of its surroundings. In his message addressed to the Intercontinental Conference of New Delhi, in 1953, Shoghi Effendi announced preliminary steps taken to acquire the land, made possible by the munificent donation of one hundred thousand dollars by the Hand of the Cause Mrs. Amelia Collins. I was at that Conference and remember the joy and enthusiasm of the friends who voted to send Mrs. Collins the following telegram: 'Conference joyfully voted one voice express admiration abiding gratitude your generous gift land Mashriqu'l-Adhkár holy mountain.' The difficult and protracted negotiations for the land led almost nowhere as the owners were reluctant to part with even the smallest fraction of their possession. I became somewhat involved in the matter because of some contacts made with the head of that

* See Appendix VI for additional information on the history of this land.

171

religious order who resided in Rome, but without any conclusive results. It was the deep esteem on the part of some officials of the Israeli Government for Shoghi Effendi, and their appreciation of all the beautification he had accomplished in and around Mt. Carmel, redounding to the attraction and prestige of the city of Haifa, that brought a direct intervention on the part of the Israeli authorities in the negotiations, leading to the purchase of approximately twenty thousand square metres of land, at the very head of the Mountain of God.

With great rejoicing, the Guardian announced the selection of the site and the availability of the needed funds in his message of April 1954 to the twelve National Conventions of the Bahá'í world. In this message there is far greater promise than may appear at first sight, for it reads: 'The site for the first Mashriqu'l-Adhkár of the Holy Land has been selected...'²⁸ It brought to my memory some of the enlightening statements he had made at table, some years before, on the future glory of the Holy Land and the significance of properties purchased at Bahá'u'lláh's bidding near the Sea of Galilee—forerunners of 'noble and imposing structures throughout its length and breadth to be dedicated to the worship and service of the one true God'.

Fulfilling to the letter his most cherished wish, the Faith now owns that land in the close vicinity of the blessed spot trodden by the footsteps of Bahá'u'lláh at the time He revealed the Tablet of Carmel—His Charter for the World Spiritual and Administrative Centres of the Faith—and near the ancient cave made famous by the presence of the Prophet Elijah.

On the last pilgrimage we made in December 1954, Angeline and I were highly privileged to be driven in Shoghi Effendi's automobile, at his invitation, to the Temple site, to pray on that hallowed spot and to visualize the luminous edifice which in time to come will rise in its loftiness on that holy mountain. When we saw him that same night, and he asked us our impressions of the location and the surroundings, his dear face was beaming with pride and joy.

THE OBELISK

Even before the site for the first Ma<u>sh</u>riqu'l-A<u>dh</u>kár of the Holy Land was purchased, Shoghi Effendi knew that it would be impossible to erect the edifice for many years to come. He planned therefore to place a marker in the middle of the land to indicate the hallowed spot on which the Temple would rise some time in the future. He sent word to me to ask my idea of what would be an appropriate manner to mark and celebrate such a future enterprise. I answered that the Romans used to celebrate men and events by erecting either a column or an obelisk, many examples being still visible in the Roman Forum and throughout the Eternal City. His decision was in favour of an obelisk, and a simple drawing was sent to me to secure an estimate of cost which was requested from four different firms. The choice fell upon the firm of Enrico Pandolfini, of Pietrasanta, whose bid was the most reasonable and was accepted by Shoghi Effendi on 12 April 1954. A final project was then prepared by Professor Ugo Mazzei, the architect of that firm, which the Guardian approved on 29 April by cablegram.

The structure consists of a quadrangular base surmounted by a pyramidal pillar tapering to a point, made of solid blocks of travertine,* with a mosaic on one side of the pillar—facing south—bearing the symbol of the 'Greatest Name'; the base is hollow and made of large slates of marble. The total height of the obelisk, from the lower plinth of the base to the tip of the needle, is eleven metres (thirty-six feet).

Within the next few months, all the marble, more than twenty tons contained in many heavy wooden cases, was shipped to Haifa. It was not possible, however, to erect the obelisk during the remaining years of the Guardian's life, because the Israeli Government, for security reasons, would not allow the raising of such a visible structure during the years of unsettled relations with neighbouring countries. Permission came finally in 1971,

---

* Travertine (Italian *travertino*) is a marble typical of Rome itself; most of the great ancient monuments and more recent buildings are built with this versatile marble which is found in the vicinity of the city. It is soft and easy to work when freshly quarried, but hardens on exposure. Both the Colosseum and the façade and colonnade of St. Peter's Basilica were built of this material.

and an announcement of the successful conclusion of the project was given by the Universal House of Justice on 19 December 1971 in these terms:

'After many years difficult negotiations erection obelisk marking site future Mashriqu'l-Adhkár Mount Carmel completed thus fulfilling project initiated beloved Guardian early years Crusade.'[29]

Epilogue

... and when he shall die,
Take him and cut him out in little stars,
And he will make the face of heaven so fine,
That all the world will be in love with night,
And pay no worship to the garish sun.

Shakespeare[30]

Events connected with the passing of Shoghi Effendi written a few days after his funeral 9 November 1957

Monday, November 4th. This being a national holiday in Italy I am at home. The telephone rings about 2.10 p.m. and I am told by the operator to stand by for a long-distance connection. At 2.15 I hear the voice of Rúḥíyyih Khánum, calling from London. 'The Guardian is dead!' Reeling under the impact of such crushing news, with little strength and reason left, I manage to book an air passage by telephone, to prepare a bag, and reach the airport in time to board a plane leaving Rome for London at 4.55 p.m.

The journey is uneventful until we reach Switzerland; after that the weather becomes bad and we land in London half an hour later than scheduled, with the elements raging all around us.

One and a half hours later I join Rúḥíyyih Khánum, Hasan Balyuzi and John Ferraby, and together we go to the Ḥaẓíratu'l-Quds at 27 Rutland Gate. The wind and the rain lash London all night; it is impossible to rest or accept with one's reason the reality of such a catastrophic situation.

Tuesday, November 5th. Dawn brings more rain and a deeper sense of despair, as we are faced by many complex problems to be dealt with at once. The morning is devoted to communications either by cable or by telephone to all parts of the world. A special call is

175

made to Stuttgart to request Dr. Mühlschlegel to come to London to assist in the final preparation of the Guardian's earthly remains, before burial. A call is sent to all Hands of the Cause [and] National Assemblies [about the funeral] to be held on Saturday, the ninth.

At night the first Hands of the Cause arrive, namely, Milly Collins from Haifa, which she had reached from America only twenty-four hours before, Adelbert Mühlschlegel and Hermann Grossmann from Germany.

In the afternoon Rúḥíyyih Khánum, accompanied by myself and Hasan Balyuzi, visits two London cemeteries to select an appropriate burial plot. The rain keeps falling steadily and after visiting one cemetery, which proved absolutely unsuitable, we reach the Great Northern London Cemetery a few minutes after 4.30 p.m. It is immediately felt by all that this spot possesses all qualifications as to beauty and upkeep, to be worthy of entrusting to it the most precious of all earthly remains in over a generation. With the assistance of the superintendent, Mr. Stanley, a very suitable plot is selected in which the grave is to be prepared. It lies between one of the main paths and a row of graves, in the shadow of two ancient trees which in the springtime form a bower, a protecting canopy, over the tomb.

We leave the cemetery at dusk and drive to the office of Mr. Leverton, the funeral director, for the selection of an appropriate coffin. The choice falls upon a solid and sombre coffin of polished bronze, lined with a sheeting of lead, to be hermetically soldered, so as to render possible the transfer of the Guardian's body anywhere, if conditions will in the future permit it. Then and there it is also decided to order a bronze plate to be placed on the upper lid of the coffin, with an inscription, the text of which is communicated to Mr. Leverton the next day.

In the evening believers from many parts of Europe and England start to arrive. The faces I remember, among the first, are those of Bahíyyih Varqá, Miss Fatheazam and her brother. Telegrams and telephone calls are coming to the Ḥaẓíra without interruption, and the British National Spiritual Assembly has set up a body of volunteers to handle messages and the throng of visitors.

Sorrow, despair and anguish are depicted on every face; human bodies moving without will or control; unspoken words of incredulity are on every lip. Can it be true that God has removed His Sign from this earth?

Wednesday, November 6th. This morning Rúḥíyyih Khánum and Milly Collins have gone to purchase the silk cloth for the shrouds. This forenoon many more believers arrive in London and there is a continuous stream of visitors at the Ḥaẓíra.

In the afternoon Rúḥíyyih Khánum, accompanied by myself, Hasan Balyuzi and the funeral director, go to make official declaration of the passing of the Guardian. Certificates of his death are issued immediately.

This night the Iranian Hands of the Cause, Khádem and Faizí, arrive, but are not seen on account of Khádem's illness.

Thursday, November 7th. Rúḥíyyih Khánum and Milly Collins have gone to make the floral arrangements for the chapel at the cemetery and for the floral blanket of roses, gardenias and lilies of the valley to be placed on the coffin. I bring the silk cloth to the Ḥaẓíra to have the Iranian ladies prepare the shrouds to be used this afternoon. Rúḥíyyih Khánum having again visited the chapel at the cemetery, to make final arrangements for the floral decoration, has purchased a large piece of green velvet which is to be used to cover the platform or catafalque on which the casket will rest. The sewing of this covering is also done by the Iranian ladies gathered at the Ḥaẓíra.

In the afternoon Rúḥíyyih Khánum, accompanied by Adelbert Mühlschlegel, has gone to the place where the Guardian's body is being kept, and in about two hours Adelbert completes the washing of the body and its placement in the first shroud. Then he, together with Rúḥíyyih Khánum, places the body of the Guardian in the second shroud and then in the coffin. Attar of rose given to me by the Guardian, some time ago, and brought by me from Rome, is used to anoint the body. A Bahá'í ringstone which I carried in my pocket is placed in the Guardian's mouth. His body, entirely shrouded with the exception of the face, is covered with rose petals brought by Milly from the Shrine of the Báb. I have been told that in the stillness of death the body of Shoghi Effendi irradiated an unusual beauty. Never during his life had his countenance been so luminous or so hieratic. His expression, often travailed by adversity and sufferings during the long thirty-six years of Guardianship, is now that of beatitude; the saintly glow of him who, for the sake of humanity, immolated himself to the great Cause, emanated from his brow. Glory, eternal glory, to him who led a life of sacrifice for the whole of humanity!

Friends are still arriving. The entire American National Spiritual Assembly, with the exception of Horace Holley,* will arrive tomorrow.

Telegrams by the hundreds and telephone calls are still coming to the Ḥazíra.

Friday, November 8th. The sealed casket has been brought to the chapel of the funeral director. The Hands of the Cause present in London keep vigil by the casket, banked with flowers, the entire day. The bronze plate is in place at about the middle of the upper lid of the casket. It is engraved in good characters. Final arrangements are made for the funeral cortège which will take place tomorrow.

The afternoon is spent in attending to other pressing matters and to arranging transportation back to Haifa. The members of the American National Spiritual Assembly have arrived. Leroy Ioas has telephoned that he will arrive early on Saturday; he was told to bring a rug and a silk covering from the inner Shrine of Bahá'u'lláh.

In the evening there is a meeting of all the Hands of the Cause present: Rúḥíyyih Khánum, Mason Remey, Milly Collins, Ugo Giachery, Paul Haney, William Sears, Adelbert Mühlschlegel, Hermann Grossmann, John Ferraby, Hasan Balyuzi, A. Q. Faizí and S. 'Alá'í, to make a definite programme for tomorrow's ceremony. It is quite late at night when we disband.

---

* Mr. Holley was then in hospital and unable to travel.

Saturday, November 9th. Mr. and Mrs. Mottahedeh have gone to the airport to meet Leroy Ioas and have brought him to town. He has the rug, a piece of Persian silk brocade, a large bouquet of jasmine from 'Akká and a box of petals and flowers taken from the various Bahá'í gardens in the Holy Land. Mr. Samandarí has brought some olive and orange branches from the Riḍván Garden in Baghdád.*

The convening hour at the Ḥaẓíra is 10 a.m. I walk there with Leroy Ioas and Paul Haney; we are taking the flowers from the Holy Land with us. A large gathering of friends is in the street in front of the building. It is almost impossible to enter; the hall, the stairs and all the ground floor rooms are filled to capacity. Sorrow and despair are on everyone's face; a mass of human beings waiting to be told what to do. This morning the weather is better (around 35 degrees), the sun is shining, lending a note of solace to eyes that have no more tears. At 10.30 word is passed to start to board the sixty or more automobiles waiting nearby. Rúḥíyyih Khánum, Milly Collins and Mason Remey enter in the first car. Myself, Leroy Ioas, Paul Haney, Hasan Balyuzi, Adelbert Mühlschlegel and T. Samandarí in the second car. It is impossible for me to see who enters the other cars. Slowly all automobiles are filled and, after some irrelevant delays, the first car moves, crossing from Rutland Gate to Hyde Park, followed by the rest. Some constables on motorcycles pass us by in both directions, keeping the traffic moving and preventing stoppage of the cortège. It is so strange to drive through London, a city so unaware of the tremendous drama which we are living moment after moment!

At a good pace we go through streets, squares, avenues in the immensity of this metropolis basking in the sun of a clear morning. At a certain point of our journey, at a place called Swiss Cottage, we stop for a few minutes; two large vehicles waiting on a side street move in front of the first car. I look at my watch.

---

* Other Hands of the Cause who arrived in time for the funeral, or soon after, depending on the distances they had to travel, were: Dhikru'lláh Khádem, Músá Banání, Enoch Olinga and Raḥmatu'lláh Muhájir.

It is 11.40. We start again, preceded by a side-glass-windowed car filled with wreaths of flowers, followed by the funeral car bringing the precious body of the beloved of our hearts, Shoghi Effendi, our Guardian. Smoothly, without any further delays or stops, we cover the remaining distance to the Great Northern London Cemetery in about twenty-five minutes.

After passing the gate we reach the esplanade in front of the chapel. A large crowd of believers is already there; they are waiting on the left side of the door, bareheaded and in tears. For five or more minutes we wait for the arrival of all the cars of the cortège. Some of the friends have already gotten out, almost impatient to get near to the coffin which is still kept in the special car. Now eight men in sombre dark clothes have come and are taking the casket down. We leave our cars; moaning and sobbing are heard from every side. We must be strong; we cannot let our feelings overcome us at this moment and throw confusion among these heart-broken friends. The casket moves into the chapel; we follow closely. It is placed to rest on the catafalque covered with the green velvet. Upon the casket a large blanket of red roses and gardenias and lilies of the valley—the flowers, I am told, the Beloved preferred—is the symbol of the love of all the friends the world over. The rear wall of the chapel is banked with row upon row of chrysanthemums of different hues and colours. On the transom of the alcove in which is the catafalque there is the 'Greatest Name'; on both sides, on a little higher level than the floor of the chapel, there are several rows of chairs. Rúḥíyyih Khánum sits at the right side, Milly beside her; all the Hands are immediately behind. In the second row, with the Hands, sits the Chargé d'Affaires of the Government of Israel, Mr. G. Avner. The chapel is now full. There are not enough seats for everyone; one-third of the friends are standing. The air is cold inside the chapel, cold enough to keep us conscious. Someone is lamenting quite loudly. It is Ṭarázu'lláh Samandarí; somebody is quieting him. Now all is still; oblivion is what we want most. It is not true, I keep repeating to myself; it is only a bad dream which I must forget!

At once the chant of Abu'l-Qásim Faizí, steady, but interwoven

180

with deep emotion, is in the air. It is the Prayer for the Dead of Bahá'u'lláh. It becomes our cry, our imploring. I cannot stand it, my heart is pounding to the breaking-point. Will God have mercy on us?

The rhythm of the chant rises and falls. I cannot understand the Arabic words but keep on repeating the refrains in Italian; I want to feel very near to the departed spirit. I repeat prayer after prayer almost unaware of the place and the surroundings. Betty Reed, Borrah Kavelin, Adib Taherzadeh, William Sears, Elsie Austin, Ian Semple and Enoch Olinga succeed each other with prayers and other selections from the Sacred Writings. It is now 12.50. Again the pall-bearers take hold of the coffin and place it in the funeral car. We follow on foot, slowly, broken in body and in spirit. This is the end; we only have a few more minutes and the earth will take its trust forever! The sun which shone in the early morning has disappeared; dark clouds are coming up from every direction. We have now reached the site of the grave. The opening on the ground is about seven by four feet. Mats of green straw imitating grass are placed all around. It gives the illusion of being early spring. The grave itself is lined with boughs of cedar studded with flowers. Everyone crowds around it; there is hardly any space to move. It looks like a human fortress, the last stand to prevent the earth from claiming its price. Can it be true that his separation must now take place?

The inevitable moment of a final farewell is at hand. The coffin is being lowered from the car; it is placed at the head of the grave. There is a moment of hushed silence, and then moaning and sobbing are heard again, this time much louder and more widely spread. It is a struggle to remain standing erect, when the weight of sorrow bends us down, down to the soil, nearer to him whom we loved so much. One by one, with an unprecedented demonstration of supreme love, wanting to empty our hearts for the last time to the hidden, lifeless, beloved Guardian of God's Faith, the friends fall on their knees, sobbing in despair, at the head of the casket. Flowers, attar of roses, kisses, tears, prayers, supplications, promises, vows are the offerings made at such a parting. Women, children, men in the prime of life, old bent men, all believers, pass for well two hours under the drizzling rain to pay the last homage, the last tribute, to him who for thirty-six years gave to them his whole life, his love, his guidance and the inspiration to arise above human limitation. What a debt of gratitude we owe him; it is too late now, our conscience well tells us how much gratitude we placed silently in the balance to recompense him for his labours! The pall-bearers who stand by the grave have a strange expression on their faces. Surely they have seen hundreds of interments, but none like this. They cannot remain untouched by the waves of sorrow and love, of grief and devotion, which are overpowering everyone. Their eyes are filled with tears, their limbs trembling. The Israeli Government representative is stunned. Deep grief is on his face, kindness and sympathy emanate from his body; he is deeply moved and does nothing to conceal it. Rúḥíyyih Khánum is the last one to kneel down; then she places the green pall over the casket and above it, in the centre, the small piece of blue brocade, from the Tomb of Bahá'u'lláh. The friends are pressing in from every side; there is no space for the eight bearers to move. Inching their way, they slowly lift the casket with strips of hemp passed under it, until they reach the opening of the grave. The rug from the inner Shrine of Bahá'u'lláh is already on the bottom of it. It gives an air of domesticity, like a corner of home; a bit of Persia, a symbol from the cradle of the Faith, to receive the great-grandson of Him Who, one hundred and four years ago, was compelled to leave His native land, never to see it again!

The merciless hand of time is at work again. The coffin is lowered to its final rest, the last step of the last journey! Moaning and sobbing are heard again, this time uncontrolled, heart-rending; who can console us now? The jasmine from Bahjí is being placed on the casket, in the grave, all around; it will be sealed in the earth as soon as the vault is closed. A female voice intones a chant in Persian; it was not planned, but I understand from her broken tones that she wants to do something unusual, quickly, afraid we may forget him whose love was our solace. As she terminates her chant, 'Alí Nakhjavání intones one of Shoghi Effendi's own orations. Hasan Balyuzi, the Afnán Hand of the

THE SHRINE OF BAHÁ'U'LLÁH AND THE MANSION OF BAHJÍ
An aerial view showing development of the gardens since 1952

Cause, ends with a prayer in English. We must leave the graveside now; we must go somewhere. The masons need much space to work to seal the vault with two large stone slabs. All the Hands of the Cause, the members of the Auxiliary Boards and National Assemblies slowly move away. We enter our cars waiting near by. The mass of believers disbands. We drive out of the cemetery; around we go without purpose, long enough to give time to the masons to complete their work. In twenty minutes we are back; the grave is sealed, some believers who never left are standing by as in a trance, motionless, with deep sorrow engraved on their faces. We gather around the two large stones which are now between us and him who, only a little while ago, was still a living reality to us. The flowers gathered from all the Bahá'í gardens in the Holy Land are now being placed in little clumps by the Hands of the Cause, upon the stones. The members of the Auxiliary Boards and of the National Assemblies follow, one by one, bringing with tender delicacy the very last offerings that can be made. In turn, prayers in many tongues are recited; I say a prayer of the Báb in Italian. The rain has stopped; the sun comes and goes. We stay around the grave. Some attendants are now bringing flowers: wreaths, bouquets, sprays, which have been sent by the hundreds and kept aside during the morning. They are being placed over and around the grave; it is a fragrant carpet of many colours, of brilliant hues, with a strong scent pervading the cold autumn air. So many flowers! There is no room for all of them. The four little cypress trees which Rúḥíyyih Khánum had planted the day before at the four corners of the grave are dwarfed by the height of these floral mementoes.

It is well after 4 p.m. The light of day starts to fade. One last farewell with tears and sobs; our hearts are throbbing without regularity. Life seems meaningless. Where are we going now? Into a world without guidance, in the darkness of despair until God in His mercy will show us the way, heal our hearts and set firm our steps in His service again.

THE SHRINE OF THE BÁB ON MT. CARMEL
The superstructure erected under the guidance of Shoghi Effendi

The Sepulchre of Shoghi Effendi

After the passing of Shoghi Effendi one of the urgent tasks to be accomplished was the final embellishment of his grave in the Great Northern London Cemetery. What could be more appropriate than an artistic memorial—simple but impressive—erected above the grave itself? Unfortunately the possibility of bringing his precious remains to the holy mountain* he had so greatly beautified had to be discarded—even if seriously discussed —because no means of transportation was available at the time that would allow the transfer of the body to the Holy Land in one hour's time, a requirement for Bahá'í burial laid down by Bahá'-u'lláh Himself.

Amatu'l-Bahá Rúḥíyyih Khánum conceived the idea that a memorial of the finest Italian marble, in the form of a column,† would most fittingly glorify the existence and honour the labours of the Guardian of the Cause of God. The design was to be simple and yet impressive, denoting in its graciousness some of the characteristics possessed by Shoghi Effendi. After preliminary drawings and inquiries concerning the marble and other details, a meeting was arranged in Rome between Rúḥíyyih Khánum and Professor Rocca—the architect for the marble of the Shrine of the Báb and the International Archives. During this conference, ideas were exchanged and technical and artistic details discussed. A final project was drafted and approved, the work to be executed in less than six months in and around the marble capital of the world, Carrara.

Little can this writer understand why the hand of fate made it imperative that he should witness the sad days immediately following the passing of his beloved Guardian and then be called upon to supervise the preparation of the marble and other material

---

* Mt. Carmel, in Haifa.
† In ancient Rome, from the beginning of the Kingdom through the Republic and the Empire, when a personage was to be highly honoured or an event glorified, the State would erect columns, triumphal arches or statues of rare marbles, adorned with gilded bronze, in the city proper or in the Forum. It is reported that at one time, hundreds of columns and triumphal arches had been erected in the centre of Rome.

needed for the erection of the memorial to the one he so deeply loved and venerated.

The marble chosen was 'Carrara Statuary', from a quarry which has provided the finest stone for countless works of art throughout the world.

The memorial to Shoghi Effendi called for a low platform rising from the ground in three steps, in the centre of which the column would be placed, topped by a beautifully carved Corinthian capital. A model was chosen from the finest and rarest examples of Corinthian art still in existence in the City of Rome.*

Placed upon the capital is a globe of the same marble, representing our planet, and traced in low relief with the various continents. It is oriented in such a way that the continent of Africa faces east towards the Qiblih of our Faith, for Africa was one of the continents visited and much loved by Shoghi Effendi. Perched on top of this globe is a gilded, bronze adult eagle, ready to start its flight, with one wing fully extended and the other in the process of opening. Both the eagle and the inscription engraved on the body of the column, half-way between the base and the capital, also face the Qiblih.

The reason the eagle was placed there is twofold: Shoghi Effendi deeply admired eagles because, as he often stated, 'the eagle is the symbol of victory', and for this reason he had placed many marble and lead eagles upon pedestals around the Bahá'í gardens both on Mt. Carmel and at Bahjí. Moreover, in his room he had a silver eagle of Japanese origin, mounted upon a piece of hardwood simulating a rock, and this he much admired for its beauty, faultless execution and verisimilitude.

Later, this decorative trophy was brought to Italy and delivered to me. I entrusted it to a sculptor who reproduced the eagle—enlarged six times—first in clay, and then in gypsum. It was then cast in bronze, electroplated in silver, and taken to Florence for fire-gilding.

* A Temple initiated by Augustus in the heart of Rome, and completed by his son-in-law, Marcus Agrippa, in the year 27 B.C., is still in existence and is known as the Pantheon. In the Middle Ages it was converted into the Christian church of Santa Maria Rotonda. The sixteen huge columns of its front portico hold aloft the capitals taken by Professor Rocca as a prototype.

While the marble work was being executed in Italy, Rúḥíyyih Khánum purchased in England a large quantity of Dover-stone balustrade—possibly from some lordly estates now being dismantled—to enclose the plot of land where the monument was to be erected. The balustrade was of fine workmanship with a strong Palladian influence, much resembling the balustrade chosen by Shoghi Effendi for the balconies of the International Archives on Mt. Carmel.

Stone urns—similar to those in the gardens around the Tomb of Bahá'u'lláh—were also purchased by her for the corners of the enclosure, and a beautiful wrought-iron monumental gate for the entrance to the sacred enclave.

During the month of October 1958, hardly one year after the Guardian's passing, Rúḥíyyih Khánum was in London to supervise the erection and completion of the sepulchre.

The text of the inscription on the column is taken from the Will and Testament of 'Abdu'l-Bahá, as follows:

Shoghi Effendi
3 March 1896 — 4 November 1957

'Behold he is the blest
And sacred bough that has
Branched out from the
Twin Holy Trees. Well is it
With him that seeketh the
Shelter of his shade that
Shadoweth all mankind.'

'Abdu'l-Bahá

Appendices

Early Descriptions of Shoghi Effendi

MR. MOUNTFORT MILLS

The first of the recently returned pilgrims to speak at the Feast of Riḍván, during the Fourteenth Annual Bahá'í Convention, 22 April 1922, Chicago, Illinois, as reported by Louis Gregory.[31]

. . .We met Shoghi Effendi, dressed entirely in black, a touching figure. Think of what he stands for today! All the complex problems of the great statesmen of the world are as child's play in comparison with the great problems of this youth, before whom are the problems of the entire world. He is a youth of twenty-six, left by the will of the Master as the Guardian of the Cause. No one can form any conception of his difficulties, which are overwhelming.

We received his joyous, hearty hand grasp and our meeting was short. A bouquet was sent to our room in the form of a young tree filled with nectarines or tangerines. It was brought by Mr. Fugeta. We awoke without any sense of sadness. That feeling was entirely gone. The Master is not gone. His Spirit is present with greater intensity and power, freed from bodily limitations. We can take it into our own hearts and reflect it in greater degrees. In the center of this radiation stands this youth, Shoghi Effendi. The Spirit streams forth from this young man. He is indeed young in face, form and manner, yet his heart is the center of the world today. The character and spirit divine scintillate from him today. He alone can today save the world and make true civilization. So humble, meek, selfless is he that it is touching to see him. His letters are a marvel. It is the great wisdom of God in granting us the countenance of this great central point of guidance to meet difficult problems. These problems, much like ours, come to him from all parts of the world. They are met and solved by him in the most informal way. Again it came to us with great force that the powers of the Universal House of Justice, when organized, would be limitless. Its sole purpose would be to solve all human problems.

The great principles laid down by Bahá'u'lláh and 'Abdu'l-Bahá now have their foundation in the external world of God's Kingdom on earth. This foundation is being laid, sure and certain, by Shoghi Effendi in Haifa today. Yet it is all futile unless throughout the world each one will make this foundation safe in his own heart and life. The House of Justice and the Hands of the Cause are given that his hands may be upheld and the Cause of God may be selflessly established. He wishes us to sense the largeness of these great things, avoid sectarianism and work for the deepening of the Cause of God before its expansion. Largeness of heart and spirit is his wish and will. As the will of 'Abdu'l-Bahá says, 'Universality is of God and limitations are of the earth'. . .

MR. ROY C. WILHELM*

He had been summoned to Haifa with Mr. Mills, and was another speaker at this Feast of Riḍván (1922).[32]

. . .'Abdu'l-Bahá says: 'God created the world; man worked out the boundaries.' No one in the world today, except the Bahá'í who has the universal, selfless mind, can see without prejudice. He has no interest save the happiness of all.

When one reaches Haifa and meets Shoghi Effendi and sees the workings of his mind and heart, his wonderful spirit and grasp of things, it is truly marvelous. Our world boundaries must fade!

MRS. MAY BOLLES MAXWELL

From informal notes taken in Haifa in 1924.[33]

. . . Shoghi Effendi discusses the affairs and conditions of the Cause with astonishing openness and frankness; he does not like secrecy and told us many times that this openness, frankness and truthfulness among the friends constitutes one of the great remedies for

---

* After his death in 1951, Shoghi Effendi accorded Mr. Wilhelm the rank of Hand of the Cause of God.

many of our difficulties, and he sets us the example of free and open consultation, with a modesty and simplicity which one must see in order to appreciate because it is foreign to our American temperament; he invites suggestions and consultation from the visiting friends and from those around him.

He listens to every suggestion with the utmost courtesy and seriousness and brings to bear upon it the light of his wonderful lucid mind, his clear all-comprehensive thought, his powerful and penetrative judgement.

The spirit of criticism is abhorrent to Shoghi Effendi. . .

ALAINE LOCKE, A.B., PH.D.
From 'Impressions of Haifa'.[34]

. . . It was a privilege to see and experience these things. But it was still more of a privilege to stand there with the Guardian of the Cause, and to feel that, accessible and inspiring as it was to all who can come and will come, there was available there for him a constant source of inspiration and vision from which to draw, in the accomplishment of his heavy burdens and responsibilities. That thought of communion with ideas and ideals without the mediation of symbols, seemed to me the most reassuring and novel feature. For after all the only enlightened symbol of a religious or moral principle is the figure of a personality endowed to perfection with its qualities and necessary attributes. Earnestly renewing this inheritance seemed the constant concern of this gifted personality, and the quiet but insistent lesson of his temperament.

Refreshingly human after this intense experience, was the relaxation of our walk and talk in the gardens. Here the evidences of love, devotion and service were as concrete and as practical and as human as inside the shrines they had been mystical and abstract and superhuman. Shoghi Effendi is a master of detail as well as of principle, of executive foresight as well as of projective vision. But I have never heard details so redeemed of their natural triviality as when talking to him of the plans for the beautifying and laying out of the terraces and gardens. They were important because they all were meant to dramatize the emotion of the place and quicken the soul even through the senses. It was night in the quick twilight of the East before we had finished the details of inspecting the gardens, and then, by the lantern light, the faithful gardener showed us to the austere retreat of the great Expounder of the teaching. It taught me with what purely simple and meager elements a master workman works. It is after all in Himself that He finds His message and it is Himself that He gives with it to the world...

MRS. KEITH RANSOM-KEHLER

From 'Excerpts from My Diary', published in 1926.[35]

The unique and outstanding figure in the world today is Shoghi Effendi. Unique, because the guardianship of this great Cause is in his hands and his humility, modesty, economy and self-effacement are monumental. Outstanding because he is the only person, we may safely say, who entrusted with the affairs of millions of souls, has but one thought and one mind—the speedy promulgation of peace and goodwill throughout the world. His personal life is absolutely and definitely sacrificed. The poorest boy in America struggling for an education would consider himself hardly used to have no more than those bare necessities which this young man voluntarily chooses for himself. The ladies of the household typify the Cause of Love and Faith. Shoghi Effendi adds to this the *élan* of the New Day—ACTION and Progress.

So to comprehend and administer all the relationships in a huge organization that only satisfaction and illumination result; never to see anything smaller than the world-wide import of all our movements, no matter how parochial; to clarify with a word the most obscure situations; to release in countless souls the tides of energy that will sweep the cargoes of these glad-tidings round the world; to remain without one moment's cessation so poised in God as to be completely naturalized into His attributes—these are some of the characteristics that make of Shoghi Effendi the unique and outstanding figure of our time. And this without reference to his surpassing mental capacities that mark this spiritually superb person as a penetrating thinker and brilliant executive. The world, its politics, social relationships, economic situations, schemes, plans, aspirations, programs, defects, successes, lie under his scrutiny like infusoria beneath a microscope.

... Shoghi Effendi is the Commander-in-chief of this great new army of faith and strength that is moving forth to vanquish the malevolent forces of life.

MRS. HELEN BISHOP
Part of a letter written to Mr. Alfred E. Lunt.

The Guardian is an example of how intellect can serve the spirit in a manner we of the West have never known. He is a perfectly controlled and mature personality. I have never heard him recite an incident in which he was the major figure, or say anything which would in any way give him a chance to excel. This may sound very naïve; but the point is that Shoghi Effendi simply refutes all those theories with which our academies are surfeited, that every ego is trying merely to maximate itself.

Shoghi Effendi is very impersonal, and he speaks only of the Word and the Faith. His speech is rapid and his English is stunning. When he speaks the hours pass tirelessly. I should say that his most obvious characteristic is power, but there is nothing arbitrary or even personal about it. Again and again he seems to convey to one that the Cause of Bahá'u'lláh will reach its aim, and that we have only to be superlatively faithful and to be active and obedient. There is something about him that makes one believe that one can do anything if he requires it...

MR. O. Z. WHITEHEAD*
Excerpt from an unpublished diary of his pilgrimage to the World Centre of the Bahá'í Faith, January, 1955.

... At least fifteen minutes before dinner-time the members of the household and the pilgrims gathered in the sitting-room. Rúḥíyyih Khánum wore a becoming white dress with a white shawl

* Mr. Whitehead, an American Bahá'í and actor. Although not an 'early description' of Shoghi Effendi, this vivid account calls for inclusion.

over her head. She did not seem conscious of her great beauty and enormous charm. After we had sat together for a short time, a sweet-looking Arabian maid came to the door and bowed to Rúḥíyyih Khánum. The maid spoke softly. I could not hear what she said. Rúḥíyyih Khánum said: 'The pilgrims go first.'

The staircase was very narrow. Only one could go down at a time. After I had reached the lower floor, I looked towards the dining-room. On the other side of the table from the door, the Guardian sat entirely still. If I had not known who he was, but had just seen him sitting somewhere else, I would have been greatly drawn to him. He had a greater magnetism than I had felt before in anyone. He had an indescribable attraction. I was not afraid to go near to him. On the contrary I could not get near to him soon enough.

Shoghi Effendi had on a black fez, a black suit and a black necktie. As we approached the dining-room, he stood up. I felt as if a light was all around him. . . The Guardian turned to me. I bent over and kissed him on the cheek. I felt that he filled the universe . . . He showed the rest of us where to sit. . . He had a warm and delightful smile. He held my entire attention. . . I looked intently at his warm and deeply sensitive eyes that mirrored many different thoughts and that kept constantly changing expression. He turned a little in my direction and smiled. His eyes were like pools of light. I noticed his wonderfully expressive hands.

. . . After dinner was over, the Guardian sat with us for awhile, then rose from his chair. After he had left the room everyone was quiet. He had filled the room with a great energy that I had never felt before. He had given us some of his infinitely precious time.

. . . As on the previous evening, we waited in suspense for the maid to appear. I feel sure that none of us could bear to think that Shoghi Effendi might not be able to come for dinner that night. After a few moments our suspense grew stronger. There was very little conversation. The maid appeared at the doorway. We all hurried downstairs.

The Guardian had on an English polo coat. I thought he looked a little tired. He said with slight concern, 'I have a little cold'. . . He continued to speak in his unique and delightful accent of unsurpassed charm and at the same time made graceful gestures with his expressive hands. His face was as always lighted up with the beauty of clear and penetrating thought. . . he spoke as if he could see vividly the many tortuous events that would take place over hundreds of years, but as if, too, he was reconciled to this inescapable fact. . .

On the last night, the Guardian sat in his usual place across the table from the door. As soon as I had come into the room, he said: 'This is your last night, isn't it? I am glad to see that you do not look unhappy. . . you will return here.' He took a vial out of his pocket and handed it to me. 'First tell the believers in New York to disperse and then anoint them with this "attar of roses",' he said.

I was so moved by this gift that I could hardly say 'thank you, Shoghi Effendi'. . . I felt that the atmosphere in the room became even stronger than before and as if it had taken on the light of another world.

APPENDIX II

Letters to Angeline Giachery

Excerpts from letters addressed by the author to his wife immediately after his arrival in the Holy Land.

4 March 1952—7.30 a.m., Haifa, Israel

Yesterday the plane arrived at Lydda two hours late and I found a message from Rúḥíyyih Khánum, to proceed on my own. I went to Tel Aviv and took a seat in a cab, arriving here around 3 p.m. Everyone is well; Milly* was truly happy to see me and so were the Revell sisters and Larry Hautz. Rúḥíyyih Khánum came to see me; she was kind and friendly and regretted you could not be asked now. The Guardian is not too well—I have not seen him yet—he is burdened with a thousand cares and lots of sorrows. He has just appointed seven more Hands to make nineteen altogether: Corinne True, Músá Banání, Clara Dunn, Fred

* Mrs. Amelia E. Collins, Hand of the Cause of God.

Schopflocher, Adelbert Mühlschlegel and two Persians (one thirty-three years old).* We got up at 4.30 a.m. and prayed together with the Revells. Here it is heavenly; there is such an air of purity and holiness in this house;† I am so happy and feel so well, I have a beautiful room and everything is comfortable and charming. I am waiting for the Guardian to call for me in a while.

4 March, a second letter written the same day

Around 8 o'clock Rúḥíyyih Khánum sent for me and I visited her in the Guardian's house which was 'Abbás Effendi's house. It is a lovely building with a very large central hall from which one can see the door of the room where 'Abdu'l-Bahá passed away. The door . . . is closed and no one is allowed therein except on special occasions. I sat for awhile with Milly who came a little later—in the small sitting-room where the Guardian receives visitors. It is an oblong room with two windows; it has the type of furnishing prevalent some eighty years ago; of course all the rugs are beautiful and the atmosphere is one of great repose. One feels happy to enter this room because there is a spirit of great holiness that hovers around you. On the wall there is a picture of 'Abdu'l-Bahá and a few hangings; the ceiling, as in all the other rooms, is very high and the walls are painted a warm buff colour. From the windows one can see the garden which goes around the house and the peacocks strutting in a special pen at the end of the garden. After awhile Rúḥíyyih Khánum came in and said that the Guardian felt better and that she was to take me to the gardens and the Shrine of the Báb. We drove in the Guardian's car to the gardens and arrived at the same time that some American tourists were arriving from the cruise ship *Constitution*, which will remain in port for three days. The gardens are beautiful beyond description; I have seen many gardens in many parts of the world, but these gardens are unique. The layout, the arrangements of the plants, shrubs and trees are so completely original that there cannot be anything like them anywhere. Rúḥíyyih Khánum told me that

* General Shu'á'u'lláh 'Alá'í and Mr. Dhikru'lláh Khádem.
† The Western Pilgrim House, on Persian Street, now the temporary seat of the Universal House of Justice.

some prominent personage sent word that he wanted to have the same gardener of the Persian Gardens to lay out his own garden! Of course you do know who the gardener is! The Shrine is truly beautiful, the word should be majestic or enchanting. It seems one of the fairy-tale dream castles made into reality. The Baveno columns glisten in the sunlight; the fresh clear spring air renders the sight of the bay and the great harbour even more brilliant. The green of the grass is like emerald and the geraniums are in bloom. The wife of Manṣúr, the custodian,* spread a carpet under the colonnade on the west side of the Shrine. We take our shoes off, and one after the other we enter the antechamber of the Báb's Tomb. Magnificent carpets are spread on the floor; my eyes are transfixed on the central spot of the central room, where a small rare rug marks the sacred spot above the real tomb. Three chandeliers give a brilliant light and there are flowers everywhere. We stop at the threshold which is covered by an embroidered white cloth, literally covered with flowers which the custodian places there fresh every morning. We prostrate ourselves on the floor with our faces upon the holy threshold and pray with all our hearts. I remained praying for a long time until I realized that Rúḥíyyih Khánum and Milly were standing up. I got up, our faces were bathed with tears; one feels that he is unable to leave that Holy Place again! Rúḥíyyih Khánum chanted then the Visitation Tablet in Persian, and left slowly, walking backwards. We left that room, going outside and entering the antechamber of the Tomb of 'Abdu'l-Bahá. Here again we prostrated to the floor and prayed. This time, Dr. Ḥakím chanted a prayer. On leaving both Tombs I picked up one flower each time and shall keep them as a memory of my first visit here. Rúḥíyyih Khánum also picked some flowers and gave them to me to bring to you personally, as a special gift because you could not be invited to come.

Haifa, 9 March 1952

Dearest Angeline: I am taking advantage of the stop in Rome of three Iranian pilgrims, to send this letter to you. The love and

---

* Manṣúr Írání, extremely devoted to Shoghi Effendi; he died a few weeks after the Guardian's passing.

consideration showered upon me by the Guardian cannot be fully and adequately described. Our meeting was something preordained by God; he waited for me alone, in the dining-room, and said: 'At last you are here, Ugo!' and hugged and kissed me three times and tears were in his eyes. During the dinner he praised me with every word he uttered, and when I said, 'Angeline, my wife, has shared in all this work,' he answered 'I know that.' He has appointed me member at large of the International Council and will name the last remaining door of the Shrine of the Báb after me. 'Your full station is not yet revealed,' he said, 'but I shall see that it is.' His eyes poured love upon me, and his tender attentions have rent my heart. He has called me here because he wants to consult about some work for Bahjí, the preliminary steps for the construction of the Sepulchre of Bahá'u'lláh, and for the establishment of a joint National Spiritual Assembly for Switzerland and Italy . . . planning for next year the Convention to elect the third European National Assembly. 'Another great pillar to support the dome of the Bahá'í Administration,' the Guardian said. 'I want you to be independent and original, and I know that the Italians and the Swiss are capable of striving for achievements.' He is pleased with our work (mine and yours) in a tremendous measure and attaches great importance to Rome, as Rome will take the leading place in all of Europe.

Haifa, 29 June 1952

Dearest Angeline: Yesterday I received a letter from . . ., giving news of you and of your activity. He tells me that you are well and very busy; that, I have imagined all the time. Between visitors and meetings, you must be busy from early morning to late evening. The Guardian knows this and he appreciates it immensely. He told me that he has written you a letter; I am sure it must have made you very happy. Life here is a continuous sacrifice; one has to let away many ideas and be remissive, obedient and extremely active. The life the Guardian leads is an example of what he expects from every one. He gets up at 4. a.m. and goes to bed at midnight, and often eats only once a day. Really I cannot yet understand how he can carry on his work which would normally require about twenty persons to do it. Only the mail would bewilder anyone; he opens and reads everything—that is the mail addressed to him—and arranges for the answer. To this you must add all the reports of the eleven National Assemblies, the work of the Council, the construction of the Shrine, the extension of the terraces, the beautification of Bahjí and the general planning ahead for the development of the Faith. The assistance we can render him is infinitesimal, and this worries me very much. I cannot tell you yet when I will be back, but it will be sometime around the first ten days in July.

APPENDIX III

The Writings of Shoghi Effendi

BOOKS

1938 *The Advent of Divine Justice.* (Published 1939.)

1941 *The Promised Day is Come.*

1944 *God Passes By.*

TRANSLATIONS

1923 *Prayer of Bahá'u'lláh; Prayers and Tablets of 'Abdu'l-Bahá.* (Booklet.)

1923 *Words of Wisdom*, revealed by Bahá'u'lláh.*

1923 *Tablet revealed by 'Abdu'l-Bahá to Dr. Auguste Forel*, 21 Sept. 1921.†

1925 *The Hidden Words of Bahá'u'lláh.* (Revised 1932.)

1931 *Kitáb-i-Íqán* (*The Book of Certitude*), by Bahá'u'lláh.

1932 *The Dawn-Breakers.* Nabíl's Narrative of the Early Days of the Bahá'í Revelation.

* *Star of the West*, vol. XIV, pp. 99–100. Reprinted in *Bahá'í World Faith* (Wilmette, Illinois, 1956), pp. 140–2.

† *Star of the West*, vol. XIV, pp. 101–9. Reprinted in *The Bahá'í Revelation* (London, 1955), pp. 220–31, and *Bahá'í World Faith*, pp. 336–48 (except for two introductory paragraphs and one line to close).

1933   *Tablets Revealed in Honor of the Greatest Holy Leaf*, by Bahá'u'-lláh and 'Abdu'l-Bahá. With Introduction by Shoghi Effendi.

1935   *Gleanings from the Writings of Bahá'u'lláh*.

1938   *Prayers and Meditations by Bahá'u'lláh*.

1941   *Epistle to the Son of the Wolf*, by Bahá'u'lláh.

LETTERS PUBLISHED IN COLLECTIONS

21 January 1922–27 November 1924. *Letters from Shoghi Effendi*. (Published 1925, and included in the next collection.)

21 January 1922–17 July 1932. *Bahá'í Administration*. Letters addressed to the National Spiritual Assembly of the Bahá'ís of the United States and Canada and to the Bahá'ís of the North American Bahá'í Community as a whole. (First published 1928; revised edition 1945.)

27 February 1929–11 March 1936. *The World Order of Bahá'u'lláh*. Letters addressed to the National Spiritual Assembly of the Bahá'ís of the United States and Canada, and to the Bahá'ís of the West. (Published 1938.) These letters were first published individually under the following titles:

27 February 1929. The World Order of Bahá'u'lláh.

21 March 1930. The World Order of Bahá'u'lláh: Further Considerations.

28 November 1931. The Goal of a New World Order.

21 March 1932. The Golden Age of the Cause of Bahá'u'lláh.

21 April 1933. America and the Most Great Peace.

8 February 1934. The Dispensation of Bahá'u'lláh.

11 March 1936. The Unfoldment of World Civilization.

21 June 1932–21 July 1940. *Messages from the Guardian*. Letters and cablegrams received by the National Spiritual Assembly of the Bahá'ís of the United States and Canada. (The actual text of the cablegrams is given, interpolations made for clarity being noted.)

21 June 1932–3 December 1946. *Messages to America*. Letters and cablegrams addressed to the National Spiritual Assembly of the Bahá'ís of the United States and Canada, to Annual Bahá'í Conventions and

to the North American Bahá'í Community. Two of the longer messages, 'The Spiritual Potencies of That Consecrated Spot' and 'A God-Given Mandate', were separately published in 1940 and 1946.

15 June 1946–8 March 1952. *World Order Unfolds.* Letters and cablegrams to the American Bahá'í Community. (The actual text of the cablegrams is given, interpolations being noted.)

25 April 1950–October 1957. *Messages to the Bahá'í World 1950–1957.* Major communications addressed to the Bahá'í world. (Published 1958; revised edition 1971.)

20 January 1947–21 September 1957. *Citadel of Faith.* Messages to America. (Published 1965.) The long letter entitled 'The Challenging Requirements of the Present Hour' was published as a booklet in 1947, and the message of 8 November 1948 was also separately published.

2 January 1923–18 July 1957. *Messages to Canada.* Apart from the first letter, the messages were sent between 1948 and 1957, when the Canadian Bahá'ís had established their own National Spiritual Assembly and independent Bahá'í Community. (Published 1965.)

2 December 1923–19 July 1957. *Letters from the Guardian to Australia and New Zealand 1923–1957.* Apart from the first letter, these are messages addressed to the National Spiritual Assembly, which was formed in 1934. (Published 1970.)

9 January 1923–6 March 1957. *Dawn of a New Day.* (Messages to India 1923–1957.) Messages addressed to the National Spiritual Assembly, to the Bahá'í youth of India, and to individual Bahá'ís in India and Burma. (Published 1970.)

COMPILATIONS

1944   *A World Survey: The Bahá'í Faith 1844–1944.* (24 pp.)

1950   *The Bahá'í Faith 1844–1950: Information Statistical and Comparative.* (36 pp.)

1953   *The Bahá'í Faith 1844–1952: Information Statistical and Comparative;* supplement entitled 'Ten Year International Bahá'í Teaching and Consolidation Plan 1953–1963'. (80 pp. and map.)

MESSAGES SELECTED BY SHOGHI EFFENDI FOR INCLUSION IN *THE BAHÁ'Í WORLD**

VOLUME II – 1926–1928

7 October 1926. 'To the Bahá'ís of the West', citing words of Queen Marie of Rumania (pp. 173–4).

VOLUME III – 1928–1930

25 October 1929. 'The Spiritual Significance of the Mashriqu'l-Adhkár' (pp. 159–63). (Repeated in vols. X, XI, XII; also in BA, pp. 180–7.)

VOLUME V – 1932–1934

17 July 1932. 'A Tribute to Bahíyyih Khánum, the Most Exalted Leaf' (pp. 174–9; see also BA, pp. 187–96).

VOLUME VIII – 1938–1940

These messages are in pp. 245–53 and 344–57, and are included in *Messages to America*, except as noted.

1938: 5 July, 10 September, 24 September, 27 November (BN, Jan. 1939, p. 2).

1939: 28 January, 17 April, 22 May, 28 May, 4 July, 28 July, 5 December (BN, Jan. 1940, p. 1), 21 December, 26 December (BN, Feb. 1940, p. 9), 30 December.

1940: 15 April (repeated in vol. IX, pp. 315–17).

VOLUME IX – 1940–1944

These messages are included in a section entitled 'Messages from the Guardian', pp. 315–36, and are published in *Messages to America*, except as noted.

1940: 15 May, 13 June, 29 October, 3 December.

1941: 25 May, 12 August, 22 November.

1942: 15 January, 9 February (BN, Feb. 1942, p. 1), 14 March (BN, April 1942, p. 1), 26 April, 26 May, 14 July (BN, Aug. 1942, p. 1), 15 August, 3 October (BN, Annual Reports, 1942–3, p. 7), 30 November.

* References are abbreviated as: BA (*Bahá'í Administration*), BN (*U.S. Bahá'í News*), CF (*Citadel of Faith*), MA (*Messages to America*), MBW (*Messages to the Bahá'í World*, 1971 ed.).

1943: 8 January, 18 January, 15 March (BN, April 1943, p. 1), 28 March, 14 April, 27 May, 8 August, 5 October, 16 November.

1944: 4 January, 15 April (repeated in vol. X, pp. 288–9).

VOLUME X – 1944–1946

These messages are included in a section entitled 'Important Messages from Shoghi Effendi to the American Believers 1944–1946', pp. 286–96, and are published in *Messages to America*, except as noted.

1944: 9 May, 15 May, 25 May (BN, July 1944, p. 3), 18 August, 21 November, 24 December.

1945: 29 March, 8 May, 12 May, 10 August, 20 August.

VOLUME XI – 1946–1950

These messages are included in a section entitled 'Messages from Shoghi Effendi to the American Believers 1946–1950', pp. 181–206; the first four are published in *Messages to America* and the others in *Citadel of Faith*.

1946: 25 April, 5 June, 20 July, 3 December.

1947: 28 April, 25 October, 15 December.

1948: 16 April (last paragraph), 26 April, 18 May, 3 November, 8 November.

1949: 25 April, 18 August.

VOLUME XII – 1950–1954

These messages are included under seven headings, as follows: 'The Centenary Celebrations of the Birth of the Mission of Bahá'u'lláh, 1953' (pp. 115–19); 'The African Intercontinental Teaching Conference Held in Kampala, Uganda, February 1953' (pp. 121–4); 'Important Messages from Shoghi Effendi 1950–1954' (pp. 337–73); 'Appointment of the Hands of the Cause of God' (pp. 374–8); 'Formation of the International Bahá'í Council (pp. 378–9); 'The All-America Intercontinental Teaching Conference Held in Chicago, Illinois, U.S.A., April 29–May 6, 1953' (pp. 133–41); 'The Completion of the Construction of the Sepulchre of the Báb in the Holy Land, 1953' (pp. 238–9.) Most of the messages are published in *Messages to America*, *Messages to the Bahá'í World*, and *Citadel of Faith*, except as noted.

1946: 15 June (excerpt, MA).

1950: 21 March (CF), 25 April (MBW), 4 July (CF), 5 July (CF), 20 July (BN, Oct. 1950, p. 1).

1951: 9 January (MBW), 29 March (CF), 25 April (MBW), 7 August (BN, Nov. 1951, p. 3), 23 November (CF), 23 November (through his secretary, BN, Feb. 1952, p. 2), 30 November (MBW), 24 December (MBW).

1952: 29 February (MBW), 8 March (MBW; corrections BN, June 1952, p. 2), 26 March (BN, May 1952, p. 4), 23 April (MBW; corrections BN, July 1952, p. 4, and August 1952, p. 7), 11 June (MBW), 30 June (MBW), 23 August (BN, Nov. 1952, p. 1), 8 October (MBW; corrections, BN, Dec. 1952, pp. 2–3), 12 November (MBW; corrections, BN, March 1953, p. 5), 15 December (MBW).

1953: February (to the African Intercontinental Conference, MBW), 29 April (CF), 30 April (MBW), 3 and 4 May (to the All-America Intercontinental Conference, MBW), July (to the European Intercontinental Conference, MBW), 18 July (CF), October (to the Asian Intercontinental Conference, MBW), 7 December (MBW).

1954: 19 March (MBW), 6 April (MBW).

IMPORTANT MESSAGES AND STATEMENTS NOT PUBLISHED IN COLLECTIONS OR IN *THE BAHÁ'Í WORLD*

References are to *Star of the West* or the American *Bahá'í News*, abbreviated as *Star* and BN.

16 December 1922. On his return to Haifa after a long absence. (*Star*, vol. XIII, p. 265.)

December 1923. Concerning The Universal House of Justice. (BN, July 1963, pp. 5–6.)

October 1924. *ibid.*

3 March 1925. Persecutions in Persia. (BN, May–June 1925, Insert.)

24 and 30 April, 2 May 1928. Cablegrams to Annual Bahá'í Convention. (BN, June 1928, p. 1.)

25 and 28–29 April 1929. Greetings to Annual Convention and gift to Bahá'í Temple of silk carpet. (BN, May 1929, pp. 1, 3.)

30 May 1930. The New History Society. (BN, August 1930, p. 3.)

April 1931. Greetings to Annual Bahá'í Convention. (BN, May 1931, p. 1.)

14 July 1947. 'The Faith of Bahá'u'lláh: A World Religion'. Statement prepared for the United Nations Special Committee on Palestine. (Published in *World Order*, A Bahá'í Magazine, October 1947, and as a separate pamphlet.)

April 1953. To First Italo-Swiss Convention. (BN, June 1953, p. 3.)

5 June 1953. Final stages in erecting the Báb's Shrine. (BN, July 1953, p. 1; corrections BN, September 1953, p. 6.)

20 September 1953. Pioneer Roll of Honour (No. 1). (Corrections BN, February 1954, p. 2, to message included in *Messages to the Bahá'í World*, p. 51.)

October 1953. To New Delhi Intercontinental Conference, including Pioneer Roll of Honour (No. 2). (BN, November 1953, pp. 2-4; corrections February 1954, p. 3.)

October 1953. Message to the Hands of the Cause at Intercontinental Teaching Conference, New Delhi. (BN, November 1953, p. 4; corrections February 1954, p. 3.)

1 October 1954. 'A succession of victories' and Pioneer Roll of Honour (No. 7). (Corrections BN, February 1955, p. 3, to message included in *Messages to the Bahá'í World*, pp. 69-73.)

15 August 1955. To the All-France Conference, announcing the National Convention for 1958. (BN, October 1955, excerpt, p. 8.)

April 1956. To four African Regional Conventions. (BN, August 1956, p. 1.)

The author is deeply grateful to Mrs. Beatrice Owens Ashton, whose compilation of the Guardian's writings has provided the material for this Appendix.

APPENDIX IV

Genealogy of Shoghi Effendi

Shoghi Effendi Rabbani was born in Acre ('Akká), Palestine, in the year 1314 A.H. (1 March 1897).*

His great-great-grandfather was Mírzá Buzurg-i-Núrí, a

---

* After the erection of the Guardian's sepulchre, Amatu'l-Bahá Rúḥíyyih Khánum found in one of Shoghi Effendi's boyhood notebooks a notation in his own hand stating that he was born on 1 March 1897. This accounts for the discrepancy with the date shown on the column of the monument.

nobleman of 'one of the most ancient and renowned families of Mázindarán', who was closely associated with the court of Fath-'Alí S̲h̲áh, and descended from Yazdigird III, the last king of the Sásáníyán dynasty (A.D. 226–651) who was reigning at the time of the Prophet Muḥammad's birth.*

His Great-Grandfather was Mírzá Ḥusayn-'Alíy-i-Núrí (Bahá'-u'lláh), who was born in Ṭihrán the second day of Muḥarram 1233 A.H. (12 November 1817).

His Grandfather was 'Abbás Effendi ('Abdu'l-Bahá), who was born in Ṭihrán the 5th day of Jamádíyu'l-Avval, 1260 A.H. (23 May 1844).

His father was Mírzá Hádí S̲h̲írází Afnán, a relative of the Báb, who was born in S̲h̲íráz, Persia, in the year A.D. 1864.†

His mother was Díyá'íyyih K̲h̲ánum, daughter of 'Abbás Effendi ('Abdu'l-Bahá), and born in Palestine.

His Great-Grandfather and Grandfather were exiled to the prison-city of 'Akká, Palestine, in 1868 and the family continued to make its home in Palestine after their deaths in 1892 and 1921, respectively.

In March 1937 Shoghi Effendi contracted marriage with Miss Mary Maxwell of Montreal, Canada.

The Family of the Báb‡

His wife was K̲h̲adíjih-Bagum, daughter of Ḥájí Mírzá 'Alí of S̲h̲íráz (the paternal uncle of the Báb's mother), and a descendant of Imám Ḥusayn. She was surpassed only by Ṭáhirih in devotion to the Báb, Who gave her a special prayer to recite 'ere you go to sleep'. (See DB, pp. 191–2). She died in 1299 A.H. (October 1882). Her brothers were Ḥájí Mírzá Siyyid Ḥasan (whose son, Mírzá Muḥsin married Túbá K̲h̲ánum, daughter of 'Abdu'l-Bahá), and

---

* Yazdigird III died c. A.D. 651; his daughter S̲h̲ahrbánú married the Imám Ḥusayn and was known as 'The Mother of Nine Imáms'.
† See sub-section entitled 'The Family of the Báb', first paragraph.
‡ The information was gleaned from Shoghi Effendi's Genealogy of the Báb in Nabíl's The Dawn-Breakers, his book God Passes By, and his translation of Bahá'-u'lláh's Epistle to the Son of the Wolf (abbreviated as DB, GPB and ESW, respectively).

Ḥájí Mírzá Abu'l-Qásim (whose grandson, Mírzá Hádí, married Díyá'íyyih, eldest daughter of 'Abdu'l-Bahá; their eldest son was Shoghi Effendi).

His mother was Fáṭimih-Bagum, granddaughter of Mírzá 'Abid of Shíráz, who was a descendant of Imám Ḥusayn. She did not realize the significance of the Báb's Mission until after His death (DB, p. 191). She died in 1882.

His father was Mírzá Muḥammad Riḍá, a descendant of Imám Ḥusayn, who died when the Báb was very young.

His maternal uncles (brothers of his mother) were:

Ḥájí Mírzá Siyyid 'Alí (surnamed Khál-i-A'ẓam), who reared the Báb after His father's death, and was one of the Seven Martyrs of Ṭihrán. His only child, Mírzá Javád, died at the age of nineteen.

Ḥájí Mírzá Siyyid Muḥammad (surnamed Khál-i-Akbar), to whom Bahá'u'lláh addressed the Kitáb-i-Íqán (GPB, p. 138). His children were:

Ḥájí Mírzá Muḥammad 'Alí. (The identification of his grave with the transfer of his remains, was a goal of the World Crusade, 1953–63.) He had one son, Mírzá Áqá.

Ḥájí Mírzá Muḥammad Taqí, 'Vakílu'd-Dawlih', chief builder of the Temple in Ishqábád. He is buried in the Bahá'í Cemetery at the foot of Mt. Carmel. (GPB, p. 300.)

Ḥájí Mírzá Buzurg, who had no children.

Bíbí-Ján-Ján-Bagum, wife of Ḥájí Mírzá Siyyid Ḥasan (the Great Afnán), and mother of Mírzá Muḥsin (nephew of the Báb's wife).

Khadíjih-Sulṭán Bagum.

Ḥájí Mírzá Ḥasan-'Alí (surnamed Khál-i-Aṣghar), whose children were:

Ḥájí Mírzá Áqá, who had five sons.
Ḥájí Siyyid Mihdí, who had six children.
Ḥájí Siyyid Ja'far, who had one child.
Ḥájí Siyyid Ḥusayn, who had four children.
Bíbí-Zahrá-Bagum, wife of Ḥájí Mírzá Muḥammad-Taqí, 'Vakílu'd-Dawlih'.

A paternal cousin, Mírzá 'Alí-Akbar, was assassinated in Ba<u>gh</u>dád when Bahá'u'lláh was absent from that city. (See GPB, p. 165, and ESW, p. 176.)

The descendants of the two brothers of the wife of the Báb and of the three brothers of His mother are known as the Afnán (the Twigs).

APPENDIX V

The War in Africa[36]

Mr. Churchill to General Alexander,* Commander in Chief in the Middle East.

British Embassy, Cairo.

'*Most Secret*

'1. Your prime and main duty will be to take or destroy at the earliest opportunity the German-Italian Army commanded by Field-Marshal Rommel together with all its supplies and establishments in Egypt and Libya.

'2. You will discharge or cause to be discharged such other duties as pertain to your command without prejudice to the task described in paragraph 1, which must be considered paramount in His Majesty's interests.

'10.8.42.'

'General Alexander to Prime Minister. Sir,—The orders you gave me on August 15,* 1942, have been fulfilled. His Majesty's enemies together with their impedimenta have been completely eliminated from Egypt, Cyrenaica, Libya and Tripolitania. I now await your further instructions.'

'*The date should have been the 10th, not the 15th.'

Commenting on the developments of the African campaign, in his handbook *The Bahá'í Faith 1844–1952*, Shoghi Effendi states: 'The invading Forces of Field Marshal Rommel, whose threat to Alexandria constituted the gravest danger to the Holy Land, and

---

* Later Field-Marshal Earl Alexander of Tunis. This directive was written with his own hand by Mr. Churchill. It was fulfilled on 13 May 1943.

whose victory would have precipitated the direst crisis in the fortunes of the Faith and its World Centre, and imperiled its institutions, were routed from the continent of Africa and the peril of a régime inimical to the Faith removed forever'. (p. 24.)

APPENDIX VI

The Tablet of Carmel

The Tablet of Carmel, which appears as section XI of the editions in English of *Gleanings from the Writings of Bahá'u'lláh* (translated by Shoghi Effendi), represents the 'Charter of the World Spiritual and Administrative Centres of the Faith on that mountain.'[37] The reader should take the time to study this Tablet with diligence and passion, because it is very revealing and affords much assurance to the heart and tranquillity to the mind.

Since ancient times Mt. Carmel has been considered the Garden of God, the literal translation from both Hebrew and Arabic being the 'Vineyard of God'. Numerous references have been made to it in the Old Testament; a poignant one, indicating its destiny, occurs in the Book of Amos. Bahá'u'lláh Himself designates this mountain as the seat of God's Throne.

Even before I met Shoghi Effendi in person he had sent word to me, by a visitor coming to Rome from Haifa, that it would be important for me to become well acquainted with this Tablet. After I reached the Holy Land some time later, and came into the presence of the Guardian and learned from him the details of the projected development of the surroundings of the Báb's Shrine, I was able to understand the greatness destined for that Holy Spot, as well as the eagerness of the Guardian to carry out the magnificent plan for its beautification and the prestige of the Faith.

In *Epistle to the Son of the Wolf*, Bahá'u'lláh, after citing the prophetic references made in the Psalms and the Books of Isaiah and Amos, concerning Zion, Jerusalem, Palestine and 'Akká, states:

'Carmel, in the Book of God, hath been designated as the Hill of God, and His Vineyard. It is here that, by the grace of the Lord of Revelation, the Tabernacle of Glory hath been raised. Happy are they that attain thereunto; happy they that set their faces towards it. And likewise He saith: "Our God will come, and He will not be silent." '38

This Epistle, the last outstanding Tablet revealed by Bahá'u'lláh, was penned about a year before His death. There is a vital connection between the passage just cited and the Tablet of Carmel, which was revealed under extraordinary circumstances on that mountain. Shoghi Effendi, in *God Passes By* (p. 194), refers to the visit of Bahá'u'lláh to Mt. Carmel when He pitched His tent, the 'Tabernacle of Glory', in the vicinity of the Carmelite Monastery, Stella Maris, near the cave of Elijah. One evening when I was in Haifa, Shoghi Effendi related that it was in the course of this visit that Bahá'u'lláh revealed His Tablet addressed to that holy mountain, to which, according to Isaiah, 'all nations shall flow'. Shoghi Effendi said that Bahá'u'lláh chanted the Words of that Tablet with supreme majesty and power; that 'the forceful tone of His exalted language sounded all around, so that even the monks, within the walls of the monastery, heard every word uttered by Him. Such was the commotion created on that historical occasion,' the Guardian said, that 'the earth seemed to shake, while all those present were overpowered by His mighty and wondrous spirit.'

He, the true 'Lord of the Vineyard', had consecrated the earth and that land to become the seat of the Spiritual and Administrative Centres of His Mighty Revelation.

'Haste thee, O Carmel, for lo, the light of the countenance of God, the Ruler of the Kingdom of Names and Fashioner of the heavens, hath been lifted upon thee. . .

'. . .Rejoice, for God hath in this Day established upon thee His throne, hath made thee the dawning-place of His signs and the dayspring of the evidences of His Revelation. Well is it with him that circleth around thee, that proclaimeth the revelation of thy glory, and recounteth that which the bounty of the Lord thy God hath showered upon thee. . .

'Call out to Zion, O Carmel, and announce the joyful tidings: He that was hidden from mortal eyes is come! His all-conquering sovereignty is manifest; His all-encompassing splendour is revealed. Beware lest thou hesitate or halt. Hasten forth and circumambulate the City of God that hath descended from heaven, the celestial Kaaba round which have circled in adoration the favoured of God, the pure in heart, and the company of the most exalted angels. . .'

Towards the end of the Tablet, He unveiled future events, some of which have already materialized under the Ministry of the Master, 'Abdu'l-Bahá, and some under the stewardship of Shoghi Effendi. These and yet others will 'resistlessly' continue to be developed and to flourish, under the guidance of the Universal House of Justice. 'Ere long will God sail His Ark upon thee, and will manifest the people of Bahá who have been mentioned in the Book of Names.' The 'Ark' sailing upon that holy mountain, Shoghi Effendi has explained, is a reference to the 'establishment of the World Administrative Centre of the Faith on Mt. Carmel',[39] and the 'people of Bahá' are the members of the Universal House of Justice.

Thus, with the Sepulchre of the Báb—'the Spot round which the Concourse on high circle in adoration'—established permanently on that holy mountain, near the cave of Elijah, facing the white city of 'Akká, with the Most Holy Tomb, the Shrine of Bahá'u'lláh, in its vicinity, and with the International Archives, the gardens and the Bahá'í endowments in their neighbourhood, there is no doubt that the Spiritual and Administrative Centres of the Faith have been gloriously established on the Mountain of God for ages to come.

Most of Israel is situated along the thirty-third northern parallel, the same latitude as that of southern California. It has been reported that when 'Abdu'l-Bahá visited that part of America in 1912 he marvelled at the great physical similarity of those two parts of the world, both being located near two vast deserts. The flora, too, is much alike, and the climate almost identical. Date palms, citrus trees, cactus plants and the 'casuarina' so often mentioned in the Old Testament are common to both regions.

Mt. Carmel is about twenty-two miles* long and stretches from east to west, coming to an abrupt end on reaching the Bay of Haifa where it presents a steep rampart, falling away to sea level. On the summit of the western end of this rampart the newly-created religious order of Our Lady of Mount Carmel built, in the twelfth century, the monastery Stella Maris, on land granted by King Baldwin of Jerusalem after the conquest of that city in 1099. He was the brother of Godfrey of Bouillon, one of the leaders of the First Crusade. There is no doubt that during all the intervening centuries the voices of those pious monks were raised daily in songs to the Glory of God, invoking the coming of the Kingdom of God on earth. Seven centuries were to elapse before the realization of mankind's hope, with the appearance of Bahá'u'lláh, the Redeemer, on that spot and the establishment of the 'throne' of God on that holy mountain.

It may also be noted here that in the years to come, on the ridge of that same mountain and very near the monastery, the great Mashriqu'l-Adhkár of the Bahá'í Faith will be erected, on land consecrated by the footsteps of the Blessed Beauty, Bahá'u'lláh, land that came into Bahá'í possession through the wise and timely purchase by Shoghi Effendi in 1955, with the munificent assistance of the much-loved and distinguished Hand of the Cause of God and vice-president of the Bahá'í International Council, Mrs. Amelia E. Collins. In the future that holy Temple will be filled with the joyous chants of pilgrims of every race, coming from every continent and from all the lands of the world, singing praise and thanksgiving to the Glory of God.

Guido M. Fabbricotti, the Marble Firm

The firm was founded in Carrara in 1800 by Bernardo Fabbricotti. He was a man of deep culture and skill, who started a marble trade with the United States of America, Canada and the United

* Approximately thirty-five kilometres.

Kingdom. He was a generous patron of the arts and established three annual prizes for students at the *Accademia delle Belle Arti*, of Carrara, for excellence in sculpture, architecture, and ornamentation. Many monuments throughout the world were executed by this firm. A son, Guido Murray Fabbricotti, established the firm of Guido M. Fabbricotti, Successori, calling into partnership, in 1918, his son Andrea, and later his sons-in-law, D. Orlando, A. Lazzareschi and A. Bufalini. Colonel Bufalini, a former officer in the Royal Carabinieri, was the one who dealt personally with Mr. Maxwell and later with Dr. Giachery in the work on the Sepulchre of the Báb. He passed away after a brief illness on 10 September 1949, and was succeeded in the firm by his two adult sons, Enrico and Maurizio. In the last few moments of his life, speaking to his sons at his bedside, he said:

'Take good care of the work for the Shrine of the Báb; do your best, as this is the greatest work of our lives.'

APPENDIX VIII

Giacomo Barozzi, the Architect Vignola

Giacomo Barozzi (1507–73) was a great architect of the Italian Renaissance, contemporary with Michelangelo, whom he succeeded as the architect of St. Peter's in Rome. He became known, and passed into history, as Vignola, the name of his birthplace, a small town some twenty miles west of Bologna. He was a champion of the neo-classic school of architecture and became famous for his handbook, *The Five Orders of Architecture*, which describes the orders (styles) of columns. It has exerted considerable influence on the work of many succeeding generations of architects. The Vignola column is not a complete cylindroid, as are the Greek and Roman columns; it tapers upward from about three-quarters of its length, like a hand-dipped candle.

Names of the Doors of the Shrine of the Báb*

Names given by 'Abdu'l-Bahá to the five doors of the original Shrine

Báb-i-Amín

The door leading to the antechamber of the Báb's Tomb from the western side of the Shrine. Ḥájí Abu'l-Ḥasan-i-Ardakání, more commonly known as Ḥájí Amín, was, in the days of Bahá'u'lláh, the second Trustee of Ḥuqúqu'lláh. He had assisted Ḥájí Sháh Muḥammad Man_sh_ádí, the first Trustee, until the latter's death, when Bahá'u'lláh appointed him as Trustee, a service which he discharged with exemplary loyalty and enthusiasm during the latter part of the ministry of Bahá'u'lláh, throughout the ministry of 'Abdu'l-Bahá and up to the early years of the Guardianship.

Báb-i-Faḍl

The door leading to the antechamber of 'Abdu'l-Bahá, also on the western side of the Shrine, named for Mírzá Abu'l-Faḍl of Gulpáygán, Persia, the most erudite teacher of the Cause of Bahá'u'lláh, who served the Faith in his native land, in Russia up to the borders of China, in India, Turkey, Europe, America and the Middle East. He was the author of many books in which he gave with courage and clarity the most logical proofs of the advent of the Manifestation of God. He was persecuted and imprisoned many times, and was infinitely loved by Bahá'u'lláh and the Master, whom he assisted both in the Holy Land and in Egypt. He was born in 1844 and passed away in Cairo in 1914 amidst the grief of all those who knew and loved him.

Báb-i-A_sh_raf and Báb-i-Bálá

Two doors, one facing north towards 'Akká and the other on the eastern side of the Shrine. They are named for Ustád Áqá 'Alí-A_sh_raf and Ustád Áqá Bálá, sons of Mullá Abú-Ṭálib. These two brothers were master-masons who went on pilgrimage from

* The Chart at the end of this Appendix gives the locations of the doors.

their native town of Baku, Russia, and with 'Abdu'l-Bahá's permission remained for some time in the Holy Land. During this period, they devoted their efforts to the construction of the Shrine and offered financial contributions towards the project.

Báb-i-Karím

The door on the eastern side leading to the antechamber of the Tomb of 'Abdu'l-Bahá is named for Ustád 'Abdu'l-Karím from Persia, who was also a mason and served in the construction of the Shrine.

Names given by Shoghi Effendi to the three doors of the rooms which he added, and to the octagon door.

Báb-i-Qaṣṣábchí

A door on the eastern side, named for Ḥájí Maḥmúd Qaṣṣábchí of 'Iráq, donor of the contributions to build the three additional rooms.*

Báb-i-Maxwell

The central door on the south side of the Shrine is named for Hand of the Cause William Sutherland Maxwell of Montreal, Canada, architect of the superstructure of the Shrine.†

Báb-i-Giachery

This door on the western side is named for Hand of the Cause Ugo Giachery, appointed by the Guardian as his representative in Italy to supervise the purchase, cutting, carving and shipment of all the marble needed to erect the superstructure of the Shrine.‡

Báb-i-Ioas

The octagon door, located on the south side of the first storey of the Shrine, is named for Hand of the Cause Leroy Ioas of the United States of America who, from March 1952, supervised the construction and completion of the Shrine. He was secretary-general of the International Bahá'í Council.§

---

* See page 61.   † See chapter VI.   ‡ See page 8.
§ See pages 106–7.

Shrine of the Báb on Mt. Carmel

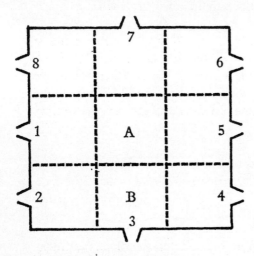

Names given by 'Abdu'l-Bahá to five of the doors of the Shrine:

1. Báb-i-Bálá
2. Báb-i-Karím
3. Báb-i-Ashraf
4. Báb-i-Faḍl
5. Báb-i-Amín

COLONNADE
(Ground Structure)

A: Tomb of the Báb
B: Tomb of 'Abdu'l-Bahá

Names given by Shoghi Effendi to the doors of rooms and octagon, which he added after the passing of 'Abdu'l-Bahá:

6. Báb-i-Giachery
7. Báb-i-Maxwell
8. Báb-i-Qaṣṣábchí
9. Báb-i-Ioas

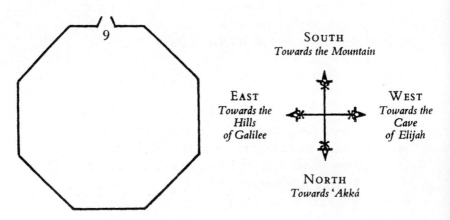

SOUTH
Towards the Mountain

EAST
*Towards the
Hills
of Galilee*

WEST
*Towards the
Cave
of Elijah*

NORTH
Towards 'Akká

OCTAGON (First Storey)

Andrea Palladio, Founder of Neo-Classic Architecture

Palladio, the most famous architect of the sixteenth century, 1518–80, originated a neo-classicism in architecture which inflamed the fantasy of European architects of his age and the British in particular. Born in Vicenza, he lived between that city and Venice, built many magnificent villas for the wealthy merchants of Venice and produced four books on architecture which were later translated into English, reaching England at the beginning of the eighteenth century.* The Earl of Burlington, who had returned from Italy at that time, was determined to rebuild Burlington House in the Palladian style. Colen Campbell became its architect and, when his fame spread, the Hon. John Fane commissioned him to design Mereworth Castle in Kent, which was almost an exact copy of the Villa Almerico of Vicenza, known as 'La Rotonda'. This building, considered the most beautiful and important work by Palladio, is famous for its circular salon, of exquisite design and the true expression of grandeur and architectural symmetry. The balustrade in question is on the balcony of the upper floor of this central hall.

Plants Used by Shoghi Effendi

Shoghi Effendi used a wide variety of highly decorative and beautiful trees and plants to embellish the Most Holy Places of the Bahá'í Faith on Mount Carmel and at Bahjí. Many of the plants were native to Palestine, while others came from the Mediter-

* Inigo Jones had already in the seventeenth century introduced the Palladian style to England.

ranean, Africa, America and Australia, including some from the islands of the Pacific. Although the writer does not presume that the following list is complete, for many other plants may have escaped his observation, the purpose in adding this Appendix is to make the reader aware of the fertile imagination of Shoghi Effendi in choosing this wide range of trees and plants to develop the Bahá'í gardens.

The genus is given only if it differs from the name of the plant.

TREES

Araucaria (Pine family)

Carob (*Ceratonia siliqua*)—its fruit is sometimes called Locust.

Casuarina—of several species.

Eucalyptus—of many species; known also as the Gum tree.

Cypress (*Cupressus sempervirens*)

Flamboyante (*Poinciana regia*)

Jacaranda

Olive (*Olea europaea*)

Orange (*Citrus aurantium*—bitter, and *C. sinensis*—sweet)

Palm—including the Date palm.

Palmetto (*Chamaerops humilis*)

Pine (*Pinus*)—of several species.

Frangipani (*Plumeria alba*)

Tamarisk (*Tamarix*)—including the Manna tree; manna is the exudation of *T. gallica*.

Mandarin (*Citrus reticulata*)—including the Tangerine.

SHRUBS, VINES AND HEDGES

Acacia

Mimosa—of several species.

Bougainvillaea—a woody vine in several colours.

Cycas

Honeysuckle (*Lonicera*)

Jasmine (*Jasminum*)—several varieties and colours of other

genera, such as *Gelsemium sempervirens* (yellow jasmine) and *Gardenia jasminoides* (Cape jasmine).

Syringa (*Philadelphus*) and Lilac (*Syringa*)—a Persian species of Lilac used for hedges and pompoms.

Yucca (Lily family)

DWARF HEDGES, FLOWERS AND GRASSES

Anemone

Azalea

Broom (*Genista*)

Calendula—Marigold

Crocus

Daisy (*Bellis perennis*)

Geranium—see Pelargonium.

Gladiolus

Hibiscus

Iris

Lupine (*Lupinus*)

Narcissus

Pelargonium—commonly known as Geranium, although it is a different genus.

Ranunculus

Rose (*Rosa*)—of many species.

Thyme (*Thymus serpyllum*)—used for low hedges.

Grasses (*Agrostis* and *Eragrostis*) —the grass used by the Guardian came first from the Jordan Valley, then from Turkey, and from 1953 to 1957 it was purchased in Italy.

SUCCULENT AND CACTI PLANTS
(*Crassulaceous* and *Cactaceous*)

By using these plants, Shoghi Effendi developed admirable and artistic plots of land quite close to the Shrine of Bahá'u'lláh and in the vicinity of the Shrine of the Báb.

Agave (*Agave americana*)-known as American Aloe.

Echeveria

Echinocactus—Barrel cactus

Gasteria (Lily family)

Mammillaria—Pincushion cactus

Cereus (*Selenicereus grandiflorus*) —Night Blooming cactus

Opuntia—Prickly Pear

Saguaro (*Cereus giganteus*)— Giant cactus

Sansevieria—Snake plant

It is also important to mention the great contribution made by Shoghi Effendi in improving the gardens of Riḍván, near 'Akká, and of Mazra'ih. He also created, in a few days, the small garden in front of the Master's house in Haifa.

Glossary of Architectural and Building Terms
used in this book

Some plural forms are given in brackets.

Acroterion (a)	a pedestal or ornament at the top or side angle of a pediment.
Amphora (ae)	a two-handled jar or vase for holding liquids (used by the Greeks and Romans); a garden ornament.
Antefix (es, a)	an ornament concealing the ends of roofing tiles.
Anthemion (a)	the so-called honeysuckle ornament in ancient art, a conventionalized plant-form more like a palmetto.
Abacus (i)	a level tablet on the capital of a column, supporting the entablature.
Architrave	the lowest division of the entablature resting immediately on the abacus of the column.
Baluster	the small pillar supporting a parapet coping.
Balustrade	a row of balusters surmounted by a rail or coping.
Bas-relief	sculpture in which the figures do not stand far out from the ground on which they are formed.
Capital	the head or top part of a column or pillar.
Cavetto	a hollowed moulding whose curvature is a quarter of a circle, used chiefly in cornices.
Cella	the body of the temple, as distinguished from the portico.
Clerestory	the upper storey or part with its own row of windows; also known as the drum.
Colonnade	a range of columns placed at regular intervals.
Congé	a type of concave moulding.
Coping	the uppermost course of masonry or brickwork in a wall, usually of a sloping form to throw off rain.
Corbel	a projection from the face of a wall, supporting a weight.
Corinthian, *adj.*	the lightest and most ornate of the three Grecian orders, having a bell-shaped capital adorned with

220

rows of acanthus leaves, giving rise to graceful volutes. See Ionic.

Cornice — the uppermost member of the entablature, surmounting the frieze; a projecting moulding along the top of a building, window, etc.

Corniche (Fr.) — a cornice.

Dowel-pin — a headless pin, peg or bolt of wood, metal, etc. serving to fasten together two pieces of wood, stone, etc., by penetrating into the substance of both pieces.

Drum — an upright part of a cupola; a cylinder, used alternatively with clerestory.

Entablature — in classic architecture, the part which surmounts the columns and rests upon the capitals, including the architrave, frieze and the cornice.

Façade — the exterior, front or face of a building.

Faience — glazed coloured earthenware.

Fascia — any long flat surface of wood, stone, or marble, *esp.* in the Ionic and Corinthian orders; each of the three surfaces which make up the architrave.

Finial — an ornament placed upon the apex of a roof, pediment, or gable, or upon each corner of a tower, etc.

Frieze — the part of the entablature between the architrave and cornice, often ornamented with figures.

Ionic, *adj.* — name of one of the three orders of Grecian architecture (Doric, Ionic, Corinthian), characterized by the two lateral volutes of the capital.

Lamina (ae) — a thin plate, scale, layer, or flake (of metal, etc.).

Motif, motive — a distinctive feature or element of a design or composition.

Moulding — an ornamental edging or band projecting from a wall or other surface.

Octagon — a plane figure of eight sides and eight angles; hence, applied to material objects of this form.

Ogee — a moulding consisting of a continuous double curve, convex above and concave below; in cross section, its outline is a sort of S shape. Hence, an ogee arch is a pointed arch having on each side a reversed curve near the apex.

Order	one of the different ways in which the column and its entablature with their various parts are moulded and related to each other.
Parapet	a low wall or barrier, placed at the edge of a platform, balcony, roof, etc.
Pedestal	the support of a column, statue, vase, etc.
Pediment	a triangular structure crowning the front of a Greek building; a similar structure over a portico, door, or window.
Pilaster	a square column, partly built into, partly projecting from, a wall.
Plinth	the square block under the base of a column; a block serving as a pedestal; a flat-faced projecting band at the bottom of a wall.
Podium	a continuous projecting base or pedestal.
Portico (s, es)	an ambulatory consisting of a roof supported by columns placed at regular intervals, usually attached as a porch to a building; a colonnade.
Socle	a low plain block or plinth serving as a pedestal to a statue, column, vase, etc., also a plain plinth forming a foundation for a wall.
Spiracle	a small opening by which a confined space has communication with the outer air; *esp.* an airhole or air-shaft.
Stereotomy	the art of cutting stone or other solid bodies into measured forms as in masonry.
Torus	a large convex moulding, of semicircular or similar section, used especially at the base of a column.
Trabeation	an entablature: a combination of horizontal beams in a structure.
Tympanum (a)	the vertical recessed face of a pediment, often adorned with sculpture.
Vestibule	a forecourt: an entrance hall.
Volute	a spiral scroll used especially in Ionic capitals; a spiral conformation; a thing or part having such a shape.

The author has been greatly assisted, in compiling these definitions, by permission to quote from *The Shorter Oxford English Dictionary* (3rd ed., 1967) and *Chambers's Twentieth Century Dictionary* (new ed., 1964 and 1970), kindly granted by the Clarendon Press, Oxford, and W. & R. Chambers Ltd, Edinburgh and London, respectively.

References

Abbreviations for references cited

BA   *Bahá'í Administration*, Shoghi Effendi. Wilmette, Illinois: Bahá'í Publishing Trust, 5th ed., 1945.

BN   *Bahá'í News*. Published monthly by the National Spiritual Assembly of the Bahá'ís of the United States. Wilmette, Illinois.

BW   *The Bahá'í World*. An International Record. Vol. II, 1926–1928. New York: Bahá'í Publishing Committee, 1928. Vol. XII, 1950–1954. Wilmette, Illinois: Bahá'í Publishing Trust, 1956.

CF   *Citadel of Faith*, Shoghi Effendi. Messages to America, 1947–1957. Wilmette, Illinois: Bahá'í Publishing Trust, 1965.

DB   *The Dawn-Breakers*, Nabíl-i-A'ẓam. Wilmette, Illinois: Bahá'í Publishing Trust, repr. 1953.

ESW   *Epistle to the Son of the Wolf*, Bahá'u'lláh. Trans. by Shoghi Effendi. Wilmette, Illinois: Bahá'í Publishing Trust, repr. 1953.

GPB   *God Passes By*, Shoghi Effendi. Wilmette, Illinois: Bahá'í Publishing Trust, 5th repr. 1965.

KI   *Kitáb-i-Íqán*, Bahá'u'lláh. *The Book of Certitude*. Trans. by Shoghi Effendi. Wilmette, Illinois: Bahá'í Publishing Trust, 3rd repr. 1960. London: Bahá'í Publishing Trust, 2nd ed., 1961.

MA   *Messages to America, 1932–1946*, Shoghi Effendi. Wilmette, Illinois: Bahá'í Publishing Trust, 1947.

MBW   *Messages to the Bahá'í World, 1950–1957*, Shoghi Effendi. Wilmette, Illinois: Bahá'í Publishing Trust, rev. ed., 1971.

SW   *Star of the West*. The Bahá'í Magazine. Published from 1910 to 1933 from Chicago and Washington, D.C., by official Bahá'í agencies.

Tablets   *Tablets of Abdul-Baha Abbas*. Vol. II. Chicago: Bahai Publishing Society, repr. 1919.

TN   *A Traveller's Narrative*, Edward Granville Browne (ed.). Cambridge University Press, 1891.

WOB   *The World Order of Bahá'u'lláh*, Shoghi Effendi. Wilmette, Illinois: Bahá'í Publishing Trust, rev. 1955, 2nd imp. 1965.

The author acknowledges with warm thanks permission to quote from the copyrighted publications of the Bahá'í Publishing Trust, Wilmette, Illinois. These include Gleanings from the Writings of Bahá'u'lláh (1935; repr. 1969), from which extracts from the Tablet of Carmel are quoted in Appendix VI.

References

1. Tablets, vol. II, p. 484.
2. This statement is included in WOB, pp. 150–2.
3. MA, pp. 8–9. The cablegram is dated 30 March 1937.
4. *ibid.*, p. 89.
5. Cited GPB, p. 194.
6. *ibid.*, p. 275.
7. MA, p. 72.
8. BW, vol. XII, p. 239.
9. KI, p. 148 (Brit. ed.), p. 231 (U.S. ed.).
10. CF, p. 80.
11. See MBW, pp. 5–7.
12. See BW, vol. XII, pp. 226–30.
13. MBW, p. 9.
14. *ibid.*, p. 6.
15. *ibid.*, p. 50.
16. See BW, vol. XII, p. 239.
17. See BA, p. 74. (In earlier editions, p. 65.)
18. For a similar written statement, see Shoghi Effendi's reply (through his secretary) to a question on this subject, as reported in BN, February 1950, p. 4. The second part of the quotation is taken from his reply to a Bahá'í, 13 November 1944 (through his secretary), kindly shared by the Department of Research, Bahá'í World Centre.
19. See MBW, pp. 45–6.
20. *ibid.*, p. 32.

21. Cited GPB, p. 193.

22. *ibid.*

23. See TN, vol. II, xxxviii–xl.

24. *ibid.*, xxxix.

25. KI, p. 161 (Brit. ed.), p. 252 (U.S. ed.). See DB for the translation here used, which appears on the title page.

26. See MBW, pp. 73–5.

27. *ibid.*, p. 108. From Shoghi Effendi's Riḍván Message, April 1957.

28. *ibid.*, p. 63.

29. BN, February 1972, p. 2.

30. *The Tragedy of Romeo and Juliet,* III ii.

31. SW, vol. XIII, p. 68.

32. *ibid.*, p. 69.

33. These notes were issued by Mrs. Maxwell as a booklet in duplicated form.

34. BW, vol II, pp. 125–7.

35. SW, vol. XVII, p. 259.

36. From *The Alexander Memoirs: 1940–1945,* ed. John North. New York: McGraw-Hill Book Co., Inc., 1962, pp. 10 and 34.

37. MBW, p. 63.

38. ESW, p. 145.

39. MBW, p. 64.

Index

Titles of books and Tablets are italicized. Footnotes are indicated by the abbreviation n. after the page number; if the name or subject occurs both in the text and in a note, this is indicated by 'p. — and n.'. Principal themes are shown by bold figures. No attempt has been made to index Appendices III, IV and XI, or the Glossary.

Lightning Source UK Ltd.
Milton Keynes UK
UKOW02f1952250515

252259UK00001B/33/P